LONGMAN OPEN LEARNING

Evaluating Open and Distance Learning

by Mary Thorpe

Longman

Longman Group UK Limited
Longman House, Burnt Mill, Harlow, Essex, CM20 2JE

© Longman Group UK Limited, 1988

British Library Cataloguing in Publication Data

ISBN-0-582-90119-7

Thorpe, Mary.
Evaluating open and distance learning
Distance study courses. Assessment
371.3

Printed and bound in Great Britain by
Biddles Ltd, Guildford and King's Lynn

For my Parents

Contents

ACKNOWLEDGEMENTS   ix

INTRODUCTION   xi

PART I   OPEN LEARNING AND EVALUATION   1

CHAPTER 1:   OPEN LEARNING AND EVALUATION   1
    Is evaluation necessary?   1
    Summary   4
    What is evaluation?   5
    A definition of evaluation   5
    Different kinds of evaluation   7
    Formative and summative evaluation   9
    Conclusion   13

CHAPTER 2:   EVALUATION FOR PRACTITIONERS   16
    Practitioners in open learning   16
    Who is practitioner evaluation for?   18
    Evaluating open learning versus conventional
    provision   19
    Less open to inspection?   20
    More to be evaluated   20
    Different criteria for success?   21
    A Team approach to organisation   22
    Case studies of evaluation for practitioners   23
    Case Study A: The OPTIS evaluation of
        open learning in two years
        YTS   25
    Case Study B: Programme review in YTS,
        and a trainee centred
        programme review team   28
    Case Study C: Continuing Education for
        Pharmacists. An NEC project
        evaluation   33
    Case Study D: Birmingham Open Learning
        Development Unit   38
    Case Study E: The Taster Pack Project:
        Open University Regional
        Evaluation   40

PART II EVALUATION IN PRACTICE   47

           INTRODUCTION   47

CHAPTER 3: LEARNER SELF EVALUATION   51
            Preparing to learn   51
            During and at the end of learning   54
            Conclusion   59

CHAPTER 4: TUITION   61
            The role of the tutor   61
            Learner perceptions of tuition   66
            Correspondence tuition   69
                Turnround   69
                Grading reliability   70
                Tutor comments and correspondence
                teaching   73
            Face to face tuition   76
            Conclusion   86

CHAPTER 5: COUNSELLING AND LEARNER
            PROGRESS   88
            Counselling and its role   88
            Issues in counselling evaluation   92
            The provider perspective   94
            Behaviour   94
                Routine records   95
                Interview   96
                Questionnaires   97
            Perceptions   98
            The perspective of the user – enquirer,
            applicant, learner or client   102
            Behaviour   102
                Drop out   107
            Perceptions of counselling   114
            Conclusion   117

CHAPTER 6: COURSE AND LEARNING MATERIALS   111
            What is a course?   111
            The course context   120
            Learner performance   124
                Job performance   124
                Assessment   126
            Learner feedback   127
                Piloting course materials during
                production   128
                Developmental Testing   130

Materials evaluation during presentation
  or delivery   131
  Quantitative data   131
  Qualitative data   140
      *Exploring learning from the
      learner's perspective*   141
Peer and tutor feedback   142
  Peer commenting during materials
  production   144
    The design stage   144
    The 'advanced draft' stage   145
  Evaluation of existing materials prior to
  learner use   146
  Tutor commenting during materials
  presentation or delivery   148
Conclusion   152

PART III   THE PROCESS OF EVALUATION   155

INTRODUCTION   155

CHAPTER 7:   PLANNING AND DATA COLLECTION   157
The social organisation of evaluation   157
  The evaluation team   158
  Planning Tools and Procedures   158
    Minutes and chairing   158
    Equality of contribution   158
    Information needed by the team   159
    An evaluation plan   160
    Summary   160
A strategy for planning evaluation   161
  Regular, baseline evaluation   167
  Issue – specific evaluation   169
    Summary   170
Data collection   171
  Routine record systems or monitoring   171
  Feedback   172
  Interviews   174
    Sampling   174
    *Types of interview and the timing of
    interviews*   175
    Interviewing skills   176
    Face to face interviews   177
    Telephone interviews   178
    Group discussions   178
  Questionnaires   179
  Conclusion   180

CHAPTER 8:   ANALYSING AND USING EVALUATION
              FINDINGS   183
              Evaluation users   183
                 The learner   184
                    Summary   184
                 The author of learning material   186
                    Summary   187
                 Receptionist in an open access centre   188
                    Summary   188
                 Tutors   189
                    Summary   190
                 Managers   191
                    Summary   193
              Making the best use of an evaluation   193
                 Planning   193
                 Contexts – politics, interests and
                    identities   193
                 Interpretation of data   194
                 Staff development   196
                 Communication skills   196
                 Consultation and collaboration with
                    'outsiders'   197
                 Conclusion   197

CONCLUSION: Beyond quality control, towards
              excellence?   199

REFERENCES   205

INDEX   209

Acknowledgements

This book would not have been written if I had not spent the period between 1975 to 1980 solidly engaged in attempting to co-ordinate and develop regional research by practitioners at the Open University. For this I must thank David Grugeon, whose optimism about and political commitment to the regional experience of teaching and learning never failed. Rick Powell, Eleanor Wright, Pat Kelly and Steve Ryan worked with me as researchers in Regional Tutorial Services, as it then was, and most of what I know about evaluation stems from my collaboration with them and with colleagues in the regions. Roger Mills in particular generated more collaborative projects for the practical evaluation and development of student support services than anyone else I know. His commitment to the quality of student learning, and encouragement of the work of others continues to sustain one's conviction that the effort of evaluation and development is worthwhile.

I am indebted to a very large number of people for contributions they have made to this book directly. Lorna Unwin, Tim Burton, Hilary Read, Colin Russell and Ormond Simpson contributed case studies in Chapter 2 and many valuable comments. Glenys Crossland, Norman Dow, Gordon Estell, Gwen Harris, Ronnie Ogier, Erland Polden, Angie Lilley, Ros Morpeth, Judith Fage, Jackie Robinson, Derek Fordyce, Peter Bowen, Julian Jordan, Steve Ryan, Jack Field, Bob Womphrey and Rosemary Welchman all provided examples of evaluation and development of open learning.

Hilary Whiteley, Roger Lewis, Terry Hamilton, Roger Candy, Diane Bailey, Derek Rowntree, Pat Kelly, Jack Field, Clive Lawless, Alan Woodley, Betty Swift, Tony Clark, Ian McNay and Rosemary Melling all commented on the book in draft and I am tremendously grateful for the time they gave me. Rosemary Melling also helped me by the keen personal interest she has taken in encouraging my efforts. John Cowan was generous enough to give me the most thorough and thought provoking feedback I have ever had on anything I have ever written, including Open University course material. His comments, together with those of Pat Kelly and Ian McNay, provided that essential stimulus of all good colleague friends: the challenge of critical argument which forces us to re-examine the easy assumption and the idea that will do, in order to develop ideas more sharply argued, and perhaps even, better. It is this kind of stimulus, of course, which helps generate the energy required for the achievement of excellence in learning and teaching. I am now more than ever aware that even the aspiration towards excellence requires the creative support and collaboration of the colleagues with whom one works. I include within that my colleague Brenda Parish who typed the book in all its various stages and worked many unsocial hours to do so. Any imperfections, omissions or inadequacies it contains are of course entirely my own.

Material in chapter 4, table 1 and figures 1 to 4 was taken from Clarke, A., Costello, M. and Wright, T. (1984/5) *The Role and Tasks of Tutors in Open Learning Systems* with the kind permission of the Industrial Training Research Unit in Cambridge.

Figures 9 and 10 in chapter 4 were supplied by the Mathematics Workshop at Bradford and Ilkley Community College and are reproduced with their kind permission.

Figure 4 in chapter 3 was supplied by Bury Metropolitan College and reproduced with their kind permission.

Figure 13 in chapter 6 was supplied by North East Open Learning Network, Newcastle-upon-Tyne and reproduced with their kind permission.

Figure 1 in Introduction to Part II is reproduced with the kind permission of the National Institute for Careers Education and Counselling, Sheraton House, Gloucester Street, Castle Park, Cambridge.

The extract by Gray in chapter 7 is reproduced with the kind permission of the Times Education Supplement, Priory House, St John's Lane, London.

The extract from 'Approved Training Organisations: Training for Skill: YTS' in Chapter 2 is reproduced with the kind permission of the Training Commission.

Introduction

I have written this book for practitioners of distance and open learning, with two main aims in view. First, I hope to convince practitioners and those who fund distance and open learning that evaluation is important for the achievement of goals which matter to them, such as the quality of the learning experience they provide and the effectiveness of their programmes or courses. Second, I hope to encourage more practitioners to incorporate evaluation as a regular set of practices in what they do. I have tried to achieve both goals by outlining a particular approach to evaluation and by providing practical examples of evaluation which could be applied and developed in distance and open learning.

Why then do I believe that practitioners ought to evaluate, and that evaluation ought to be useful in practice? The answers to both questions are interdependent. To the first, my answer is that the kind of evaluation which is directly useful to practice requires a considerable degree of practitioner involvement and cannot be wholly subcontracted out to some other group or individual, even though an 'external' evaluation may be highly desirable on some occasions and for some purposes.

My answer to the second question derives from a commitment to learning, teaching and training. The rationale for evaluation in this context, is that it should be applied to practice and make a difference to that practice by (it is to be hoped) leading to better ways of doing things. In short, evaluation needs practitioner involvement if it is to be useful in practice, and must be applied to practice if it is to serve the interests of learners and practitioners primarily. Evaluation which does not involve practitioners directly is probably more likely to serve the interests of the evaluator/ researcher and of communities (whether funding bodies, learned societies or government departments) remote from the implementation of education and training.

I am not suggesting that evaluation which does serve the interests of these last two groups is not a legitimate activity, nor that there is a necessary opposition between the needs of these two groups and those of practitioners. I do believe however that evaluation is not a neutral tool, that it can serve different interests, and therefore that we need to be clear in whose interests any evaluation is being undertaken.

Evaluation and research carried out solely by full-time professionals may achieve high standards but have a poor record for application to practice. Issues are formulated in terms which can be researched rather than in a form which matches the practitioners' experience of problems. The evaluation design produces findings too late for decision making or when circumstances have changed and new problems arisen. Very few people are aware of the findings when they appear, or know what to do with them in any case. These problems have been identified and discussed most particularly in relation to research, (Nisbet and Broadfoot, 1980. Ashton et al, 1983) but also apply to evaluation the more it approaches the characteristics of research.

The value of practitioners being involved in evaluation is not to replace the professional evaluator, but to spread the benefits more widely. There are benefits to be gained both in understanding practice and in developing it. First, one of the common starting points for evaluation is a wish to find out what causes something, or what the results are of a particular decision we have taken. Whether we find the answer or not, in the process of looking for it we learn more about the kind of people who are our learners or students, the attitudes of our colleagues, the way other institutions cope with similar problems, and so on. Evaluation can be a form of continuous in-service staff development, which makes us, the practitioners, more aware and probably better informed.

Second, when practitioners carry out an evaluation, it can lead to procedures which improve practice, even before the findings are applied. The need to decide what to evaluate in the first place, may prompt a more careful definition of programme goals which would otherwise have been left implicit. Procedures for recording events, queries, attendances and so on, have to be organised, and create opportunities for discussion and enhanced awareness of the programme involved. Evaluation can generate a more deliberate decision making process generally, from the initiation of a programme through to its completion.

Third, when practitioners are directly involved in evaluation, they have access to the findings as these accumulate and can respond to them directly by applying some new idea or information in the way they carry out their role, whether as manager, trainer, teacher or administrator.

I am not suggesting that the practitioner-evaluator approach is 'better than' professional evaluation. The practitioner needs the professional who has expertise which can save time and the needless difficulties we can get into by a poorly designed project. If possible therefore, practitioners should attempt to consult or perhaps collaborate with full-time evaluators able to advise them in this way. Many of the examples used in this book are the work of professional evaluators. They are included not because they are models for practitioners to imitate exactly, but because they offer useful experience which can be adapted to very different circumstances.

At a personal level, commitment to practitioner evaluation comes out of roughly 13 year's involvement in the evaluation of tuition and counselling at the Open University, working collaboratively with academic staff leading developments in each of the regions of the United Kingdom. Although by far the largest proportion of evaluation at the Open University has been contributed by full-time evaluators in the Institute of Educational Technology, academic staff in the regions are continuously involved in monitoring support services and have more formally evaluated a wide range of issues — tutorial attendance, study groups, counselling, the failure of students to make progress in their studies, and so on. Many of these evaluations were useful in the development of better local support for students.

The legacy of this experience which is important here is not so much the findings that were contributed but the model of practitioner as evaluator, where those who are in touch daily with learners and the development of a system which supports learning are also concerned to evaluate it themselves and to improve it through evaluating it.

To those who ask why there are not more examples of evaluation done *outside* the Open University, I can only say that I made every effort to find such examples. Those that I discovered have been included in Part II and in the case studies at the end of chapter 2. Having followed up every single contact suggested, whether in Further Education, industry or elsewhere, I have come to the conclusion, however, that there is not a great deal of non-OU evaluation to discover. If this book is successful in its aim, it is to be hoped that a more representative body of evaluation findings will exist in future.

I have included both open and distance learning in the title of the book as a whole, to signal to readers still unsure about the relationship between these two terms, that it is relevant to both. Outside the United Kingdom of course, it is still the distance learning form of open learning which is dominant. Both terms were introduced and defined in the first book in this series:

> distance learning if surely a sub-set of open learning – not synonymous with it, but a particular example of one type. 'Open learning' is an umbrella term which refers to a whole series of varied educational initiatives and provision.
> (Thorpe and Grugeon, 1987)

Open learning is more a movement than a particular model, towards opening up education and training, particularly for those who have not traditionally participated after initial education. As in the preceding volume, I am concerned to identify common or generic concerns in open learning, this time in relation to its evaluation. I have not drawn attention to different open learning systems hereafter, and have tried to provide ideas and examples in a form accessible to a readership with experience of very different systems, so that they might apply and develop those which interest them in their own work context.

Evaluation is an activity which practitioners can profitably undertake, whatever their initial training but with effective preparation and a willingness to learn from and to use those who do have professional expertise. I suggest that practical approaches to evaluation are more dependent on what David Jenkins calls '*an intelligent use of existing skills and competences* than on "learning" the novel tricks of some alleged definitive paradigm be it positivist research or whatever'. Jenkins (1978) (my emphais)

I hope this book encourages practitioners to feel that they do have 'existing skills and competences' which could be used (or used more) in evaluating what they do, and that the ideas it contains stimulate 'an intelligent use' which rewards their efforts and improves the quality of the learners' experience. For that, in the last analysis, is what it is all for.

PART I OPEN LEARNING AND EVALUATION

1 Open learning and evaluation

Main themes: *The need for evaluation in open learning, and the roles it can play. Defining evaluation and the different approaches to it which reflect the variety of purposes for which it is undertaken. Differences between summative and formative evaluation. The importance of formative evaluation for practitioners.*

Is evaluation necessary?

Evaluation has not been one of the most frequently mentioned topics in the literature on open learning which has mushroomed in the last five years. This is puzzling, when we consider that open learning is *an innovatory approach* to education and training, still in its early development stages. Surely we cannot be so confident about an innovation that there is no need to check whether aims have actually been achieved and our expectations justified?

Part of the problem may lie in the way open learning has been defined at the general level, as an approach to put right all the mistakes of conventional education and training which keep people out of the system and make learning difficult for the few who get in. Open learning has so often been defined in terms of the desirable effects which are its goal, and which incorporate values it would be difficult to reject, like learner centredness and autonomy. If open learning is the removal of institutional barriers is there any need to prove that it works, when there is so much evidence of the damage these barriers cause?

The problem is that this is not the goal of open learning, but one of the means it uses. Its goal, surely, is twofold. First, to increase rates of participation in education and training, especially among groups with low rates of participation hitherto; and second, to improve the quality and extent of learning achieved by those who do participate. Both goals relate to the achievement of efficiency and effectiveness of provision. While we may not need to be convinced of the desirability of the general goals, there is every need for evaluation at the level of particular examples of open learning precisely in order to find out whether barriers to learning have been removed, or at least lowered, and whether learning has in fact occurred. The arguments which justify evaluation of conventional provision apply with equal force to open learning provision. The fact that open learning is defined in terms of highly desirable goals does not mean that we no longer need to evaluate it *as a set of practices, differing quite widely according to the various contexts in which it occurs.*

At its most general level, evaluation is about finding out the effects of our own actions, so as to judge their value. Its importance for learning is that it is an essential technique for fine-tuning our own behaviour as teachers or trainers, so that the learner is able to learn or learn better from us or from the materials we prepare. Any successful teacher engages in informal evaluation: responding to the expressions of the group, listening to their conversation, taking note of the ideas that are still causing difficulty and so on. All these activities during routine contact with learners give a 'feel' for how things are going and will certainly affect the way the individual teaches. 'Responsiveness' is one of the determining characteristics of good teaching, but is only possible if we first have information about the learner and the learning to which we can respond.

The desirability of responsiveness applies with at least as much force to open learning, and means that the transaction between provider and learner is not completed by the improvement of access alone, even less by the sale of a set of materials There is a responsibility to check out the quality of the learning process thereafter. However this raises a problem particular to open learning, where it is often difficult to get hold of information about the learner, and therefore to be responsive, because much of the learning occurs as private study. Evaluation as a formal activity becomes more important therefore, because it is one of the few ways of finding out learners' reactions in order to tailor provision for a closer fit with their needs.

A second major justification for evaluating open learning stems from the fact that it is still an innovation and in the early stages of its development. Different models and systems are being tried out and providers need comparative evidence of their effectiveness. Regular evaluation can produce this evidence, and a means of learning why some things work better than others. There may be an irreducible element of trial and error, in the early stages of innovation, but evaluation can provide a structure for the process and prevent its being purely random.

Evaluation can also make a contribution to the effectiveness with which a programme is implemented, because it encourages those involved to think rather more about what they are trying to achieve and how to measure its success. These are key issues for the kind of evaluation this book is about, and also for successful project implementation. Evaluation is central to good management, though it has other purposes as well.

Evaluation is also essential for development, and open learning practitioners can learn from the best practices of some of their clients in industry and business of all kinds. Just as the most successful entrepreneurs are always following up good sales figures to check out customer needs, so open learning providers must continue to develop the quality of the service they provide. There may be a temptation to assume that sales figures tell the whole story: 'the customer buys it so it must be alright.' Unfortunately, buying a course or enrolling on a training programme does not lead automatically to learning and the transaction in open learning is not completed at the point of sale — it has only just begun. In the short term evaluation consumes resources, but in the long term, it contributes to satisfied customers and new developments.

Evaluation therefore is necessary to open learning because it is an essential component in the range of practices we establish so as to provide effective opportunities for learning. It is certainly possible to manage without it, but some of those who have are no longer 'in business'.

The findings of evaluation are also likely to suggest areas where the competence of practitioners needs to be developed. It can (and should) feed in to the in-service training or staff development work of organisations providing open learning. In the longer term also this developmental role of evaluation can enable us to build up a better understanding of the complex nature of barriers against learning. Many of these barriers are not so easily removed because they exist within the learner. Strang for example speaks of the 'hidden barriers' which exists in the form of inappropriate ideas of what learning is and how best to go about it. (Strang, 1987) The integration of evaluation into the learning process can help to identify some of the more intractable problems learners face, especially if they are encouraged to evaluate their own learning as they go about it (see chapter 3).

Last, and by no means least, evaluation may be unavoidable as a way of meeting requirements set by external bodies. The board of a company may demand proof that a new approach to training works. The College may ask its open learning unit for performance indicators to contribute to an educational audit of its activities. Corporate clients may want to see the success rate of previous cohorts of open learners, or to know what other training managers have said about the programme. Funding agencies may require that projects are evaluated, or that continued funding depends on some evidence of success.

The Training Commission (formerly the Manpower Services Commission, and probably the single largest funding source for open learning development) has recently emphasised the necessity of evaluation in the projects it funds, as an aspect both of accountability and effectiveness. In December 1987, the Commission launched a handbook for practitioners and users of open learning, titled 'Ensuring Quality in Open Learning'. The handbook incorporates a code of practice for the achievement of quality in open learning, in which the role of evaluation is central:

> *Quality in Open Learning from market research through to design, production, dissemination and suppport services — never arises automatically, just by accident or good fortune. It needs to be planned for and built into our systems. Hence this 'Handbook for Action' puts forward a Code of Practice, based on the quality systems of the most experienced providers and users of Open Learning. It should help all of us who are involved in Open Learning to evaluate and improve our own activities and those of others . . .*
>
> Manpower Services Commission (1987)

Summary

Summarising this section therefore, I have argued that evaluation of open learning is needed because:

— as with the provision of any learning opportunities, it is necessary to find out whether the means used have achieved their goal, and to prevent the danger of taken for granted assumptions about their effectiveness;

— it provides the basis for responsive and therefore learner-centred provision;

— it is integral to the improvement of quality in open learning which is still very much in the research and development phase;

— it has an important development role, not only for the quality of the learners' experience, but for the competence of practitioners and the programmes and courses offered by organisations;

— it contributes towards understanding of how people learn and in particular how to help adults learn while fulfilling other social and work roles for which they are responsible;

— it is an important mechanism for effective programme implementation and management and may be required by external bodies and clients.

What is evaluation?

In summarising the reasons for evaluation, I have suggested some of the different purposes it can have — helping to improve learning, finding out the effects of actions, understanding other people's perspectives, improving efficiency and management and offering 'proof' of the value of materials and services we have provided. Clearly I have been using evaluation to cover a very wide range of activities and before going further, I shall outline more clearly what I mean by evaluation in the context of this book. There is an extensive literature in educational evaluation which highlights differences among evaluators in the way evaluation is defined and even greater differences in how it is done (Jenkins, 1978). The definition I offer below is not intended to be universally applicable, but to provide a working definition of the kinds of activity and the purposes of evaluation which are the focus of this book.

A definition of evaluation

Evaluation is the collection, analysis and interpretation of information about any aspect of a programme of education and training, as part of a recognised process of judging its effectiveness, its efficiency and any other outcomes it may have.

This definition has a number of characteristics which require opening out in more detail, so that their implications are not missed.

• *inclusiveness:*
The definition means that activities nor normally thought of as evaluation — recording attendances, meeting local sponsors, interviewing tutors etc — *can* become part of one if so planned. It certainly includes all those activities called 'monitoring' which Lewis defines as — 'The critical examination of a scheme, or any part of a scheme, as it is running, checking the effectiveness of management procedures, learner support and learning materials.' (Lewis, 1985) He distinguishes between monitoring and evaluation in terms of the 'greater degree of detachment' implied by evaluation, and its being an event rather than a continuous activity, happening therefore at intervals during a course, or only at the end. Monitoring he defines as a practical activity, the aim of which is to put things right that are obviously going wrong. This resembles the distinction made below between formative and summative evaluation and underlines Lewis's point that evaluation and monitoring are often

used interchangeably. I have chosen to use a single term to cover the whole field of activity rather than several terms which can reify differences between activities that are rarely precisely delimited in practice. There are plenty of adjectives which can be used to qualify 'evaluation' and indicate more exactly what we mean — formative, summative, continuous, illuminative, goal based, and so on.

• *not synonymous with assessment*
One of the terms evaluation is *not* synonymous with is assessment, which is the procedure of assigning value to the learning achieved during and at the end of a course. Examination results and continuous assessment are of course very relevant data for most evaluative purposes because they are a measure of outcomes. Like most other indicators, however, they do not so much provide the answers as suggest the need for further information and explanation.

• *component activities*
Whatever form evaluation takes,it typically has three components — data collection, analysis, and interpretation. I use the term 'components' rather than 'stages' because they are often not distinct phases but overlapping, and in some approaches there may be several rounds of collection, analysis and interpretation where issues for evaluation become progressively more focused.

• *a planned activity, capable of being made public*
Although a very inclusive definition of evaluation has been proposed, the methods used must be deliberate and recorded if they are to count as part of an evaluation.

Routine monitoring, discussion and decision making can be harnessed to an evaluative exercise but only *if they are scheduled within an evaluation plan and their outcomes recorded.* Though much of the management of open learning involves the analysis and interpretation of information about how a programme is going, I would argue that this can not simply be re-labelled evaluation. It only becomes an evaluative activity if it has been integrated into an evaluation plan which, however provisional and generalised it may be, is known to others and assigns some role in the evaluation to this routine activity or data collection.

What distinguishes evaluation from other related activities is not just that judgements and opinions are made, but that they are seen to be made. *Evaluation is essentially a public act — not necessarily published or publishable, but open to inspection by an outsider and therefore capable of being made public.* Hence in Part III, stress is placed on the social arrangements for setting up an evaluation and on careful record keeping.

This is particularly important because evaluation can contribute to decisions which directly affect the actions of a number of individuals and groups. If the procedures and outcomes of evaluation are capable of being made public, it follows that there must be a deliberate decision to undertake an evaluation, however minimal, and a framework of actions and events planned.

- *Both intended and unintended effects*

The scope of evaluation is not limited to checks on the overt goals of a programme but can encompass any of its aspect and their effects. Equally, an evaluation does not have to be comprehensive, or even close to it; it can be legitimately focused on only a narrow selection of the possible issues provided this is made clear in the reporting and use of findings.

Different kinds of evaluation

I referred earlier to the variety of purposes which evaluation serves and which have generated a variety of traditions rather than a single tradition for evaluation. The subtlety of the distinctions between these different traditions is less important than an understanding of how the different approaches they use relate to the purposes for which evaluation has been undertaken.

Some of the purposes for which evaluation is commonly undertaken are as follows:

(a) measurement of achievement of objectives of a programme as a whole;
(b) judging the effectiveness of courses or materials;
(c) finding out what the inputs into a programme were — number of staff, number and content of contact hours, time spent by the learner, and so on;
(d) 'mapping' the perceptions of different participants – learners, tutors, trainers, managers etc;
(e) exploring the comparative effectiveness of different ways of providing the same service;
(f) finding out any unintended effects of a programme, whether on learners, clients or open learning staff;
(g) regular feedback on progress towards meeting programme goals;
(h) finding out the kinds of help learners need at different stages;
(i) exploring the factors which appear to affect the outcomes of a programme or service.

This is not a comprehensive list of purposes, nor are the individual items mutually exclusive. Taking items from the above list, for example, measuring the achievement of objectives of a programme as a whole (a) is likely to involve finding out what participants thought of it (d) and measuring inputs (c).

The development of different approaches to educational evaluation traces the effort to provide data about learning and processes of teaching which are richer and more informative than those provided by psychometric testing alone.

Tyler's 'Basic Principles of Curriculum and Instruction' (1949) was one of the earliest benchmarks here. It stressed instructional objectives (preferably expressed in behavioural terms) as the measure of student progress and thereby the worth of the programme. One of the limitations of this approach was its narrow focus on quantitative assessment of student achievement, and its over-simplification of the school process as the context in which most of this evaluation occurred. Subsequent approaches have picked up one or more of the perspectives which it ignores. Some evaluators have stressed the importance of subjective accounts of practitioners and learners as valid findings and seek to promote understanding of the programme, rather than to measure outcomes.

Others have linked evaluation very closely to decision making within the institution, focusing on specifying objectives and reviewing performance. This approach has also been criticised for its inward looking orientation and for an over-emphasis on intended effects. Evaluation should also explore outcomes in areas which the policy makers have ignored, or which are important to others. The effects of a programme may have wider and different reverberations than those predicted by the staff who implement it. One of the roles of evaluation is to remove the blinkers of those who are too close to a project to see some of its less obvious effects and implications.

These developments in evaluation generated much debate within the literature on educational evaluation about what should be its proper tasks and purposes. These arguments came to a head (in the UK at least) in a paper which drew together many similar approaches under the title of 'illuminative evaluation'. The authors of the paper, Parlett and Hamilton, challenged all approaches to educational evaluation which seek to bring research principles from the natural sciences into an arena of social interaction as in learning and teaching. Their charge against experimental controls, psychometric testing, the statistical manipulation of highly complex variables and dependence on quantitative assessment of learning, is that these methods are inappropriate for their subject matter and a missed opportunity. They ignore the social values which influence action within institutions of education and training and fail to illuminate the meaning of processes and events from the point of view of the key participants. They often remain remote from the decision making and development within institutions.

This critique of what Parlett and Hamilton refer to as the 'agricultural-botany paradigm' leads in to their outline of illuminative evaluation, which gives a greater role and status to qualitative evaluation. This offers a means of discovering competing interests among the various actors involved in institutional provision of education and training and of comprehending the complexity of the learning process.

I have included this reference to the differences of approach which exist within the field of evaluation not only to point out that there is no consensus around a 'best model' among the professionals, but also to hint at the variety of approaches and methods which are available. The aim is not to pick the winner from a league table but to emphasize that this variety exists, that there is no one right model, and that we can and should choose one or a combination of approaches appropriate to the purposes and resources available to us at the time.

The procedures of an evaluation should be designed therefore to satisfy within a particular timescale the local purposes for which it was set up, which will vary according to the course or programme being evaluated. But there is a more general distinction of purpose which applies to any evaluation, whatever its more specific goals, whether these are to do with materials development, course review or whatever. This is the distinction between formative and summative evaluation, and I shall explain what each involves more fully.

Formative and summative evaluation

Formative evaluation is concerned with the evaluation of progress towards achieving programme goals, during implementation. It typically answers the questions — 'how are we/they doing?' 'What should we be doing next?' Its aim is not to measure the effectiveness of a programme but to identify any changes it requires which will improve it, and make it more likely to achieve its goals eventually.

'Summative' evaluation is usually aimed at assessing the effectiveness of a programme on completion, and typically aims to answer the questions 'Were aims achieved?', 'Was it worth doing?', 'Is it worth continuing?' Formative evaluation focusses on how well goals are being achieved rather than whether they were the right ones in the first place. One of the by-products of formative evaluation though is (often) heightened goal awareness among practitioners, and one should see formative and summative evaluation as occupying different positions along a spectrum, rather than as categorically distinct. (Figure 1)

Although there is no rigid division between formative and

summative evaluation in relation to the kinds of data and data collection methods that are used, each does place very different constraints on the evaluator. In a summative evaluation, for example, it matters very much whether feedback comes from a sample truly representative of the total population of a course or package. If we wish to make relatively final judgements about outcomes, rather than provisional, temporary ones, there is much greater pressure to provide data which are comprehensive and reliable according to each of the perspectives of the different decision makers involved. They may be one reason why summative evaluation is often a large-scale and costly exercise.

Figure 1.1

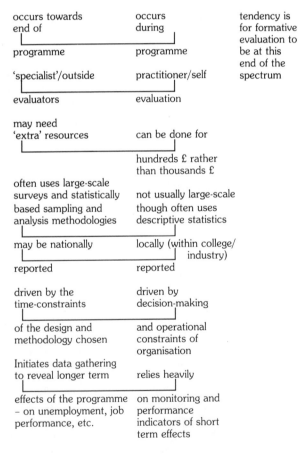

| tendency is for summative evaluation to be at this end of the spectrum | occurs towards end of | occurs during | tendency is for formative evaluation to be at this end of the spectrum |

programme — programme

'specialist'/outside — practitioner/self

evaluators — evaluation

may need 'extra' resources — can be done for

hundreds £ rather than thousands £

often uses large-scale surveys and statistically based sampling and analysis methodologies — not usually large-scale though often uses descriptive statistics

may be nationally — locally (within college/industry)

reported — reported

driven by the time-constraints — driven by decision-making

of the design and methodology chosen — and operational constraints of organisation

Initiates data gathering to reveal longer term — relies heavily

effects of the programme – on unemployment, job performance, etc. — on monitoring and performance indicators of short term effects

Formative evaluation may or may not be costly, but the key difference from summative evaluation is that it should feed into, and thus help to shape, subsequent practice. Findings are not meant to be definitive but indicative; to provide preliminary indications of progress or problems which we can use (along with other inputs) to decide on appropriate action in response. It is the immediacy of the impact on action which makes formative evaluation of interest to practitioners on a day to day basis. Summative evaluations can be enormously interesting and influential but they are not something that most practitioners can engage in directly, on a regular basis. For this reason, it is formative evaluation I have in mind when advocating that practitioners involve themselves directly in evaluating their own work.

Before turning to the next chapter for a fuller account of what practitioner evaluation might mean, there are a number of issues arising from what I have just said which need comment.

These issues have generated a large literature, which the interested reader may follow up by looking at the further reading suggested at the end of this chapter. However, some of the most important need to be clarified because this book incorporates a particular view in relation to them. They can be summarised in the form of a number of questions:

How should evaluators negotiate the trade-off between feeding into decision making versus methodological purity?

Should evaluation incorporate value judgements or only the evidence on which others may make such judgements?

Who should evaluate whom? Can practitioners be sufficiently objective about their own work to be relied on as evaluators?

How systematic and 'scientific' should data collection methods be? Are qualitative accounts of events and attitudes valid material for evaluation?

Where does monitoring end and evaluation begin? What's the difference between evaluation and research?

The debates around these issues are not easily resolved — perhaps they are irresolvable — and I do not claim to have found 'solutions' to the very real problems behind them. My answers are in the form of a number of 'working resolutions' of these debates, which I have listed in a series of points below:

— Much of what this book is concerned with is *formative evaluation*, the purpose of which is to modify and improve programmes while they are running, and thus must feed into decision-making schedules. This kind of evaluation is an essential mechanism for improving quality in open learning and (it is argued) needs to be a regular and integral component in its provision. It has to be undertaken by practitioners, even if specialists are also involved, on occasion, or as collaborators.

— In the likely event that specialist evaluators will not be available, regular formative evaluation will only happen if practitioners themselves are committed to doing it. Inevitably therefore, they will be involved in many instances in both data collection and in making judgements based on that data.

— Some aspects of data collection must be systematic and reliable, otherwise the goals of providing accurate baseline information will not be achieved. However, 'openness' in data collection methods is at least as important as 'scientific' standards for practitioner evaluators. The fact that data are being collected should be made clear to those involved and the status of the findings should be asserted whenever they are published or made use of. For example, if a survey is returned by only 20% of those surveyed, it should be emphasised that information exists for a minority of the population/sample, 80% of whom chose not to return the questionnaire. Similarly, when comments or feedback are reported, it should always be clear who is saying what and in what circumstances. For example, when tutors collect the opinions of those who are regular attenders, we must be aware that these are the comments of a particular sub-set and a very different picture might come out of a more representative canvass of opinion. Neither quantitative nor qualitative data can be 'taken on trust', they have different strengths and weaknesses and neither is intrinsically 'more valid' than the other.

— Monitoring provides much essential data from which value judgements may be formed. It is perhaps the single most important method for formative evaluation and is often crucial for summative evaluation (i.e. end of programme evaluations which review outcomes and assess what has been achieved overall). Monitoring is *one* of the components of evaluation.

— Some evaluations may be very similar to research, or may feed into it. If there is an essential difference however, it is that research focuses on the exploration of issues or hypotheses selected by the researcher, manifested variously in different forms and learning contexts. Evaluation accepts as given a particular context and its learning forms, and often the particular issues of inquiry.

— Practitioners need not work in isolation. They can collaborate with others whose professional interests are not directly affected by the outcomes of the evaluation. Outsiders free of the taint of bias can advise and act as a reminder of 'external' standards and audiences. No evaluator (professional or otherwise) and no audience can claim absolute neutrality, and a professional evaluator may have perspectives or views which are as narrow as some practitioners.

Nonetheless, practitioners are increasingly required to be accountable — to 'prove' their programme's effectiveness, or provide performance indicators of various kinds. They need therefore to develop some of the skills of the evaluator, and to be familiar with some evaluative tools and strategies which suit their purposes. They may not achieve complete objectivity — who does anyway, and how would we know? The outsider, or the client, is still free to question or to take issue with the results of an evaluation which has been carefully recorded and reported, and is thus *open for inspection*.

Conclusion

Having argued for the importance of evaluation in open learning I defined evaluation and drew attention to a number of its features which are important. Evaluation is characterized by the distinctive activities of data collection, analysis and interpretation and can also make use of existing activities in administration and management if these are specifically integrated within an evaluation plan. Evaluation is a public process which should be open to in spection, not least by those directly involved or affected by it.

Evaluation can be undertaken to meet very different purposes and this is one of the reasons for the variety of approaches in the way it is implemented. One of the most important distinctions here is that of formative versus summative evaluation. The kind of evaluation which practitionrers are likely to find most useful on a day to day basis is formative, because as it name suggests, it contributes to the formation of practice, providing evidence during programme or course implementation which can be fed back into practice. This need not exclude some aspects of summative evaluation because data collected *during* a programme can be relevant to an account of its outcomes on completion. Some kinds of summative evaluation however involve very large-scale data collection which are beyond the usual means of most practitioners in open learning, though their findings may be of use when they are available.

Further reading

Curriculum Evaluation (1982) Units 19, 20 and 21 of Open University Course E203 Curriculum Design and Development, Milton Keynes.

Provides an excellent introduction to the different contexts in which evaluation is used, and an outline of six alternative models of evaluation.

Ruddock, R. (1981) *Evaluation: A Consideration of Principles and Methods*. Manchester Monographs 18. Dept. of Adult and Higher Educatin, The University, Manchester M13 9PL.

An overview of a large number of evaluation methods, including participant observation, life histories, action research, participatory research, critical incidents as well as interviewing and surveys.

Evaluation in Action: a journal of evaluation and appraisal for further, higher and professional education, edited by Roy Cox and Mike O'Neil, available from the Society for Research into Higher Education. Published in the Spring and Winter. 'The aim of the journal is to foster experience and idea exchange among practitioners in this field. "Evaluation" is to be interpreted broadly as including appraisal of courses, individuals, departments, institutions, teaching-learning methods and the assessment of student learning.'

Ensuring Quality in Open Learning: A Handbook for Action. Produced by the Manpower Services Commission, Sheffield.

'The Quality Handbook represents the accumulated experience of a good number of experts in industry and education who have successfully operated quality open learning systems. These include the Open University, National Extension College, WH Smith, ICI and others . . . Observance of the Quality Handbook is voluntary, but it has been developed for open learning based on the requirements of the UK National Quality Management Standard — BS5750.'

Scottish Training and Support Unit (1986) *Training Course in Evaluating Open Learning Schemes*. Dundee College of Education, Gardyne Road, Broughty Ferry, Dundee DD5 1NY.

A course offered by SCOTTSU, incorporating five tutor assessed assignments. Designed to enable a practitioner to choose appropriate methods for the evaluation of the teaching/learning and operational aspects of an open learning course. Focuses on materials, tutoring and administration and has a good section on sources of information. A very good introduction for the practitioner.

Open Learning. A journal co-produced by the Open University and Longman Group UK Limited. Appears three times annually, in February, June and November. The Editorial Group (based in the Open University) draws on a wide range of expertise in training as well as education, and aims to include articles of both a theoretical and practical nature, whether from Britain or elsewhere. A valuable source of accounts of experience, some of which include evaluative elements.

Tavistock Institute of Human Relations (1988) *Open Tech Programme Final Development Review Report.* Available from the Tavistock Institute, 129 Belsize Lane, London.
The Tavistock Institute carried out an independent evaluation of the MSC funded Open Tech Programme. This report describes the origins of the programme, the various projects and their performance and survival, relations with MSC and the impact on LEA provision and users of OTP training — organisations and individuals.
Hamilton, D., Macdonald, B., King, C., Jenkins, D., Parlett, M., (1977) editors. *Beyond the Numbers Game: A Reader in Educational Evaluation* Macmilan, UK.
An immensely thorough and readable account of evaluation in education with chapters on illuminative evaluation, the evaluation of learning objectives, formative and summative evaluation, case study and fieldwork. Considers in depth the issues raised at the end of this chapter.

2 Evaluation for practitioners

Main themes: *Who are the practitioners in open learning and what are the implications for evaluation?. Who is practitioner evaluation for? Is there any difference between evaluating open learning and conventional learning? Are there any examples of evaluation for practitioners? Case Studies A to E.*

Practitioners in open learning

Thus far I have referred only very generally to 'practitioners' in open learning, but there are of course several different kinds of practitioner and this has important implications for evaluation. Open learning is growing so rapidly that it would be unrealistic to attempt to produce a comprehensive list of practitioner titles. Those listed in figure 1 are only an indication of the range of organisations using open learning and the variety of staff with an open learning responsibility, either as a full-time requirement or as part of other responsibilities.

Figure 1 points towards a number of general points about the relationship between practitioners and evaluation. First, each has a different role in open learning provision and offers a different perspective from which to contribute to an evaluation. The receptionist is likely to be aware of some aspects important for learners but which they might consider too trivial or too difficult to mention to a manager or tutor – the difficulty of using public transport to get to a centre, the fact that one tutor explains things better than another, or always returns assignments quicker, the lack of any canteen facilities in the evenings, and so on. These are important points which might be missed in an evaluation determined solely by the manager's perspective.

Similarly tutors and trainers have unique insights into how the learner has used a course or training programme, but they lack the opportunity the supervisor has to observe whether learning is being applied to the job in hand. Each of these perspectives has an important insight into different facets of the learner's experience and all are necessary to build (as near as possible) a complete picture.

Figure 2.1: Practitioners in open learning

ORGANISATION	POSSIBLE PRACTITIONER TITLES/OCCUPATIONS
1.– A department in a polytechnic, F.E. college or university	Lecturer as tutor and counsellor, lecturer as author, administrator, head of department or school, counsellor, course co-ordinator (esp. on vocational preparation courses)
2.– An industrial concern	Training manager, trainer, supervisor, mentor (may or may not be a subject expert, but able to support the learner by offering friendship, encouragement and understanding of the applicability of training to the workplace and employment more generally)
3.– An Accredited Staff Training Centre	Staff Training Co-ordinator, Staff Tutor, Administrator
4.– Training Commission Local Area Office	Area Manager, Programme Managers, Programme Assessors (disseminate open learning7
5.– Organisation producing open learning materials (may be combined with 6)	Manager, author, administrator, marketing manager
6.– Organisation delivering open learning (may be combined with 5)	Manager, receptionist, tutor/trainer, administrator, counsellor
7.– Managing Agencies (YTS, JTS, Community Programme)	Manager, Placement Monitoring Officer, Staff Trainer, Guidance Officer
8.– Open Access Centre	Manager, Receptionist, Administrator, part-time tutors

Second, each of these practitioners needs evaluation for different purposes. The author wants evaluation to suggest which parts of the materials ought to be revised, and why. The tutor wants to know if her comments on the assignment are read by learners and help improve their understanding. The trainer needs to know whether trainees are better at their jobs as well as successful in course work. If evaluation is to be useful in practice, it must be designed from the outset to meet the varied demands of each of the practitioners involved.

The third point derives from this. The work tasks of practitioners in open learning are complementary, but the demands they make on evaluation represent a call on resources that it may not always be possible to meet. Even if there is consensus about what should be evaluated, it may be necessary to set priorities in order to keep within budget. The existence of competing interests may be much more clear if there are externally imposed demands for evidence of outcomes and performance data. The request for data may be entirely reasonable, but still make additional demands on staff which mean that some of the requirements for evaluation that practitioners feel would be desirable cannot be met.

This analysis poses two very important questions which need an answer before we can continue: Who is evaluation for? Is evaluating open learning different from evaluating conventional provision? In answering these questions some important implications for evaluation will be made clearer.

Who is practitioner evaluation for?

Practitioner evaluation is for practitioners and learners. The answer comes easily but is perhaps less straightforward than it looks. Take practitioners first.

Practitioners as we have seen are a varied group, in relation to their functions in open learning. They also occupy positions of different status within organisations that are hierarchically organised. Because evaluation is associated with quality control and performance review, it may be seen as a sub-set of managerial responsibilities. It may not be directly stated as such, but in these circumstances evaluation is likely to be undertaken for management *only*, very tightly controlled perhaps by a manager. Managers do have legitimate demands for evaluation, and these are likely to be related to his or her perceptions of what is in the interest of the users of the service to which each of the practitioners contributes.

However, this in itself is not the problem so much as the tendency for evaluation to become *only* a tool for management, narrowed down to issues of efficiency and output and remote from the learning process. Whereas, as we have seen, evaluation is by no means a restricted set of practices and need not be focused on a narrow view of what the programme is all about. We need to open out a broad view of evaluation and draw on as many of the existing evaluative approaches as we can, and recognise that *it is for tutors, counsellors, receptionists — all the practitioners involved — as well as for managers*. This has important implications for the way open learning evaluation is organised. If all practitioners are to make an effective contribution, a team approach is necessary, bringing people together from different areas of an organisation, and probably cutting across hierarchical boundaries. This can be a valuable support to team building within an organisation and can help to generate a commitment to effective learning. (Case study A at the end of the chapter illustrates the value of a team approach, and the idea is further developed in chapter 7.)

Having said that, do we also need to specify that evaluation should also be for learners as well? Can we assume that what is in the interests of practitioners will also be in the interests of learners? To the extent that all practitioners are concerned to provide a better service for the learner, I think we can make that assumption. Any practitioner cynically unconcerned about the quality of the learner's experience is unlikely to be reading this book. However there are differences of interest between learners as individuals and practitioners as a group. The practitioner has a future perspective on quality of service and can use evaluation as a tool for making improvements to the way things are done in future.

The learner's perspective is obviously much more focused on the here and now, and their own progress and problems. While not unconcerned about quality in the long term, they are not in a position to postpone to some future date finding solutions to their problems. Practitioners need to set up forms of evaluation which will provide very early indication of any concerns and anxiety. It is very difficult to 'redeem' completely the negative experience of learners in the first part of a course. The sooner appropriate action is taken, the better.

In addition, practitioners can encourage learners to engage in a collaborative process of evaluation of the learning as it is taking place. This will involve the learner in a form of *self-evaluation*, as well as of the effectiveness of course materials or tutors. There may be lessons for what the learner should do in future, as well as for the organisers of the programme. This kind of evaluation is developed further in chapter 3 and is particularly important for the encouragement of independence in learning.

Evaluating open learning versus conventional provision

In chapter 1 a definition was offered of evaluation applicable both to open and conventional learning. There are generic processes in evaluation to do with goal setting, design, data collection and analysis, and the similarities are greater than the differences when we turn from conventional provision to applying them in open learning.

There is also fundamental similarity in what is being evaluated — the quality of learning, the effectiveness of materials and services provided, the suitability of courses for the needs of the area or the population served. But there are differences, some deriving from the nature of open learning itself, others more from the features of practitioner evaluation outlined above. I shall take each in turn.

Less open to inspection?

Open learning very often requires the learner to study independently of a teacher, very often in the form of private study at home. On the whole we cannot observe this process, though we might notice some of its effects on questions the learner asks, or in tests or assignments. This is very different from a course which is defined in terms of attendance of a series of classes, which can be observed and evaluated directly.

Conversely, some aspects of teaching may be very much more open to inspection than in conventional provision. Instead of teaching a series of classes open only to learners, the author of open learning courses writes material which anyone can buy and read. The Open University broadcasts course material on national networks and these are open to evaluation by experts in the field, as well as by learners. The tutor's marking of assignments takes the form of a written grade and comments, which can be made available to other practitioners as well as to the learner.

More to be evaluated

Open learning involves both a wide range of practitioner roles, and diversification of the conventional teaching roles of staff involved. In conventional provision, there is one key figure — the lecturer, teacher, or trainer. Open learning does not necessarily diminish the role of this key figure, but it changes it and it increases the importance of other staff roles. From the learner's point of view, it is just as important that she chooses the right course as that the course should be a good one. Course choice advice is likely to come from a receptionist or administrator, perhaps even a counsellor, but probably not from a tutor. Similarly the effectiveness of the tutor in facilitating learning is very much dependent on the quality of the course author's work.

In brief, successful open learning requires a team effort and each of the inputs into the learner's experience is important. In this sense, there is more to be evaluated because there is a more diverse range of inputs.

There is also more to be evaluated in that individuals have a greater degree of choice about *how* they learn. In conventional learning, the evaluator can start with a class, lecture or training programme and assume that, for the majority, this defines 'the course'. In open learning, the learner has (more or less) freedom to define their own course, and is free to attend or use the facilities offered, at times which suit them. They may decide not to take up the facilities offered, they may use all of the materials or only part of them. If there is any assessment or examination, it is up to them whether they take it. These represent different inputs on the part of learners, and it is the task of evaluation to map these inputs, as it is to map those which the organisation makes.

Different criteria for success?

Open learning is bringing back into learning individuals and groups who would not have participated in conventional provision. Their reasons for taking an open learning course are often very much wider than the narrow goal of certification as a preparation for employment. Some learners will already be in employment, perhaps sponsored by an employer, whose sponsorship depends on the learner passing an end of course examination. Others in the same group might not need to pass the examination, and elect only to complete the course to their own satisfaction. Each of these individual decisions can be represented statistically in the form of aggregate data on drop-out, course completion, examination completion, examination passes and so on. The problem comes in interpreting the data, particularly if it is presented comparatively with the results of conventional provision. Is it legitimate even to compare two very different approaches?

Legitimate or not, such comparisons are made, and it is clear that the statistics themselves cannot be left to 'tell their own story'. If there is no assessment involved, it may not be possible even to turn to a single statistic such as percentage pass rate to provide a quick (and over simple) criterion of success. Much more detailed comparative data are needed, beginning with two areas which can be derived from what has just been said.

First, data should be provided on the demographic characteristics of learners, including educational qualifications. Most forms of conventional provision exclude all those who have not already attained qualifications which provide a good basis for the course applied for. Open learning very often has a high proportion of learners who would be seen as under-prepared, or at best, not conventionally qualified for the course they are about to take. From the perspective of conventional provision, examination passes achieved by this group could be seen as having more 'value added', because of a less advantaged starting position.

Second, data on intentions and outcomes other than pass rates are necessary to provide a context and other criteria of success. If 10% of learners do not wish to take an end of course examination, this should be reflected in the statistics for examination passes. Where learners drop out in order to take up a job, or move on to other course work, this can also be included.

It may also be difficult for open learning to provide performance data which are taken for granted in conventional provision. One example will suffice. Enrolling for a conventional course is straightforward. The enquirer either enrols and becomes a 'student/

trainee', or does not and drops out of the picture. In open learning, it may be possible to participate in several different ways, for some of which the term 'student' would be misleading. The user may purchase a pack of materials from a provider like the Birmingham Open Learning Development Unit, or from the Open University, and choose not to buy tutorial support or assessment in addition. In the Open University's Community Education Sector, materials have been produced for professionals to use with groups, and in this way 'reached' thousands of users — but it would surely be misleading to include group members in a total figure of 'students enrolled'. The University has had to distinguish between these different forms of participation by defining a new set of categories. In addition to registered students, the OU's Health Education programme has 'sponsored place students', 'purchasers of study packs', 'purchasers of discussion packs', 'number of professional/ para-professional users' and book sales. Even where learners do formally enrol on a course, they may decide to drop out before final fee payment, so that we have to distinguish between them and those who do effectively embark on the full programme.

Extra mural departments of Universities engaged in outreach work may not be trying to bring learners in to the institution, but to take services out to the learners in their communities. Perhaps the idea of 'de-registered students' conveys the paradox of opening up provision to more people without necessarily increasing numbers of official students.

A team approach to organisation

I have argued that open learning requires even more than conventional provision, a team effort. It involves a variety of contributions from a number of different practitioners, all of whom should include evaluation within their responsibilities. Practitioners will be involved in different ways in evaluation, some with a heavier responsibility than others. But insofar as all practitioners share responsibility for the quality of open learning offered, so all should be directly involved in its evaluation. It is for this reason that chapter 7 in Part III emphasises the value of a planning group composed of all staff involved, irrespective of status, to design and co-ordinate evaluation from the beginning.

In this respect, evaluation for practitioners should differ from an audit (see chapter 7) which is a management tool, however creatively applied. Evaluation is *a collective practice*, not a tool used by the top level of a hierarchy to appraise the lower levels in the hierarchy. The findings of an evaluation are as likely to point towards the failures of management as they are to poorly designed materials or inadequate counselling — as likely that is, provided that *all practitioners have been given an equal opportunity to decide what they want evaluation for and the findings they need.*

Evaluation will only achieve its potential for generating a continuing responsiveness to the learner and continuing improvement to practice, if it is perceived as *a resource in the interests of all staff and learners on the programme, and if it occurs through consultative and democratic procedures.*

Summary

Although the component activities of evaluation involve the same principles whether applied to conventional or open learning, there are some important differences in evaluating open learning. Some aspects of the learning may be inaccessible for the evaluator, whereas some aspects of provision are *more* open to inspection than is the case in conventional teaching. There is more to be evaluated, because of the flexibility allowed the learner and the variety and range of inputs by a number of different practitioners. The criteria for success in open learning may be different from conventional provision, and in some respects, less easy to measure. And the importance of a team effort in the provision of open learning should be reflected to some extent in the organisation of evaluation. Evaluation should be a collective practice, perceived as a resource in the interests of all staff and learners and implemented through consultative and democratic procedures.

Case studies of evaluation for practitioners

The second half of this chapter includes case studies of evaluation which has been, or is being undertaken by practitioners themselves. Such practical examples are an essential adjunct to general description in order to find out what the author 'really means'.

A glance at the further reading list will show that others have also recognised the desirability of regular evaluation tied to practice, and two initiatives deserve special mention. The Open Tech programme was evaluated up to the end of 1987 by the Tavistock Institute of Human Relations, which also produced a guide to self-evaluation for open learning projects. The checklist of issues it includes is extremely thorough and a very useful aide memoire for any project.

More recently the Training Commission launched its code of practice of open learning providers which takes the form of a loose leaf file: 'Ensuring Quality in Open Learning: A Handbook for Action'. It is intended for three main users — producers and deliverers of open learning, corporate sponsors and individual learners — and each sub-section has important items on evaluation.

The code of practice for deliverers of open learning for example, includes six main items — attracting clients, clarifying client needs, choosing a package, agreeing the support system, operating the system, *evaluating and improving*. Under 'evaluation' the code has two injunctions for providers which suggest an approach to evaluation similar to that outlined here:

— Evaluate the operation and outcomes of the programme, both while it is in progress and when it is completed.
— Use the results of the evaluation both to improve your own support services and to give feedback to Producers about the effectiveness of their learning materials and any unexpected problems (or opportunities), that may have become apparent while using them.

(Training Commission, 1987)

The action checklists for corporate sponsors and individuals are also strongly evaluative in nature because the aim is to help them evaluate the Producers and/or Deliverers, and their future needs. Corporate sponsors are asked, for example:

How will you evaluate Open Learning?
By 'evaluation' we mean observing the effects of Open Learning, judging the extent to which they are good or bad, and deciding what (if anything) needs doing about them. There are three ways in which you may find it useful to evaluate your Open Learning scheme:
1.   *In-Programme* evaluation of each programme while it is in operation — with a view to improving its effectiveness for those Learners (and others) *currently* working on it.
2.   *End of Programme* evaluation of the effects and effectiveness of the programme — in order to improve it for the benefit of people working on *future* runs of that programme.
3.   *Long-term* evaluation of Open Learning programmes *in general*, and of your success and failures in operating them.
TC1987, Action Guides for Corporate Sponsors p.D25

The code of practice provides an essential framework for the improvement of quality in open learning; together with the items listed in Further Reading at the end of this chapter, it provides essential reference material for any team of practitioner evaluators. The case studies which conclude this chapter are essential reading of a different kind. They do not pretend to provide a blue print or a model approach; like politics, they offer an art of the possible, not perfection. These are reports of practice which help to make the general ideas of these first two chapters more concrete and which provide encouraging examples of practitioners who are already undertaking evaluation of the kind being advocated.

CASE STUDY A:
The OPTIS evaluation of open learning in two year YTS

This is an interesting example of evaluation led by an organisation specialising mainly in the production of open learning materials, working in collaboration with deliverers of the Youth Training Scheme (YTS). The development phase especially offers a useful example of evaluation generated directly by practitioners.

The Training Commission (formerly Manpower Services Commission) began funding in April 1987 for a two year project based in the Oxfordshire Project for Training Instructors and Supervisors (OPTIS). The aims of the evaluation phase of the project are to investigate four main issues:

1. The extent of use of open learning in two year YTS
2. How open learning has been integrated as a training strategy
3. How open learning has been used in support of other forms of training
4. The nature of the support open learning provides.

The Project Manager is Hilary Read, based at OPTIS but leading a management team whose members are open learning practitioners from three institutions — The Gwent Staff Training Centre, the Lincoln Accredited Training Centre and Surrey University Department of Education (where questionnaire analysis will be undertaken by I. Haffendon).

The first phase is survey based, with questionnaires distributed to two key organisations in YTS.

(a) Managing Agents of YTS schemes — 1,400
3 different questionnaires, designed for each of the key participants: manager, trainer, trainee.
(b) Accredited Training Centres — 55
(responsible for providing training for Managing Agent staff).

During 1988 the development phase of the project will be established. The results of the survey will be used to inform and communicate good practice to organisations involved in YTS, through seminars and workshops.

The main aim of the project involves a materials development exercise which is being piloted in order to develop workable methods for helping YTS supervisors to develop materials for their own schemes. There is still a need for training material tailored specifically to the requirements (both content and level) of YTS Schemes. The aim is to meet this need by helping schemes write their own material, which will subsequently be edited and produced at OPTIS. Any scheme can then buy copies of the materials, if they met their needs at the time. This approach is being piloted in Gwent, Lincolnshire and Oxford (and OPTIS itself).

At each location there will be a team working with 2 YTS schemes each on the production of materials for the schemes' trainees, using guidelines on writing materials, provided by OPTIS. Each scheme will meet together to evaluate its own progress on three occasions, in the form of a workshop. The project will be introduced at the first workshop, and the second and third workshops will be used to review progress, during and at the end of the pilot. Representatives from each team will meet between workshops I and II to ensure uniformity and to compare outcomes from the schemes at this particular stage. There will be a fourth final workshop bringing together all three teams for an overview. Trainees using the materials will also be interviewed. One of the staff members of the Gwent scheme will act as co-ordinating evaluator, helping to structure workshops, analyse feedback and design the question formats used in the evaluation. This role will be carried out by Eddy Knasel, whose evaluation design is included below. From his description it is clear that this is formative evaluation and that practitioners in each scheme will be engaged in a process of collaborative self evaluation. There will also be direct feedback from trainees.

Plan for the Evaluation Element of the Development Phase of the Project (by E. Knasel)

'The key concern of the "evaluation" element of the development phase is to ensure that the project gains the maximum amount of relevant information from the process, ensuring that the materials generation model derived from this phase is both effective and replicable.

'The approach will be to ensure that certain standard pieces of information are obtained from each of the development workshops, including both flip-chart generated material and a formal questionnaire to be completed by pilot schemes in conjunction with Workshop Three. As "evaluator" I shall attend a selection of the workshops to gain a "feel" for the data and to provide an element of standardisation across the three workshop teams. I shall also make a small number of visits to the pilot schemes themselves to make direct contact with trainees so that their views on the materials can be taken into account.'

The main tasks in the evaluation process will therefore be:

- **Flip-charts.** It is important that certain flip-charts from each workshop are fed back to me. From Workshop One the most important ones will be concerned with initial Hopes and Fears and with the workshop closing review process. This will record participants'reactions to the project model which should prove helpful both in refining the model and in planning future staff development elements linked to the project. Similar considerations will apply to Workshop Two — from which it will be necessary to obtain each scheme's detailed implementation Finally it will still be helpful to obtain flip-charts from Workshop Three to augment the information obtained from the questionnaires — note that this flip-chart data is more likely to reflect group consensus and discussion than will the questionnaires. Both kinds of data will be important.

• **Issues/problems/solutions booklets.** These should effectively be blank booklets which will be distributed to participants during Workshop One with the intention that individuals can use them as a diary of their involvement with the project. The potential value is that these booklets should give us some information on the participant's involvement between workshops.

• **Questionnaire.** The intention is that the questionnaire should be sent to participants about a week before they take part in Workshop Three. They should bring it with them (completed!) to the workshop and there should be scope within the questionnaire for participants to record any changes they may wish to make to their responses as a result of workshop discussions.

The Questionnaire will be very closely linked to Workshop Three and I shall produce the first draft of it in collaboration with colleagues in the Gwent project team working on the design of this workshop.

• **The 'peripatetic evaluator' role.** The intention is that I should attend a selection of the workshops as this should help in making the best sense of the data collected and – by choosing workshops in each of the three areas – should help in ensuring that the three teams are working along the same general lines. I propose sitting-in on at least one Workshop One, one or two Workshop Twos and three Workshop Threes.

• **Scheme visits.** The idea here is to talk to trainees, using some standard questions, about their experiences of using the materials. These visits could occur either just before or quite shortly after Workshop Three. Again I propose visiting at least three schemes chosen for their diversity.

• **Review workshop for teams.** The objective is to hold a structured workshop bringing together the three project teams so that they can share their learning from this phase of the project. This meeting will provide an opportunity to agree the content and format of the evaluation report and form basis for planning the next phase of the project.

The outcome of this process of formative evaluation will be an improved set of guidelines for materials production by YTS schemes and better procedures for the agencies leading and supporting the exercise.

> Further information from:
> Hilary Reed,
> Oxfordshire Project for the Training of Instructors and Supervisors
> Optis House
> Cricket Road
> Cowley
> Oxford OX4 3DW

CASE STUDY B:
Programme review in YTS, and a trainee centred programme review team

The procedures the MSC has introduced for the achievement of 'Approved Training Organization' status by YTS Managing Agents, require a team approach to evaluation and the establishment of regular systems of monitoring and evaluation by practitioners. Sumlock Calculating Services Ltd is using a particularly interesting approach, based directly on trainee involvement.

In 1985 the Youth Training Scheme (YTS) moved from a one year to a two year programme. In 1986 Manpower Services Commission launched ROTA — Review of Training Activities — with the aim of reviewing and improving the quality with which YTS is being delivered by Managing Agents. All existing Managing Agencies delivering YTS, and new applicants, must carry out a ROTA process according to guidelines provided by the MSC. Each YTS Managing Agency is assigned a Programme Assessor (who is a member of staff in the local MSC Area Office) who spends three months with the staff in the Agency, evaluating the scheme according to 10 criteria:

1. Arranging a two year programme —
    Once running, the programme should be able to demonstrate

    • trainee awareness of the terms, conditions and entitlements which apply

- suitability of individual training plans (taking account of trainee needs through induction and assessment)
- trainee progress in acquiring competence objectives and in preparing for suitable vocational qualifications.

2. Previous record in training —
   Evidence that previous experience is satisfactory

3. Resources of the organisation —
   Sufficient to enable satisfactory delivery of training, especially through

   - monitoring of and liaising with all work experience and training providers, on and off-the-job
   - formal review and guidance with each trainee at least quarterly
   - involvement of trainees in agreeing future training activities
   - maintaining acceptable group sizes.

4. Competence of staff —
   Adherence to MSC Code of Practice on selection, briefing and development of staff employed by the scheme.

5. Premises and equipment —
   satisfactory and safe for the type of training and accessible to the trainees.

6. Assessment of trainees —
   regular and consistent assessment on and off-the-job, of trainee progress towards competence objectives.

7. Effective programme review —
   Adherence to MSC Code of Practice (see below)

8. A positive commitment to equal opportunities —
   In advertising, recruitment and during training

9. A positive commitment to health and safety —
   With reference to all training locations and work practices of the programme

10. Financial viability
    Including the use of effective financial systems.

At the end of the three month's review, Managing Agencies apply for ATO Status. Completely unsatisfactory agencies are refused, and the Scheme is closed. Others are either awarded ATO Status outright, or given provisional status for six months, during which they are given support by their local Accredited Staff Training Centre and MSC Area Office, to remedy deficiencies identified in the Review. At the end of the six months, the ROTA is repeated and the Scheme is either awarded ATP status or closed down.

More details can be provided on this process by contacting any YTS Managing Agency.

The seventh listed criterion in the ROTA process is of particular interest here because it requires that evaluation becomes a regular feature of the Managing Agency's work after ROTA has been completed. This was the criterion that most schemes had to put in the most new effort to achieve, since many were already meeting most of the other criteria set. The code of practice introduced by the MSC here was as follows:

Programme Review in YTS
A Code of Practice

1. Designing a training programme is not a once and for all activity. Trainees, trainers and circumstances change. So do training techniques and industrial requirements. A mark of a proficient training organisation is that it keeps its training programmes under review, and changes them in response to identified internal weaknesses or external changes. For this reason MSC, in awarding the status of Approved Training Organisation to providers of YTS, will want to be satisfied that the organisation has mechanisms for reviewing its own operations, and for instituting changes to programme design which reviews of programmes suggest.

2. This code of practice details the main features which MSC would expect to see in an organisation which was undertaking serious review of its own programmes. These features, which may be complementary to any other monitoring process in operation, are as follows:

A structure for bringing together, at regular intervals, representatives of the main parties involved in training.

Many providers have instituted a 'Programme Review Team'. The title does not matter. What is important is that those most closely involved with the operation of the scheme should come together to review its operation. Key contributors will include:

- *scheme leader;*
- *one or more trainees (normally elected by trainees generally);*
- *one or more representatives of those immediately concerned with providing and supervising work experience;*
- *one or more representatives of those providing off-the-job training;*
- *representatives of appropriate and recognised trade unions.*

In addition MSC and Careers Service representatives will also be able to make a useful contribution.

It is unlikely that such teams will be able adequately to influence the development of the programme unless they meet at least three times a year.

Such teams would be expected to discuss:
• feedback about the operation of the programme to date (not only in terms of trainee achievements, but also in terms of recruitment targets, particularly monitoring equal opportunities policies);
• plans for future development.

Methods for gathering information about the operation of the programme and its results.

To review progress one needs information. Providers will need to establish mechanisms, for example, to gather information on trainee destinations after training, trainee views on certain elements of training, employer views on the relevance of training etc. One can expect that the focus for investigation will change from time to time, and methods will vary from formal surveys to informal feedback.

A stock-take on scheme progress.

As a result of Programme Review Teams and information gathered it should be possible to agree a situation report on the state of the programme, identifying strengths and weaknesses as perceived by the main parties involved.

A forward agenda for change and adaptation.

As a result of taking stock of the operation of the programme, a responsive organisation will generate items for future developments. This might well take the form of an annual plan for scheme development. Items in such a forward agenda might range from changes in instructional techniques to alterations in organisational structure. Plans for staff development and training are also likely to feature.

Interest in good practice elsewhere and developments in training techniques.

A responsive provider will keep abreast with developments outside his own scheme. Interest will range from contact with other local

providers to share good practice to awareness of national developments in YTS generally or the relevant occupational sector.
Extract from Manpower Services Commission (1986)
'Approved Training Organisations:
Training For Skills, YTS'

All Managing Agencies delivering two year YTS programmes are now required by MSC to carry out a minimum of three Programme Review Team (PRT) meetings during a year. This provides an opportunity for YTS schemes to bring together people who participate in or have a close relationship with the scheme in order to review progress and problems. Most schemes leave the organisation of PRTs to their co-ordinating staff, who contact potential participants including work placement providers, local careers' officers, trades union representatives and the MSC programme assessor. Trainees are asked to provide a representative and scheme staff also attend. A few schemes have, however, deliberately set out to use the PRT as a process for trainee development rather than simply a mechanism for discussion and, in doing so, have achieved far more in terms of positive results than the schemes that hold staff-centred PRTs.

Sumlock Calculating Services Ltd., in Stoke-on-Trent has held a series of PRT meetings over the past 18 months and regards them as a major part of the scheme's attempt to ensure the on and off-the-job training it provides are integrated as closely as possible, to record formally comments from participants, and negotiate future action following the discussion. From the first PRT meeting, Sumlock decided that the trainees themselves should play a key part in the process and not simply be invited along in the same way as staff and non-trainee participants.

At Sumlock, therefore, the trainees begin the process by electing a representative from each of the six groups of trainees that attend Sumlock's training centre for a range of business studies courses. They also elect six stand-by representatives and a 'secretary' who will take minutes at the PRT meeting. The trainees then draw up an agenda of items they wish to be discussed and circulate this to scheme staff who can add further items of their own. Letters of invitation are sent to work placement providers and other relevant parties including the scheme manager, tutors and placement monitoring officers.

After the meeting, the trainee 'secretary' types the minutes and circulates them to all participants, and the trainee representatives report back to their fellow trainees. This system has resulted in a closer relationship between the trainee groups and between trainees and scheme staff with the former feeling confident that their views and concerns are both listened to and acted upon. Some major changes have been made to the scheme's training content following recommendations made at PRT meetings. For example, the original two week induction programme for first year trainees was increased to four weeks to include basic computer skills and training as trainees felt this would help them adapt more easily to modern office environment. This request from trainees was supported by work placement providers who, in turn, asked that typing by given space in the induction programme. Another change has been the revision of a complete module in Calculating Skills, where the component tasks have been 'pulled out' and integrated through project work with the rest of the training programme.

This trainee-centred style of programme review encourages trainees to develop their inter-personal, communication, organisational and decision-making skills, thus turning a mechanism to which many schemes pay lip-service into a dynamic process for personal development.

Contact: Miss Whittaker
Sumlock Calculating Services Ltd
Stoke-on-Trent
Staffordshire

CASE STUDY C:
Continuing education for pharmacists: An NEC project evaluation

Continuing Education for Pharmacists was a project run by the National Extension College (NEC) for the Pharmaceutical Society of Great Britain for two years from April 1985. Its core was a series of three 15-hour open-learning modules and a C80 tape distributed free – without prior request – to a random sample of 3,500 practising pharmacists in the south of England. A carefully planned sequence of pre-, in-course and post-course evaluation made the project one of the most extensively evaluated that the NEC has ever undertaken. This was largely carried out at a distance and it is these distance methods which are the focus here.

Pre-course evaluation

The project team was made up of an NEC editor and five practising pharmacists, the latter working under the title of the Pharmacy Practice Group (PPG). At the start of the project the team planned a detailed survey of the perceived educational needs of the target group.

A questionnaire was planned after a series of discussions among the project team. The first draft consisted of a series of open-ended questions designed to test the validity of earlier surveys into continuing education needs. These questions were then sharpened into closed, multiple-choice questions which would give results compatible with a simple, BBC-based, software programme for statistical analyses of questionnaires.

The final questionnaire consisted of 19 questions, one of which was used simply for administrative purposes. The team considered it essential that the evaluation should be as straightforward and undemanding as possible to complete and this influenced the way the questionnaire was compiled and distributed. Specifically:

— each of the 19 questions contained on average five alternatives, which participants were required only to tick. The final question did, however, contain an open ended 'PS' that asked pharmacists to list any areas of training that had not been itemised in the questionnaire.
— the questionnaire was sent out with:
—a letter explaining the purpose of the survey and emphasising that by completing it pharmacists would be able to influence the choice of topics in the open-learning material they were later to receive.
—a reply paid envelope
— the language and style of the questionnaire was subject to the same editorial scrutiny that would later be given to the materials themselves.

The questionnaire was sent to all 3,500 pharmacists in the target area during July 1985 and 1,630 (47%) responded. Pharmacists who had not replied within a fortnight were sent a reminder card. A total of 1,200 questionnaires were analysed, which corresponded to the maximum capacity of the computer system and just over a third of the original sample. Batch analysis (in groups of 400) enabled detection of any significant differences in responders who replied immediately, compared with those who responded later. No significant variation could be detected.

The pre-evaluation identified key characteristics of the target group, knowledge of which was essential for the design of properly focussed open learning material. The principal features identified were:

— branch of profession (e.g. hospital, retail, industry)
— employment status (e.g. part-time, retired, full-time)
— existing commitment to continuing education activities and courses
— time available for study

· — preferred course structure (e.g. balance between text and audio).

While these categories were designed in the context of pharmacy, most could be usefully applied to the pre-evaluation of any open learning programme.

In-course evaluation

Module One of the course, and the cassette tape, were ready for despatch in August 1986, and the remaining two modules were sent out in October 1986 and January 1987. The materials tried to reflect as far as possible the findings of the initial survey, though the original terms of reference of the project meant that all pharmacists received materials whether or not they answered the initial questionnaire or sent in evaluation forms despatched with the modules.

Learner progress was then regularly assessed using a computer marking system known as MAIL (an acronym for Micro-Aided Learning). Answers to simple questionnaires, sent out with each of the three modules, were computer assessed and an appropriate computer generated letter returned to responders. This enabled NEC to obtain a statistical summary of results at any point in the project and regular updates of student numbers and performance were circulated among the course team.

A key, additional, component of this in-course assessment was a series of seven questions designed to provide information on participants' subjective evaluation of the course. Six of the questions required ratings using a scale of one to six, ensuring that responders were not biased towards the middle of the scale. The questions asked:

— how relevant the course was to day-to-day practice
— whether it was intellectually challenging
— whether the writing was clear
— whether the course was worth the time spent on it (i.e. the opportunity cost)
— how the course compared with face-to-face courses
— whether the estimated study time of five hours per module was correct.

By April 1987, 438 of the 3,500 pharmacists who received the course material (13% of the target audience) had responded to Module 1, 229 (7%) to Module 2 and 128 (4%) to Module 3, although a steady trickle of responses to all three modules continued throughout the remainder of the year.

Post-course evaluation

Although the response to the initial survey and the in-course evaluation had been good (particularly the former), the project team decided to increase their knowledge of what was still a silent majority, by two further techniques.

The first of these included sending each member of the target group a very short and simple survey form with Module 3. This form, with the bold heading 'Just 60 seconds of your time' was printed on an A5 card (green for prominence), the bottom half of which could be detached and used as a prepaid postcard. Only six questions were asked, the first two of which were to be answered irrespective of whether participants had completed the course. These questions established branch of profession and how much of each of the three modules they had read, on a scale of one to four. The remaining four questions looked at the perceived effect of the material on day-to-day practice, at pharmacists' interest in receiving further, similar open learning and at the areas in which they would like further training.

The green postcard was returned by 341 (10%) pharmacists within six weeks of despatch. Of these, at least 72% had read more than half the material while 62% had read the majority of the course.

The second technique was a short telephone survey which aimed to evaluate pharmacists' involvement in continuing education, irrespective of their response to the current course. A simple algorithm (see figure 2) was developed to guide interviewers and elicit the maximum information on interviewees, with particular emphasis on:

— how much of the course they had covered and in what depth
— reasons for coverage or lack of it
— other involvement in continuing education.

The survey was conducted by an NEC employee with experience of 'blind' telephone techniques and calls were made early on weekday evenings over a period of 14 days. As far as possible, the interviews sought to cover a representative sample of pharmacists from both rural and urban areas, with their varying opportunities for continuing education. In all, 134 registered pharmacists were contacted, of whom 100 were practising. Eighty of those active pharmacists were treated as an initial survey, followed by two batches of 10 to confirm the reliability of the results.

Of the 100 active pharmacists, 64 had covered the course, 44 in sufficient depth to work through most of the self-check questions in the modules. Fifty-seven stated that they had benefited from the course. Of the 36 active pharmacists who did not cover the course, 28% obtained continuing education by other means.

Figure 2.2: An extract from the algorithm used in telephone interviews in the NEC evaluation of their project: Continuing Education for Pharmacists

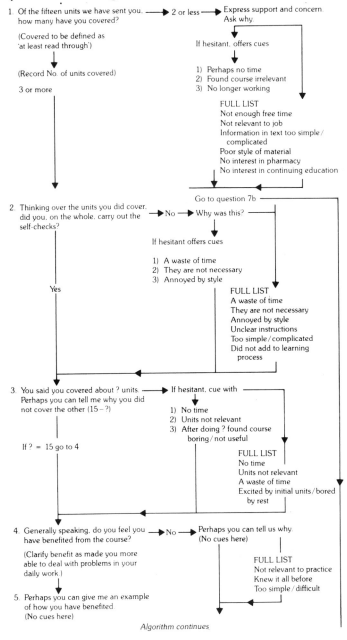

1. Of the fifteen units we have sent you, how many have you covered? ——▶ 2 or less ——▶ Express support and concern. Ask why.

   (Covered to be defined as 'at least read through')

   If hesitant, offers cues

   (Record No. of units covered)

   3 or more

   1) Perhaps no time
   2) Found course irrelevant
   3) No longer working

   FULL LIST
   Not enough free time
   Not relevant to job
   Information in text too simple / complicated
   Poor style of material
   No interest in pharmacy
   No interest in continuing education

   Go to question 7b

2. Thinking over the units you did cover, did you, on the whole, carry out the self-checks? ——▶ No ——▶ Why was this? ——

   If hesitant offers cues

   1) A waste of time
   2) They are not necessary
   3) Annoyed by style

   Yes

   FULL LIST
   A waste of time
   They are not necessary
   Annoyed by style
   Unclear instructions
   Too simple / complicated
   Did not add to learning process

3. You said you covered about ? units. Perhaps you can tell me why you did not cover the other (15 – ?) ——▶ If hesitant, cue with ——

   1) No time
   2) Units not relevant
   3) After doing ? found course boring / not useful

   If ? = 15 go to 4

   FULL LIST
   No time
   Units not relevant
   A waste of time
   Excited by initial units / bored by rest

4. Generally speaking, do you feel you have benefited from the course? ——▶ No ——▶ Perhaps you can tell us why. (No cues here)

   (Clarify benefit as made you more able to deal with problems in your daily work.)

   FULL LIST
   Not relevant to practice
   Knew it all before
   Too simple / difficult

5. Perhaps you can give me an example of how you have benefited. (No cues here)

Algorithm continues

Conclusions

The evaluation used a combination of extensive and intensive methods. The extensive method — the surveys and assessment — was most effective for gathering large amounts of quantative data. The intensive method — the interviews — provided valuable amounts of qualitative data. The methods were used with perhaps diminishing effectiveness over time. Pharmacists, like other professional groups, have limited time and energy for continuing education, and having already been extensively canvassed as a group by one intensive, pre-course evaluation, some almost certainly found subsequent similar requests a burden. It seems essential, therefore, that any open learning initiative should:

— map out a complete evaluation strategy at its inception
— ensure a balanced programme of extensive and intensive evaluation
— in extensive evaluation — minimise the effort demanded of responders and analysts by:
  • asking for simple tick-box responses compatible with a computer analysis programme
  • providing prepaid envelopes or stickers
— in intensive evaluation — plan the interviewers' strategy, using an algorithm or schedule of questions, to ensure maximum consistency of approach and of data gathered.

Above all, evaluation should not be seen as an added extra; if it is carried out at all it should be given the same detailed consideration, using the same criteria, as the open learning programme itself.

Contributed by Tim Burton, Assistant Director, Publications, NEC, 18 Brooklands Avenue, Cambridge, CB2 2HN, from whom further details of the evaluation and its results are available.

CASE STUDY D:
Birmingham Open Learning Development Unit

This is an interesting example of the use of evaluation by a former Open Tech Project to generate case studies of the use of open learning in Basic Education, and for the further development of materials and curriculum.

Birmingham Open Learning Development Unit (BOLDU) provides a location (within Garretts Green College, Birmingham) where individuals and companies can find out about open learning, buy materials and courses, and negotiate any arrangements for tutorial support. The Unit has also produced a series of eighteen units 'to assist educators intending to adopt more flexible learning systems'. The series, 'Developing Open Learning' includes 'Assessing Materials' 'Record Keeping' and 'Identifying Training Needs', all of which are aspects of evaluation.

As part of its service to Local Authorities, the Unit is evaluating the rapid growth of open learning workshops as a means of providing Adult Basic Education. Colin Harris and Joyce Bailey are leading the evaluation.

Three workshop locations have been selected, and two tutors from each location, one mathematics tutor and one English tutor. There will be a total of six tutors participating, and in each case three of their clients (learners on the programme) will be asked to participate; one for interview and two by completing a questionnaire (a total of 18 learners).

Tutors will be involved in selecting clients for interview. The evaluators have defined three categories from which clients will be selected – those who are working with high, moderate or with low success. Each tutor will be asked to suggest one client for interview, whom the tutor feels falls within the cateogory (one of the three listed above) requested by the evaluator. In all there will be two clients in each of the categories distributed across each of the workshops and subjects as follows:

Category of Learner	Workshop 1		Workshop 2		Workshop 3	
	Maths	English	Maths	English	Maths	English
High success	X					X
Moderate success		X	X			
Low success				X	X	

The remaining 12 clients will be selected by the tutor and will complete a questionnaire, an extract from which is shown in figure 3. Tutors will also be interviewed using a semi-structured approach, and will be asked to complete questionnaires using checklists similar to those included in the client questionnaire.

The outcome of the evaluation will be three case studies which will be the basis of recommendations on a range of issues, further materials and curriculum development.

Figure 2.3: Boldu monitoring and evaluation project Extract from the client questionnaire

— How many hours a week do you study?

— How far through the course are you?

| 0% | 20% | 40% | 60% | 80% | 100% |

— How much time a week do you spend with your tutor?

— How would you rate the open learning course? (1 = low, 4 = high)
Ignore any features which aren't relevant

Simulating	1	2	3	4
Useful	1	2	3	4
Relevant	1	2	3	4
Amount of self-assessment	1	2	3	4
Amount of tutor assessment	1	2	3	4
Tutor contact	1	2	3	4
Contact with other clients	1	2	3	4
Study skills materials	1	2	3	4
Accuracy of materials	1	2	3	4
Use of facilities at open learning centre	1	2	3	4
Flexibility	1	2	3	4
Ease of progress	1	2	3	4
Value for money	1	2	3	4

— I thought the two most useful parts of the course were:
   1.
   2.

— I thought the two least useful parts of the course were:
   1.
   2.

Further information from Colin Russell, Birmingham Open Development Unit, Garretts Green College, Birmingham.

CASE STUDY E:
The Taster Pack Project: Open University East Anglian Region

This is a good example of evaluation being used for the development of services to learners. In this case the project being evaluated is a local innovation in the practice of a national distance learning institution – a 'Taster Pack', designed to give applicants a chance to try out course materials before starting a course.

During 1986 and 1987, two of the Open University's 13 regions (East Anglia and West Midlands) collaborated on production and evaluation of material for applicants interested in getting a 'better feel' for an OU foundation course. These Taster Packs consisted of about an hour's work of carefully selected material from each of the five foundation courses, together with a student's assignment, tutor's comments on that assignment, and (in some cases) an examination question. In the words of the West Midlands Region: 'Taster Packs are the University's equivalent of a free sample.'

The idea of Taster Packs originated from student comments received at advisory and induction meetings and mentioned in conversations between tutor counsellors and students concerning student anxiety and desire to 'see a bit' of the course. Some tutor counsellors or advisory counsellors have no doubt 'pulled out' actual units to show students but two Senior Counsellors from two different Regions discussed the feelings that students expressed and decided to explore ways of meeting that need.

No one extract could hope to illustrate the whole course and all its sub-areas, but it was hoped to give a 'taste' and enough insight to help a student feel more confident about the chosen course and/or to enable him/her to contact an advisory counsellor to discuss problems raised.

In all, about 700 packs were sent to applicants in the East Anglian Region, and over 600 to initially registered students in West Midlands Region. Many applicants asked to borrow two packs, usually Arts and Social Sciences packs, or Mathematics and Technology packs. Each pack contained a questionnaire (see figure 4) which users were asked to return with the materials when they had finished with them. The inclusion of a stamped addressed envelope for West Midlands users appears to have made a big difference in the response rate: West Midlands had a response rate of around 90% (580 questionnaires returned) and East Anglia around 15% (101 questionnaires returned). Before analysis, all questionnaires were checked for problems or requests which needed immediate action. Questions about further preparation were the most frequent.

Almost all respondents found the material encouraging. In the West Midlands for example, only 13 found the material unhelpful or discouraging. For most people, the packs clarified their ideas of course content and the majority were confirmed in their choice of course. A small number were put off from applying because they were able to see that course work would not be as they had expected.

The questionnaire also asked which sections of the pack were most helpful, which least helpful and what else applicants would wish to see. The responses showed no significant differences arising from the different content areas of the five packs. Many found the whole pack very helpful and did not specify anything that was unhelpful. Student answers and tutor's comments were found helpful by many, with the course excerpts themselves following close behind in popularity.

Respondents wanted a general outline of the whole course, study and assignment timetables and, where not given, exam questions and model answers. The technologists were particularly anxious to gauge the level of the extract: 'Does it get harder?' was a general query.

Most recipients of the packs were very enthusiastic. Packs seemed to fulfill a great demand. These are some of the general comments made by users.

'Thank you — it has given me some idea of the course — I can't see what more you can do — other than give more samples.'

'Having read taster packs for both courses have decided my first choice was correct.'

'Thank you for the insight and for the sensitive way in which is was worded.'

'Being unsure of exactly what Social Sciences encompassed, I was particularly interested to have a taste of the lessons. It helped me to confirm my choice.'

'I think the idea of a taster pack is excellent, especially if one was unsure whether to take a particular course or not. It certainly helped me to confirm my choice of study.'

'This taster pack is a fair exemplar of what is to be expected. It is well laid out and clearly explained although I found myself reading it two or three times principally because of the wealth of information.'

'The pack has been sufficiently interesting and encouraging to give me a feeling of excitement and enthusiasm for the course.'

'I found the example interesting, although a little out of my depth. However, I shall be obtaining preparatory material to swot up on basics.'

'It whets one's appetite. In no way discouraging, it spurs one on.'

'I found it helpful to see how much work is expected in approximately one hour's studying time.'

'I found the excerpt from the course material much easier to understand than I had expected .....the student could not fail to be totally immersed in the subject.'

'I am encouraged and filled with enthusiasm to start. However . . . most people are less likely to have studied philosophy . . . perhaps the inclusion of an excerpt from that section of the course would be beneficial to prospective students.'

Many found that their appetites had been whetted for their chosen courses and although some found the standard higher than they imagined, many looked forward to the challenge presented. Several had spent longer than one hour on the extract. One asked if she might keep the pack, and many were not returned: one assumes they are still being used. A tutor at an open evening reported an enthusiastic exchange of ideas arising from the packs.

Figure 2.4: Open University Taster Pack Project Extract from the user questionnaires

We hope you have found this Taster Pack helpful. To help us assess how useful it has been to you, would you fill in a short questionnaire for us? You can return it to us together with the Pack. We may write to you again next year and ask if you would be kind enough to complete another similar questionnaire in the light of your recent experience on the course.

WHERE APPROPRIATE PLEASE RING THE RESPONSE THAT MOST CLOSELY RESEMBLES YOUR FEELING ABOUT THE QUESTION:

1) Do you feel that the Taster Pack gave you a clearer or more confused idea of what was in the course?

   CLEARER / MORE CONFUSED / NO CHANGE

2) Did the Taster Pack change your idea of what was in the course?

   VERY MUCH / SOMEWHAT / NOT AT ALL

3) Did the Taster Pack change your mind about which course you wanted to take?

   YES / NO / STILL UNDECIDED

   If YES — how have you changed your mind?

4) Did the Taster Pack put you off doing the course altogether?

   YES / NO / STILL UNDECIDED

   If YES — what was it in particular that put you off?

5) Which items in the Pack were most helpful?

6) Which items in the Pack were the least helpful?

7) Was there anything omitted that you would have liked to see?

8) Any other comments.

Outcomes

The pilots have proved that users found the packs very helpful and that the material was appropriately selected and presented.

The exercise has also been very inexpensive (some £200 in West Midlands Region in production and distribution costs, approximately £350 in the East Anglian Region for writing and editorial work with a recurring annual cost of approximately £300 for production).

The offer of Taster Packs will continue into 1988/89 in both Regions.

It was decided not to enlarge the Pack — that it was only a taste — and that although an examination question ought to be included in all packs it will not include grade and answer. It was also planned to include an advertisement for the packs in the Guide for Applicants, so that users see them while making up their minds whether to apply and for which course. Both regions would like to see these packs at Course Choice meetings, at Summer Schools and Advisory Meetings as well as in other Regions, and will continue to promote them for such ends. The East Anglian Region intends a follow-up questionnaire to users who are foundation students in 1988, to canvass their opinion of the packs in the light of their subsequent experience as students.

Further information from:

Vicky Rand at the Open University West Midlands Region
66-68 High Street
Harborne, Birmingham B17 9NB

Christine Adams, and Ormond Simpson at
The Open University, East Anglian Region,
12, Hills Road, Cambridge CB2 1PF

Further Reading

Mitton, R. (1982) *Practical Research in Distance Teaching: A Handbook for Developing Countries.* The International Extension College, Cambridge.

Do not be put off by the reference to 'research' and 'developing countries' in the title. Although the author is himself an experienced social researcher, the text is written for practitioners, with the assumption that they do not have specialist research skills. All the methods which might be used for evaluation are explained with clarity and realism — observation, surveys (by interview and questionnaire) pre-testing and monitoring. Although the context and examples are not UK based, the procedures and princples *are* applicable to open learning in the UK. Full of practical advice and *essential* reading.

Hilgendorf, L. (1984) *Self Evaluation by Open Learning Projects: A Guide for Managers and Projects in the Open Tech Programme*. Tavistock Institute of Human Relations, 120 Belsize Lane, London NW3 5BA.

The evaluation of the Open Tech programme by the Tavistock Institute led to the production of these guidelines . . . 'intended to stimulate those involved in projects to develop their strategy for evaluating their progress and achievements and to suggest methods they could use for gathering information'. Good on helping managers sort out what *they* want from evaluation, with lots of useful checklists of questions about products and services, learning outcomes, demand, quality control, costs and management and marketing. Inevitably, the section on information systems necessary to answer these questions is very brief, but the booklet as a whole is a useful overview of the management perspective on evaluation.

Bell, J., Bush T., Fox, A., Goodey, S. (editors) (1984) *Conducting Small-Scale Investigations in Education Management*. Harper and Row, in Association with the Open University.

A selection of practical articles on most of the topics that would be required in evaluating open learning — planning, action research, case study, records, questionnaire design, interviewing, observing and recording meetings; analysis and presentation of information, and report writing. A really useful and relevant handbook on techniques and approaches.

Hargreaves, J. *A Case Study of Course and Programme Review in the School of Education and Humanities at North East London Polytechnic*

Standing Conference on Educational Development Services, Occasional Paper No 9.
    A very interesting account of formative self evaluation within a department in a polytechnic. Stimulated by CNAA proposals for 'partnership in validation', it describes how one department reviews the effectiveness of its courses.

Lewis, R. editor (1984) *Open Learning in Action. Open Learning Guide 1*. Council for Educational Technology, 3 Devonshire Street, London.

Sixteen case studies of open learning programmes, three of which provide information on record keeping and evaluation: 'Sight and Sound Secretarial Training', 'The Bradford Mathematics Workshop' and 'Educational Technology at a Distance, from Dundee College of Education'.

Quality in NAFE (1987) Further Education Unit, Elizabeth House, York Road, London SE1 7PH.

A 32-page document which provides a comprehensive guide to quality, related to the context of work-related non-advanced further education. It emphasises a curriculum-led approach to quality, because of the centrality of the learner and the quality of learning for the fundamental goals of further education. Provides guidelines on quality in each of the five inter-dependent elements of curriculum — values and needs, programme design, implementation, support systems and evaluation and review.

PART II EVALUATION IN PRACTICE

Introduction

The chapters in this part provide an introduction to the evaluation of key areas in the provision of open learning — course materials, tuition, counselling and learner self evaluation. The boundaries between each of these areas are not clear cut and are defined differently in different systems. This is particularly important for evaluation, where evidence of the effectiveness of one component in the system is likely to exist in several areas. Each of the components in a system is interdependent and it is very difficult, if not impossible, to isolate the effectiveness, and the effects, of only one of its components.

Even more important, from the learner's point of view, open learning is one experience, not differentiated by the well-defined administrative concerns of the practitioner. There is a degree of arbitrariness in any choice of sub divisions within what is a set of interconnected elements, which are experienced as an integrated whole by the learner.

I hope nonetheless that most practitioners will find the grouping of content and issues in each of the chapters in Part II is familiar and a useful basis on which to follow up practical (rather than theoretical) concerns. The order in which they are read is immaterial, but each has material which impinges on issues covered in the other three. The indivisibility of tuition and counselling issues is especially important. Both are seen as components within guidance for example, according to the Unit for the Development of Adult Continuing Education. The National Institute for Careers Education and Counselling also defines 'guidance' in terms of all the functions of a learner support system, and includes both tutors and counsellors as guidance resource people. The resources within an open learning scheme complement those of the workplace, the community and the learner's immediate environment (figure 1).

A comprehensive account of guidance is clearly impossible within the scope of this text, which in any case is focused on evaluation rather than an account of how to set up open learning systems. I have narrowed down guidance issues to tuition and counselling because in many systems they offer the most significant guidance resources for learners, and because they are the components of

Figure 1: Guidance resources: people

OPEN LEARNING SCHEME

- Administrators - record keeping, advocacy

- Receptionist - preliminary information

- Tutor - subject expertise and support

- Counsellor - sustained guidance

- Writer - coaching in study skills, support built into packages

- Manager - co-ordination, advocacy, feedback

WORKPLACE

- Trainers - providing learning resources, organising time, advocacy

- Supervisors - help with practical resources, coaching

- Managers - releasing resources, sponsorship, liaison, vocational advice

- Union - vocational information

LEARNER

LEARNER

- Mentor - support negotiated with the learner

- Colleagues - subject expertise, practical help, informal support

- Peer Learners - co-operative learning, reduced isolation

- Family, Friends - confidence building, co-operation in managing study

COMMUNITY

- MSC Agencies - information on jobs and training

- Careers Service - occupational information, vocational advice/counselling

- Educational Guidance Services - information and guidance on further learning, grants

- Libraries - learning resources, space to study

- LEA Services - advice on grants

Taken from NICEC "Guidance in Open Learning" : Thinking About Resources guidance most directly within the power of practitioners to influence. I have found it more useful to think in terms of the functions of tuition and counselling rather than role titles as listed in figure 1 (tutor, counsellor, trainer and so on) because these differ so very widely in practice. Thus readers are likely to need to read both chapters 4 and 5 to be sure that they have covered the relevant issues.

Although it was not practicable to include separate chapters on the functions of administration reception and management (see the list of open learning, scheme resource people in figure 1) these are implicit in some aspects of all the chapters in this Part. All three may be variously involved in providing advice and counselling, sometimes tutorial support, to scheme users and in that respect the evaluation of their work is covered in chapters 4 and 5. All three are likely to have key roles in any evaluation because theirs is a full time concern for the effective implementation of the open learning programme as a whole. It is they in many cases who will be introducing and maintaining monitoring and feedback systems and co-ordinating the evaluation as a whole.

The work of the writer (or materials author/producer, since audio and visual media should be included as well as text) is covered largely in chapter 6, though here again, the 'boundary definition' issue is relevant. In systems like the Open University, the term 'course' is reserved for materials which include assessment (most often a mix of continuing (50%) and final (50%) assessment) and a variety of guidance features — tuition, counselling, possibly summer school, the Students' Association, and so on. If a user purchases only materials without any assessment or interpersonal guidance features, these are referred to as packs or course materials rather than 'courses'. Following this distinction, chapter six focuses mainly on the evaluation of materials, and the reader interested in course evaluation should refer to chapters 4 and 5 in addition for the relevant issues in tuition and counselling.

The first chapter in Part II however concerns none of these areas directly. Learner self-evaluation comes first as a reminder that the learner does have an important role in the evaluation process — not only as a provider of feedback and data of various kinds about teaching, but as an evaluator of their own learning and how it should best develop. If there is less to report in this chapter, it may be a result of two factors. First, the encouragement of self evaluation by learners is under-emphasised by practitioners, and thus it happens infrequently. Second, what there is to be evaluated of teaching is known about (on the whole) in advance. It is not possible to know about each learner's learning in quite the same way, and indeed it may not be necessary. The point of evaluation here is to give the learner tools with which to come to terms with the learning process they have been engaged in, and to consider what it means for them. John Cowan has expressed the importance of this in a 'credo' which would lose much, were I to re-phrase it. He asserts:

'In everything I do in evaluation, I must remember that —
at the end of the day — it is the
— effectiveness
— efficiency
— validity or worth
OF THE LEARNING that matters. It matters not how
effective or impressive the teaching. It matters not that the
pass rate is high, for this could well have been achieved
either by spoon feeding, or by highly demanding entrance
requirements, or by low standards in the final examination.
The real concern in evaluation is, and should be shown to
be, the quality of the learning experience and the extent
to which the learner learns or develops as a consequence
of the experience which is arranged for her or him'.

Cowan, 1987 seminar presentation.

One final caveat about the inevitable selectiveness of Part II. Although much of the experience it reports is derived from the Open University, it does not pretend to offer a representative let alone comprehensive account of evaluation carried out at the OU. Readers who want to follow up particular issues, or fill in some of the gaps, should start with the bibliography suggested below. One issue conspicuous by its omission is that of costs. Again, there are suggestions in the second publication below, relevant to particular areas of the educational system. It is not that financial resources are unimportant, but that this is an area where issues are difficult to discuss independently from system specific detail.

Whitehead, D. (1988) editor *The Institute Bibliography* : A bibliography of published and unpublished work by members of the Institute of Educational Technology, The Open University, Milton Keynes.

Implementing Open Learning in Local Authority Institutions: A Guide (1987) Further Education Unit and the Open Learning Branch of the Manpower Services Commission.

An extremely useful set of guidelines, including sections on resourcing, resource deployment, costing and pricing. The latter 'examines the importance of cost information in the sound management of open learning and identifies the cost elements involved. It then reviews pricing criteria and indicates some of the accounting implications'.

3 Learner self-evaluation

Main themes: *the importance of learner self-evaluation. The role of self-evaluation in preparing to learn, during learning and at the end of learning. Different approaches to initiating self-evaluation when the learner is not face to face with a practitioner. The role of assessment in self-evaluation.*

The learner can be involved in evaluating any aspect of open learning provision and it is very often their opinions and behaviour which are collected when courses, or tutors or learning systems are evaluated. However, in this chapter I shall be looking at examples of how learners can be involved in evaluating their own learning, and therefore engage in self evaluation rather than in judging the quality of someone else's work.

The two areas are not unconnected of course. Learners may be asked to comment on the effectiveness of a course and their thinking may prompt a useful review of why a particular section was more fruitful for their work, or whether they could have asked the tutor more questions and thus resolved some of their problems. However, these incidental payoffs of any kind of learner involvement in evaluation can be more effectively developed by creating a specific opportunity for the learner to reflect on their reasons for learning, what they are getting out of learning and where they want to go to next.

Preparing to learn

This is a process which can usefully begin before study, and many institutions in their initial advice prompt the learner to 'think carefully before beginning'. Enquirers do not always have a very clear idea of what to think about of course, and require the skills of a counsellor to help them work through the implications of their decision.

   Whether or not face to face counselling is available, it can also be helpful to give enquirers some thought-provoking material which they can work through on their own. Figure 1 shows an example of the kinds of questions which would prompt thinking about reasons for study, and figure 2, questions which specify some of the activities study might involve. The approach is moving the enquirer towards a review of his or her existing skills in learning, suggesting an active approach ('I shall need some practice') where skills are undeveloped.

Figure 3.1: Learner self-review: Reasons for learning

It is always a good idea to know clearly why you are donig anything. Below are some of the reasons people give when asked why they want to take an open learning course. How much does each of them apply to you? It can be beneficial to have several reasons for learning, so do not be worried if you find youself agreeing with most of them.

	Strongly Agree	Agree	Neither	Disagree	Strongly Disagree
It would help me with my job					
I would like to change my job					
I feel I missed out on my education when I was younger					
I want to prove something to myself					
I want to show my family/ friends I can do it					
I think it will be a good opportunity to meet people					
I enjoy learning					
I'm getting in a rut and need a change					
It will take my mind off other problems					

Now you have checked through the this list of reasons, write down in your own words the main reasons why you are thinking of taking an open learning course

(Checklist adapted from Simpson, O., 'Getting Going')

Figure 3.2: Learner self-review: Learning skills

If you have not been involved in any form of training or study recently, you may need to think about developing your learning skills. You are likely to need at least some of the skills listed below, and to improve your effectiveness in particular areas.

How do you rate yourself on

	Yes I can do that: how well?	No I shall need some help Any areas in particular?
Reading something to learn from it		
Concentrating for an hour or two of study		
Making notes from spoken information		
Making notes from written information		
Planning and writing reports or essays		
Using simple statistics, reading graphs		
Learning from TV or video		
Learning from audiocassette		
Taking part in discussion		

Contact your local open learning centre to discuss ways in which you can develop your learning skills.

(Checklist adapted from Simpson, O., 'Getting Going')

A small-scale evaluation of the use of this approach with Open University applicants in the East Anglian region showed that, if only for a minority, it did affect the decision to apply. Sixteen applicants who had received a booklet ('Getting Going') containing activities similar to those in figures one and two, were interviewed. Four changed their decision as a result of working through the booklet, seven found it helpful or generally a good idea and five had either not read it or did not find it relevant to them. This is a positive result for a booklet that does not have a high profile among all the literature applicants receive from the University, and this extract from the report of interviews suggests why a booklet of this kind is helpful, even though some decide against study, as a result:

(One student said that) . . . 'it played a fairly considerable part in causing me to decline. It was quite a clever piece

of paper actually . . . it put me off but then I think I would have dropped out anyway.' . . . . . . Another student accepted a place in 1982 in a positive mind, having declined in 1981 after reading 'Getting Going' and discovering that she wouldn't have enough time. . . . . . Overall the experience of 'Getting Going' for these applicants seems to have been positive. It clarified their feelings and helped them reach decisions they were happy with: 'it showed you why you wanted to do the thing'. . . . . 'it pin pointed things I'd been thinking about. Strengthened my belief in doing it . . . .'

(Gibbons, (1982))

Evaluation undertaken during the Open Tech programme also identified the importance of learner motivation and its effects on learner progress. Roffey Park Management College has produced material similar to that in figures 1 and 2, designed to stimulate the novice learner to explore their reasons for studying and to strengthen them. (Sagar and Strang, 1985)

During and at the end of learning

'Significant developments in the evaluation of teaching will not come from staff thinking about their own courses, or from students as consumers expressing their judgements about the courses which are provided for them, but **by an integration of evaluation into the learning process** *so that an important part of the students' learning is in fact coming to understand his (sic) own strengths, weaknesses, inhibitions, and styles of thinking and working in relation to the varieties of constraints and opportunities presented by the course.'* (emphasis added)

(Cox, (1978))

It is perhaps even more important to integrate learning evaluation into the open learning process because there are often few opportunities for informal discussion of how things are going. Adults in particular need to be given time in which to digest what has been communicated and to relate it to existing experience.

In the work she has developed with trainees in industry, Downs describes the use of 'ponder sessions' as a regular aspect of group work, where the trainer poses three questions: What was the purpose of the session? What have you learned? How can you apply it? (Downs, 1988). Each participant contributes to a discussion in which the role of the trainer is not to correct the learners' ideas, but to elicit them without criticism and to compare them with the trainer's own purposes for the session, especially if these do not seem to have been achieved. The value of the exercise is that the learner is given time to think about (ponder) what they have learned and how it might be applied to what they do in future. The individual learns from the group and any misconceptions can be revised with minimum embarrassment.

Many of the techniques for evaluating learning which are used in group work (see further reading) are potentially applicable to open learning, but it is also important to consider how self-evaluation can be encouraged during private study. Two approaches have been used here, the first more frequently than the second: activities based on the content of the materials, and self-review questions, where the individual reflects back on a period of learning to review it in a similar fashion to the group exercise outlined above.

Content-related activities usually take the form of questions or exercises introduced at different points in the materials which enable the learner to orient themselves to what they are about to learn, to review what they have learned and perhaps to develop it, by one or more of these methods:

• asking the learner to think ahead, or to pose questions about material they are about to learn;
• testing knowledge of the content of earlier material, through exercises of recall, re-statement, identification of concepts, and so on;
• asking the learner to apply what has just been learned to a different contex;
• asking the learners to relate what they have learned to their own experiences.

This takes us into the area of self-assessment questions and activities, where the content and style of each item are designed to be appropriate for the particular learning goals involved. One of the lessons learned early in distance teaching and open learning is the desirability of an interactive approach in the content of materials. Learners value the opportunity for regular feedback on the progress they are making and this does not have to depend on the physical presence of a teacher, but can be 'built in' to the medium being used, by using a variety of in-text questions and activities.

Much less attention as yet has been given to the second kind of self evaluation introduced above, where the individual 'sits back' and reviews more generally whether the learning experience is meeting their expectations and whether adjustments are required. Figure 3 provides one example of an approach which is used at various stages in the materials for an Open University professional diploma in post compulsory education. During one of the modules, 'Approaches to Adult Learning', students are introduced to the idea of keeping a journal during the course of their studies, in which they work on activities suggested in the text, and explore their reactions to the module, as they arise. This approach is especially valuable where the content of course work is closely related to the learner's work context or life experience, and has already been successfully used elsewhere (Walker, 1985). Keeping a journal is an important means through which the learner works with and learns from his or her existing experience and integrates it with the new learning of the course. Learners can also be prompted with explicit 'self-review' questions (as in figure 3), and these are also used in the Approaches to Adult Learning module. This is one way of recognising the importance of the learner's own involvement in the learning process, and of encouraging him or her to spend some time thinking through the outcomes and implications of their study.

Figure 3.3: An example of a self-review exercise

1. *Suggested at the beginning of study*

    Try answering these questions about the first module:

    (a)   Aspects which interested me were . . . .

    (b)   Things I would have liked more/less of . . . .

    (c)   About myself: how well did I work on this? Is it picking up my interests/work experience? . . . .

    (d)   How should I tackle the next module? . . . .

2. *Suggested at the end of study*

    (a)   Which module did I get the most from? . . . .

    (b)   Which parts shall I use in the assignment/exam? . . .

    (c)   Do I need to revise some parts/go through my own notes? . . . .

    (d)   Do I need to discuss future plans with my tutor/trainer?

          from Thorpe (1988) *Approaches to Adult Learning.*

The importance of learner evaluation has also been well recognised by the Training Commission, whose code of practice, 'Ensuring Quality in Open Learning, includes checklists for the learner to work through, both during and at the end of learning. Some of these ask the learner to evaluate the quality of teaching, as in these examples: 'Am I satisfied with what I am getting out of the package materials? Have I been able to get assignments or other work commented on by a tutor or counsellor as frequently as

I expected? Have I found it easy to contact my tutor and/or counsellor as agreed?' However other questions are included which direct the learners towards examination of their own learning, especially when the programme is completed: 'Have I had sufficient feedback (from self-assessment and/or from a tutor or counsellor) so that I can tell how much I have learned from the programme? If I do know how much I have learned, am I satisfied? If not does any fault lie with: the package? . . . the support service? Myself? Others . . . Do I myself want to do more organised studying?' (MSC, 1987)

To some extent of course, any open learning which involves formative assessment of the learner can encourage the learner to reflect on the progress they are making. This is certainly one of the hallmarks of good correspondence teaching, where the tutor not only corrects work, but comments on progress since the last assignment, explains what would be necessary to achieve a higher grade and poses questions for the learner to consider further. Bury Metropolitan College has developed the idea of self-assessment and provides all its students with a form for this purpose which they are encouraged to complete and keep in their work folder (Figure 4)

Figure 3.4: A proforma for a 'learning log'
An example from Bury Metropolitan College

				Subject
Student Name				Course Tutor
①	②	③	④	⑤
Type of Assignment	Time Taken	Student Mark	Tutor Mark	Students Comments

R. Ogier, Bury Metropolitan College

Some assignments are self-assessed, and the student puts their mark in column three of their learning log (figure 4), together with time taken to complete the work. Where the assignment has been tutor graded, the student completes columns 2 and 5, and the tutor completes column 4. The Director of Development, R. Ogier, comments on column 5, 'students' comments', as follows:

> *this is the most important column and students are encouraged to express their feelings about the work*

*completed. It can provide a useful discussion point, and can
assist in the development of a 'Learning Log'. An added value
of this comment column is that it acts as a monitoring device
on the materials themselves.*

*The tutor may, in conjunction with the student, assess the
development and progress being made by each individual
student. It can be a great value for a tutor to see the length
of time taken to complete a piece of work related to the
grades gained.*

*A further value is the acceptance of the student and the
trust in their opinions by the tutors. This encourages the
development of self esteem and helps in the broadening of
the whole person encouraging them to become self sufficient.'*

R. Ogier, personal correspondence.

This kind of activity is also a means of developing the learners'
awareness of the merit of their own work, which is a competence
more likely to be developed by learner and tutor assessment, than
by tutor assessment alone.

Where learning has been terminated by the learner's dropping
out, it is also possible to follow up with self-counselling material
of the kind shown in figures 1 and 2. The questions in this case
would be focused on reasons for withdrawal: 'did you withdraw
because the course wasn't right for you? because you didn't have
the time? because of a crisis or sudden change in your
circumstances?' and so on. The OU East Anglian Region uses
a booklet ('Bailing Out') with questions of this kind, followed by
information about sources of financial and other kinds of help,
and encouragement to come back to the University — either for
further counselling or to re-register if that seems appropriate at
a later stage.

Evaluation of the use of the booklet uncovered the strength
of feelings many students have about dropping out and the
appreciation they felt about receiving a sympathetic follow up. A
majority of the seventeen students interviewed had read the booklet
and valued it — either for themselves or as useful for others; these
are some of their comments:

'Nice to think that someone cares; will follow up and not just
let people drop out.'

'I've still got it; I was pleased that someone had noticed I wasn't
there any more.'

'Don't know if I found it helpful in practical terms, though I
think others would do. Keep sending it.'

'I'm sure there's a real need for it, but not particularly appropriate
for me. It's a support service — on other people's behalf I felt
glad.'

(Gibbons, 1984)

In one or two cases, decisions were changed, or the regional centre was able to resolve an administrative problem. However for most students, the value of this kind of contact is not that it can transform the conditions which led to drop out, but that it demonstrates understanding of their situation, and can help to alleviate some of the unpleasant feelings associated with drop out. Apart from any other consideration, such students are less likely to see themselves as failures, and more positively inclined to try learning again, if that becomes possible in the future.

Conclusion

Learner self-evaluation stands or falls on the commitment of the learner, even where self-evaluation is required by the course structure. It may often not be mandatory however, and the practitioner role will be to suggest approaches, or prompt with the right question at the right time. However, this is surely a critical intervention for the facilitation of better learning, and potentially no less important than the more time-consuming forms of evaluation introduced in the rest of Part II. Indeed it may not be less time consuming in the event, for the role of the practitioner does not end with initiation of the self evaluation process; having opened up the process, the practitioner has a responsibility to contribute to its development, if the learner requests his or her involvement.

The practitioner's other contribution is to demonstrate by example; by engaging openly in a process of self-evaluation of their own professional work, practitioners show their acceptance of personal responsibility for the quality of their own work and their commitment to continued professional and personal learning.

Further reading

Jacques, D. (1984) *Learning in Groups* Croom Helm.
   An excellent and practical guide to group work for learning purposes. Has a good section on evaluation methods for small groups.

Boyd, N. and Cowan, J. (1985) A case for self-assessment based on recent studies of student learning in *Assessment and Evaluation in Higher Education* Vol 10 No 3.

An excellent case study which illuminates the potential of self-assessment and some of the difficulties. The case in point was a course in Civil Engineering Design in the final session of a four-year degree course. The lecturer and 12 volunteer undergraduates agreed that learners would set their own goals and the lecturer's role would be to facilitate both the learning to which the student aspired and the assessment *by them* of their learning.

4   Tuition

Main Themes: *What is tuition? The diversity of tasks which may be carried out by staff designated as 'tutors'. The tutorial role of the tutor. Learner perceptions about tuition. Monitoring the performance of tutors and the quality of correspondence tuition. Unreliability in script grading. The importance of tutor comments on assignments and their role in learning. Criteria in assessing quality in tutor commenting and the correspondence role more generally. Face to face tuition and the different forms it can take. Measuring attendance at sessions and the student user rate.*

'Tuition' is used here to refer to course-related teaching/support provided by an individual for a particular learner or group of learners who are also using prepared materials as a resource. The tuition may take a variety of forms but is usually focused on *facilitating* the learning of a known group of learners not on replacing the materials. It usually involves a local tutor with whom learners are in direct (if infrequent) contact, whose role may be defined variously, for example, as interpreting course materials, enriching course content, diagnosing learning problems, helping with study skills and practical activities. The overlap with counselling may be more or less encouraged, depending on the kind of system set up, but counselling issues are treated separately here, in chapter 5.

What tutors actually do again varies widely, and they may have different titles in different systems — trainer, tutor-counsellor, learning advisor, teacher, and so on. However there are a number of major topics in tuition evaluation which provide a general introduction to the area — the tutor role, correspondence tuition and face to face tuition at workshops, resource centres and so on.

The role of the tutor

In systems like the Open University which commit very large amounts of resource to the design and presentation of multi-media packages, the question 'what is the role of the tutor?' has been from the beginning a focus of interest, research and development, particularly among regional staff and tutors themselves. The University has of course designated the role of the tutor in its staff development materials, and oriented it towards the facilitation of learning, especially for new learners, with perhaps more emphasis on a remedial role after the first year, when it is hoped that learners will be increasingly 'independent' in their approach. However there has also been evaluation of the role that tutors actually do play at the OU and in a variety of open learning systems. During 1983–84, researchers from the Industrial Training Research Unit, (sponsored by the then Manpower Services Commission) reported on the role of the tutor in the OU and in 27 vocationally oriented open learning courses: 14 in colleges, nine in companies and four

Figure 4.1: The main tasks of a tutor for the Kingston Open Learning Action Project for Industrial Supervisors

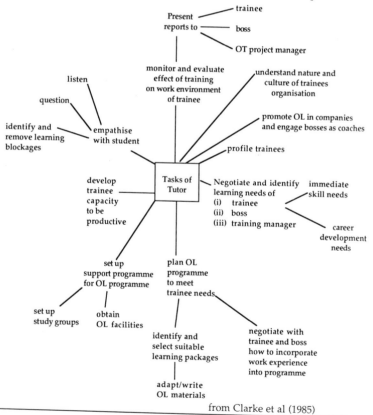

from Clarke et al (1985)

training association/ITB courses. (Clarke, Costello and Wright, 1985.)

The ITRU researchers distinguished between three main types of open learning which determine key differences between the role of the tutor:

(a)   those where tutors both prepare and deliver open learning materials;

(b)   those where bought-in materials are modified by tutors for a specific learner group and then delivered;

(c)   those where tutors deliver bought-in materials unadapted.

(Clarke et al, 1985)

Forty-eight tutors involved in the 27 courses sampled, completed a questionnaire on a wide range of aspects of their role. A selection of some of the questions together with the responses is shown in table 1. The tutors surveyed were on the whole experienced, with an average of over five years in open learning and experience of around 50 learners on average. Fourteen said they had had some training for open learning, the rest not.

Five in-depth case studies of particular courses revealed that tutors may combine marketing as well as authoring with a tutorial role, in some schemes. The authors mapped the range of tasks on each scheme and the example shown in figure 1 (the Kingston Open Learning Action Project for Industrial Supervisors) shows how all-embracing the role of 'tutor' can become, certainly by comparison with figure 2 (an Open University tutor).

Figure 4.2: The main tasks of an Open University tutor

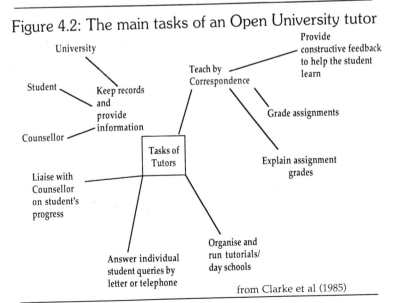

from Clarke et al (1985)

Table 4.1: Tutor responses on a selection of issues concerning their role

Industrial Training Research Unit survey of tutors on vocationally oriented open learning courses.

	Number of Responses	
	YES	NO
Are you involved in the preparation of learning materials for this scheme?	23	24
Are you involved with students before they undertake the course?	26	21
Do you arrange tutorials?	24	22

Where are you expected to be available?
    at all times   7
    at all times at work   4
    by appointment   24
    on the telephone 32		

Do you have to set assignments?	20	26
Are you responsible for marking assignments?	37	8
Do you keep records?	41	5

Are you responsible for evaluating/monitoring
    (a) the students
    (b) the course
	25
	16
		20
		23

The title open learning 'tutor' therefore can cover a very wide range of tasks, some of which have little to do with tuition, though they may influence how the tutorial role is carried out. This is summarised in figure 3.

However, whatever the job specification of tutors on different schemes, the *facilitation of learning* is often specified as at the core of *tuition* specifically. The components of this role are also varied, and not all schemes involve all of those shown in figure 4 below. One of the key 'optional' areas for example is the counselling/guidance area, which may be provided independently of the tutor in some schemes, or not at all.

Figure 4.3: A range of tasks which may be carried out by open learning tutors

Tasks	Skills/Knowledge required
Negotiation with business organisations	Marketing, interviewing, negotiating skills. Understanding of business organisation and practices.
Selection and adaption of existing OL materials	Awareness of OL databases and course materials. Content of qualifying syllabus.
Preparation of OL materials	Knowledge of target audience, learning goals and assessment needs. Ability to author and design learning materials.
Pre-course counselling (determining learning needs and assessment of ability and potential)	Knowledge of open learning material available. Skill in assessment, counselling/guidance, interpersonal relationships.
Induction	Communication, guidance, knowledge of the course and the open learning system concerned.
Supporting learning	Knowledge of what OL involves. Coaching, adapting to learning styles, teaching of study skills and examination techniques, running tutorials, telephone tutorials, assignment marking, record keeping, counselling/guidance, dealing with personal problems.
Post-Course counselling	Counselling/guidance, knowledge of career paths.

Includes material from a table in Clarke, Costello and Wright, (1985 p.43).

Figure 4.4: Component tasks of tuition in Open Learning

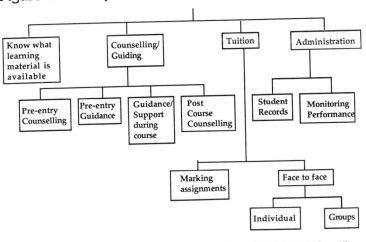

Adapted from a diagram in Clarke, Costello and Wright (1985), p.45

Learner perceptions of tuition

The role of tuition and the tutor within distance open learning has been explored in an OU project which surveyed over 5,000 students studying a variety of post-foundation courses, i.e. these students had already studied at least one foundation course at minimum, and many had studied and passed several other courses as well. They were asked to comment on their tuition on the course just completed, and on their experience of tuition in general. Kelly and Swift (1983)

The questionnaire used a five point rating scale to explore reactions to the provision of different media on the course students had just completed.

Table 4.2: Student reactions to media provision

Components:	Much too much %	Too much %	About right amount %	Too little %	Much too little %	No answer %
Correspondence materials (including units, supps., readers, set books)	2	17	76	5	0	1
Broadcasting (including TV/ video, audio cassettes)	2	11	70	12	2	3
Tuition (including TMA grades and comments, tutorials, etc., informal tutor contact)	0	1	58	29	10	1

Kelly and Swift, 1983

Of the three main components listed in table 2, tuition is the one eliciting most of the 'not enough provided' responses. Four in ten respondents noted too little provision of tuition and, when specifically asked, 45% favoured reduction in TV broadcasts if that allowed more tutor contact instead. 29% of students were also against this idea, however.

Having established something of the value of tuition relative to other media, the questionnaire then attempted to explore the quality of the role of the tutor in general. Students were asked to respond to a very wide range of statements, both about the course they had just completed (table 3) and about their experience of post-foundation tutors generally (table 4).

Table 4.3: Student perceptions of the help they need from tutors

Type of help needed from tutor:	% needing		Total requiring 'some' *or* 'a lot' of help
	A lot of help	Some help	
Analysis of the errors and deficiencies in my TMAs	21	45	66
Explanation of what a good answer to a TMA would have been	21	37	58
Clear identification of the good points in my TMAs	19	39	58
The clearing up of problems, obscurities in the teaching materials	14	44	58
Developing a fuller, more rounded understanding of the subject area than that provided by correspondence and other materials	16	42	58
Analysis/feedback on how I was progressing in my understanding of the subject	15	42	57
Human support and encouragement from tutor	19	34	53
Advice on strategies for coping with materials and set tasks	13	38	51
Identification of the requirements of TMAs/CMAs	12	38	50
Understanding the main themes and issues of the course	10	40	50
Help with preparation for the final exam	16	33	49
Development of my skills so that I can do better in the future	8	34	42
Advice on essay-writing/structuring TMA answers/ study skills	7	27	34
Help with identifying my strengths and weaknesses as a student	6	26	32
Discussion, practice in developing skills in argument	8	24	32
Support, reassurance when depressed, worried about my studies	9	21	30
Help with pacing my studies, identifying priorities	3	18	21

Adapted from Kelly and Swift (1983)

NOTE: TMA – Tutor Marked Assignment
CMA – Computer Marked Assignment

Table 4.4: Student evaluation of the role of the tutor and tuition generally

Attitude Statements:	Strongly agree %	Agree %	In between %	Disagree %	Disagree strongly %	No views %
Apart from having my TMAs graded and commented on, I don't want or need other contact with a tutor	2	5	14	36	41	2
		8*			77*	
Without a course tutor there would be no-one in the OU system to whom I could turn for help with study problems	23	46	11	14	3	3
		68			17	
A good tutor can make a course; a poor tutor can spoil one	34	32	15	11	3	4
		67			14	
Some aspects of most courses can only be taught effectively on a face-to-face basis	13	45	20	14	13	6
		58			17	
If the amount of tutor support were reduced it would adversely affect my ability to cope with OU studies	14	31	20	22	9	3
		45			31	
Without the help of a tutor I would probably have dropped out from at least one course that I stuck with	10	15	10	33	27	6
		25			59	
If there were no provision for contact with the course tutor, the OU would lack credibility as an academic institution ...	28	40	11	11	3	8
		68			14	

* Percentages are rounded up or down, as appropriate

Swift and Kelly (1983)

Students were asked whether they had needed help from their tutor on the course they had studied in 1982 and the responses are shown in table 3. On all except one of the 17 types of help listed, at least 30% of students reported needing some or a lot of help. Predictably most (two-thirds) needed help on continuous assessment (tutor marked assignments or TMAs) over half had also needed 'human support and encouragement', 'feedback on how I was progressing in the subject', and help in 'developing a fuller, more rounded understanding of the subject area than that provided by correspondence and other materials'.

Overall, it was clear from this survey that students value tuition as a whole very highly. 68% felt that without a course tutor there would be no one to help with study problems and 25% definitely felt that without the help of a tutor they would probably have dropped out from at least one course. Over two-thirds felt that 'A good tutor can make a course, a poor tutor can spoil one'. (See table 4).

It was only possible to devise these lists of attitudinal statements because individual tutors had already described their own role in accounts published in 'Teaching at a Distance' and much discussion with tutors had occurred either in interviews or through the regular staff development role of regional staff. Much qualitative 'research' had already occurred, albeit informally; this provided a firm basis for the design of the questionnaire, especially the attitudinal statements shown in tables 3 and 4.

Correspondence tuition

Many open learning providers will want to monitor and evaluate the performance of tutors in this area which remains otherwise a private transaction between tutor and learner where the learner is especially vulnerable to the effects of poor quality tuition.

Turnround

There is first the turnround issue — how quickly does the learner get back an assignment after posting or handing in, and how much of this time is taken by the tutor in marking? Many of the European correspondence schools can monitor tutor turnround very easily because learners mail their assignments direct to the institution which then mails on a batch to the tutor, who also returns marked scripts to the school. The system 'knows' therefore when the tutor should have received what, and can chase late returners, if there are any.

In a system like the OU, where students send assignments direct to their tutor, such checking is not possible. Tutors return marked assignments to the University where a record is made onto computer files for both the tutor and the student. Where no assignments have been received by 21 days after the cut-off date (the date by which tutors should receive scripts from their students for that assignment) a 'marker' against the tutor name is made automatically by the computer and the appropriate staff to investigate are notified. In 1986 for example, 20% of tutors were identified as late in this way, on one or more occasions. (Field, 1987)

This is an imperfect system but it does identify the worst offenders. In a system where tutorial staff number tens and not thousands, it would be possible to monitor tutor turnround regularly for every learner allocated to a tutor for a proportion, if not for all assignments.

Recent research at the OU confirms the assumption that students do want to get their assignments back quickly, though it reveals other issues too. The average time a student has to wait to get back their assignment from marking has varied in different years and also at different times of year. The range has been from 17 days (1983-85) up to 20 days (1986) and, an experimental study of three Social Science courses in 1987 recorded 24 days as the average number a student waits for each TMA to return. A proportion of this time is of course taken while the assignment is in the (second class) post and while it is being processed. Tutors in the same experimental study, tended to keep the assignment 9-10 days for marking. Although many other factors are involved, a majority of students in this study (59%) said they would prefer the assignment to be returned direct to them by their tutor, because they felt it would arrive more quickly by that route. (Field, 1987)

Students also commented on a number of other issues: the illegibility of some tutors' handwriting, and the particular difficulty of getting assignments back towards the end of a course, when they were needed for revision.

Grading reliability

The speed with which tutors mark and return assignments, is not the only important issue. There is also the issue of tutor reliability in awarding grades. The OU for example has a system for checking leniency/severity in tutor marking. This is based on the assumption that a norm can be created by calculating the percentage of A, B, C, D, F grades (or their numerical equivalents) awarded to all scripts submitted by a course cohort, on each assignment in turn. Each tutor's grades for her group on each assignment can therefore be compared with the national distribution of grades and the 'deviation from the norm' observed.

This system provides a performance indicator of reliability but, as is often the case with performance indicators, there are problems with its use. The most important of these is that tutor groups can be quite small – sometimes around 10 or less by the middle of a course – and one cannot assume that each group represents a 'normal distribution' of ability on the course. Some groups do have a higher proportion of really able students than others, for example. The extent to which a tutor is deviating from the mean, and whether in the direction of being 'too harsh' or 'too lenient' a marker, offers again only an indication that corrective action may be necessary. Investigation may show however that grades were justified.

Some of the most effective measures for improving reliability however revolve around opportunities for tutors to discuss their expectations together during the marking process. An OU study where tutors were able to discuss how they marked the first assignment, showed improved reliability on the next few assignments at least. Reliability among a group of markers can also be improved by the kind of procedures used in examination marking; tutors mark, say, four or five scripts independently and then compare grades and comments.

Figure 4.5: Characteristics of three types of assignment and the range in grades given by tutors

Group*	Subject(s)	Type of assignment and nature of guidance provided for the tutor	Average grade range per script (University Scale 0-100)[1]
1	Arts, Social Sciences and Educational Studies	Single essay assignments with impression grading. General guidance offered, but no marking scheme. Letter grades used (these being converted to numbers on the University's 1-100 scale for conflation purposes).	2.3
2	Physical sciences and physical science-based technology subjects	3-4 questions per assignment, each often sub-divided into part questions. More specific than those of Group 1. Analytic marking schemes using numbers always given and a numeric grade for a script derived by combining the part scores.	1.2
3	Mathematics	2-3 questions each usually divided into parts. Detailed answers given in tutor notes with an analytic marking scheme using numbers. Numeric grade derived by combining part-scores.	0.9

* Group 1 contained six assignments, Group 2 four assignments and Group 3 three assignments.

1 100; A = 93, B = 78, C = 63, D = 48, E = 35, F = 23, G = 7

Byrne, C. Tutor-marked Assignements at the OU: A question of reliability (p.37) adapted from TAAD no. 15 1979.

Why are markers 'unreliable' in the first place, you may ask? Evaluation of tutor marked assignments at the Open University in the later seventies confirmed earlier findings from other contexts, that a group of tutors marking the same set of scripts was likely to grade them differently. A selection of assignments covering all faculties was chosen and for each assignment, three tutors marked the scripts of the same 12 students. Some indication of the differences between the assignments is shown in figure 5.

The results of the study of grades awarded showed that:
• the same script was given different grades by different tutors; there was often a difference of two to three grades on scripts from group one. Variation in the grades awarded was much larger for scripts in Group 1 than it was for those in Groups 2 and 3, where Group 3 was slightly better than Group 2 (See figure 5).
• tutors also differed in their ranking of scripts, especially tutors in Group 1.
• the average (mean) of all grades awarded by each tutor showed that means often differed, indicating that tutors vary in leniency/severity
• some tutors used a wider range of grades than others
• tutors interpreted the grading scale differently; for example they might agree that a script was one of the best but grade it anything from C+ to A-.
• tutors of students in Groups 2 and 3 did tend to be more lenient in marking scripts from 'their own' students but the effects were small by comparison with the variation in grades given the same script.

It may be surprising to discover that, even in a subject like mathematics, experienced tutors do not agree absolutely on grades. This means that we would expect to find different grades for the same script even among experienced tutors, and figure 6 suggests the range based on the findings discussed here.

Figure 4.6: Approximate frequency with which two tutors would be expected to award grades differing by at least one point on a large set of scripts (expressed on a 0-10 scale)

Group	At least 4 points	At least 2 points	At least 1 point
1	1 in 25	1 in 3	2 in 3
2	Very rare	1 in 25	1 in 3
3	Very rare	1 in 70	1 in 4

Byrne (1979)

The value of this kind of evaluation is not primarily the discovery of unreliability per se since, on the basis of previous research in conventional education 'unreliability' can be expected. Its value in this case was, first, that it demonstrated that tutor unreliability on continuous assessment was no worse than that reported in studies elsewhere on examination marking. Second, it stimulated consideration of the possible causes of unreliability, and provided a very helpful form of staff development for those taking part.

Those tutors involved discussed their grades and discovered why others had judged a script differently in an atmosphere which was supportive rather than threatening. As suggested earlier, similar exercises, especially at the beginning of a course, can improve both grading and commenting on scripts thereafter.

Although the exercise demonstrated that it would be unrealistic to hope to eradicate unreliability completely, some of the reasons for unreliability became clearer, and a number were associated with the quality of assignment design, where improvements can be made. Some assignments generated more unreliability than others, because of unclear wording, poor student or tutor notes. The single essay question generally came out worst, of all question types, and can be improved by being broken down into a number of components, if that is possible. Students then need guidance on the relative importance of these parts, and problems can be created if this is not given, or if unrealistic word lengths are provided.

Evaluation of tutor reliability can therefore be as much an evaluation of the quality of assignments on a course as of the quality of tutor performances. During discussion of differences of opinion, it was possible to pinpoint aspects in the advice to students, or in the notes to tutors, which were the cause of disagreement, or to pinpoint other inadequacies. These are valuable findings for the redrafting of assignments.

Tutor comments and correspondence teaching

Although the grade awarded a script is very important to the learner, the purpose of the assignment interchange includes far more than assessment of the standard that it reaches. It may often be the case that the learner's work is not graded at all. Whether there is a grade or not, however, the learner is looking for feedback on general progress with the course and specific help with areas of difficulty. The quality of the tutor's comments on a script therefore also matter as well as the grade, and are not unconnected. A low grade for example can make it very difficult for some students to read comments carefully and learn from them, disappointment and a sense of failure making them want to push the script away and forget about it. Clearly this is a very individual matter, but survey findings suggest that there is little basis for the view that students are only interested in the grade (see table 5).

Table 4.5: The importance attached by students to provision of four types of content in their tutor's comments on assignments for the course

| | **Importance attached to attributes:** | | |
	VERY IMPORTANT	FAIRLY IMPORTANT	NOT VERY/ NOT AT ALL IMPORTANT
Attributes of TMA comments:	%	%	%
Analysis and clear explanation of where things went wrong and why.	78	17	4
Constructive criticism – helpful and encouraging comments.	68	25	6
Understanding of reasons for grade awarded to TMA.	52	30	16
Assessment of general progress at several stages throughout the year.	33	33	31

TMA — tutor marked assignment   Kelly and Swift (1983)

The 1983 OU Survey of students mentioned earlier provides conclusive evidence for the importance of correspondence tuition. Table 5 indicates that almost all respondents (over 90%) felt assignment comments were important for explaining errors and making helpful criticism. Students were also asked what they usually did with marked assignments and table 6 indicates that fewer than 10% are only interested in the grade. 72% read comments carefully and tried to use them in subsequent assignments. There seems good evidence that the quality of correspondence teaching is a vital part in the effectiveness of the system as a whole, from two points of view: the learning process and the performance of students on continuous assessment.

Table 4.6: Types of use of correspondence teaching by students

	Usually did this	Sometimes did this	Never did this	No answer
Read comments carefully and, where appropriate, tried to incorporate advice into later assignments.	72	23	3	3
Made use of comments for examination revision.	43	33	19	5
Read comments carefully and followed up references made to units, books, articles, etc.	33	45	17	4
Took up points made on TMAs in tutorials.	17	29	50	4
Did additional work on TMA in the light of comments.	12	33	53	3
Only ever took a quick look at grades and comments.	9	19	68	4
Contacted tutor outside tutorial to take up points.	5	22	70	4
Used comments in self help groups.	6	12	75	7
Looked at grades but ignored comments.	2	6	88	4

TMA — tutor marked assignment   Kelly and Swift (1983)

Given the importance of correspondence teaching, it is an important area for monitoring and evaluation. This can be done by asking students directly, as in the case of the survey findings reported above. However, it may also be particularly important to check that professional norms are being achieved by individual tutors, and this requires the judgement of professional peers. In a system like the OU, monitoring of tutor comments requires that scripts are read by a subject expert with experience of correspondence teaching. A proportion of scripts is selected from one or more assignments marked by the tutor being monitored. A tutor can expect that the scripts they mark will be monitored at least twice a year on a full credit course (440 hours and around 8 assignments) , and at least once a year on a half credit course (220 hours and around 4 assignments). New tutors, and any tutor whose work causes concern, are monitored more often.

The criteria which can be used to judge the effectiveness of an example of correspondence teaching naturally depend on the type of learning outcomes of a course, and its difficulty. Figure 7 lists a range of possible criteria.

As important as checking standards is the communication back to a tutor of the results of monitoring. During the course of an evaluation of the OU's briefing of its part-time staff, it was discovered that tutors value monitor comments and use them as an indication of whether they are meeting the University's requirements for correspondence tuition. (Thorpe, 1985) Some faculties now send the monitor's comments direct to the tutor, who has the right of reply, if necessary. The monitor's comments therefore need to be phrased with the kind of constructiveness and consideration that is expected of tutors in their comments to students.

Figure 4.7: Criteria which can be used in monitoring a tutor's scriptmarking

A tutor marked assignment can be assessed for

Efficiency: returns marked script within the period required by the
                              system
                              writes legibly
                              Completes associated records/forms in full and
                              accurately

Grading: accurate/lenient/severe
                              correct use of marking scheme (if there is one)

Relationship with   tone friendly and sympathetic
learner: Comments likely to encourage continued learning
                              Further contact suggested, where desirable

Overall appraisal of learner's work

: praise on achievement
: reasons for the grade given
: suggestions for what would have been necessary to get a higher grade
: improvements needed for next assignment
: assessment of progress in course as a whole

Detailed comments

: corrects any errors
: suggests improvements in approach/structure as necessary
: suggests course pages or components learner needs to revise
: tells learner what she is doing well/adequately
: comments on any irrelevance by referring to wording of the assignment
: shows where marks have been lost (if relevant)
: picks up over/under length, poor presentation
: points to the relevance of materials/developments outside the course for
  development of ideas the learner has expressed.

Face to face tuition

Face to face tuition takes different forms depending on the context for open learning. Figure 8 indicates some of the variety in this range.

Figure 4.8: Some of the forms of face to face tuition

Category	Duration	Learning context
On-site supervision	Mostly under 1 hour, available continuously, on demand from learner	Often 1 to 1: Job supervisor may act as tutor for employee on 'on-the-job' training
College-based 'class' or workshop	Approximately 1-3 hours	By appointment or drop in. Learners may consult a tutor for 1 to 1 help. Group work also organised
Resource Centre	By arrangement	Learner uses packages (text, video or audio based, or CBT) either on site or elsewhere. Help often available on site, on demand
Tutorials in distance open learning		
— weekday evening	1½-2 hours	Usually 1 tutor with a group of learners
— Saturday	½ to 1 day	1 or more sessions available to learners, led by different tutors
— Specially scheduled session	around 1 hour session scheduled during study to respond to needs of one or more learners which had not been predicted	Tutor with one, or a group of learners
Residential Schools	Weekend, up to one full week	Variety of group and one to one activities with several tutors. May include lab work, lectures and counselling too

In most forms of open learning, face to face tuition has a voluntary aspect; it is provided with the assumption that learners will want to use it. But do they in fact use it, and for how long and how often? There are also important managerial considerations for monitoring attendance, because buildings, rooms and salaries are costly resources to offer a group of learners. Does take-up justify provision? Could we increase take up if we re-organised provision, to better match learner convenience? These are important questions, particularly for providers like the OU which has not made tutorial attendance compulsory; although the value of face to face interaction and group tutorials is emphasised, it must still be possible to pass an OU course without having attended tutorials.

This is one of the features of 'openness', most obviously for those who are physically disabled, geographically isolated, or otherwise prevented from attending.

Reliable figures for learner attendance can only be gathered by a meticulous and systematic monitoring process. This is likely to require the co-operation of learners, clerical staff and tutors, depending on the system. In the case of a college-based workshop, the learner initiates a record of attendance which is collated and reviewed by clerical or tutorial staff. At the Bradford and Ilkley Community College (BICC) Workshops for Mathematics and Communications, learners are asked on enrollment which sessions during the week they elect to attend. This information is entered onto the microcomputer database set up for the Workshops. A new printout is produced for each day of the week, listing the names and sessions of all those who ought to attend on that day. As each learner comes in, they sign for the appropriate session against their name and at the end of the week, all the registers are entered onto the learner database.

Figure 4.9: Session Register: Mathematics Workshop

Attendances for the first ten weeks by all learners electing for the Monday afternoon session

Counsellor	Student Registration Number	Part-time/ Full-time	Name (Alphabetical order)	Monday Afternoon Week No											A* A/P
				1	2	3	4	5	6	7	8	9	10	11 etc	
ND	7099487	F	ALNASER	/	/	/	/	/	/	/	/	/	/	/	10/10
SH	7115180	F	BASHIR		/	/	/	/	0	0	0	0	0		4/9
ND	7071191	P	CHAN		/	/								X	2/2
PB	7126522	P	CLARKE	/	0	/	0	0	0	0	0	0	0	0	2/10
PB	709437A	P	CLOUGH										/	/	2/2

* – Attendance: Actual/Possible   X – indicates withdrawn

Source: N. Dow, Mathematics Workshop, BICC

Data can be taken off the database in various ways, for different purposes. Figure 9 shows a version of the printout of a cumulative register for the Monday afternoon session, showing all learners due for attendance at that session together with the number of attendances achieved out of the total possible (remembering that learners can register at any point during the year, after week one). This register would enable a counsellor scheduled to cover Monday afternoon sessions, to check the attendances of all learners who have been allocated to them and are due to attend every Monday afternoon. It is also possible to generate a printout for every learner, showing all sessions attended, and total hours (figure 10). This enables the counsellor, or a clerical assistant to pick up all who have missed for more than, say, two weeks, (or a specified number of attendances), so that a follow-up letter can be sent, offering support and asking the learner to get in touch.

Figure 4.10: GCSE Mathematics: Learner Register

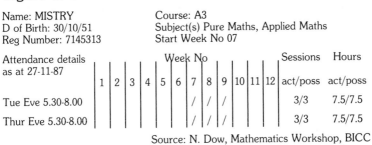

Name: MISTRY	Course: A3
D of Birth: 30/10/51	Subject(s) Pure Maths, Applied Maths
Reg Number: 7145313	Start Week No 07

Attendance details as at 27-11-87						Week No						Sessions	Hours
	1	2	3	4	5	6	7	8	9	10	11	12	act/poss	act/poss
Tue Eve 5.30-8.00							/	/	/				3/3	7.5/7.5
Thur Eve 5.30-8.00							/	/	/				3/3	7.5/7.5

Source: N. Dow, Mathematics Workshop, BICC

Where learners are using flexi-study or distance learning options, it is more likely to be the tutor who records contact. South Manchester Community College uses a proforma similar to that shown in figure 2 chapter 5, which is provided in duplicate form to flexi-study tutors who complete and return the duplicate copy to the college on a monthly basis. The open learning staff transfer the information to a cumulative form for each tutor, and also onto a computerised learner database. These records are regularly checked by the Workshop Co-ordinator; if a tutor has no contact with a learner for two consecutive months, the co-ordinator sends the learner concerned a follow-up letter.

Each of these systems could be used to produce a cumulative total of actual versus possible attendances for all learners (in the case of workshops), and number and type of contact between learner and tutor, in the case of flexi-study. The Open University has undertaken a large number of studies of this kind for two main purposes: the first to ascertain the nature and distribution across the year of tutorial and counselling tasks; the second, to provide indicators of the efficiency with which face to face tuition has been provided and its effectiveness as a medium for teaching and learner support. I shall return to the value of attendance rates as indicators, but first we need to look more closely at the methods which can be used.

Monitoring attendance can take a variety of forms but is the basis of calculating usage and therefore must be done systematically and reliably. Collecting attendance data is only the beginning though, and a review of the findings of OU evaluation in this area will serve to indicate some of the pitfalls.

Some of these arise from differences in what has been measured. For example, two measures have been used most often, and they produce quite different rates. The first measure is the *student user rate*, that is the proportion of students who have used tutorials *at least once* on a course. Three major studies since 1976 have consistently produced a figure of around 60% of students who say they have used tutorials during the course studied. In 1979, a survey of 16000 students studying 91 courses produced findings shown in table 7 below.

Table 4.7: Student use of tuition

	Percentage of students making	
	Use	Extensive Use
Correspondence tutoring	90	31
Study Centre Tutorials	59	29
Telephone Tutorials	15	02

Source: Grundin (1980)

Similarly 63% of the post foundation students surveyed in 1983 said that they used tutorials, whether evening or Saturday morning sessions. However this survey also asked students to discriminate between different forms of tuition, and to say whether they were aware that a particular form of tuition was available to them. As table 8 shows, if we take this awareness into account in calculating percentage usage, rather higher figures result. Thus 75% of those

Table 4.8: Student reported usage of tutorials

	Col. 1 % aware of tutorial programme	Col. 2[1] % using the mode	Col. 3[2] % taking up option
Types of Tuition:	%	%	%
Day/half day schools	53	33	62
Evening (or Saturday equivalent) face-to-face tutorials	83	62	75
Individual face-to-face tutorials	11	6	55
Group telephone tutorials	6	2	33
Individual telephone tutorials	26	12	46

[1] base = all respondents
[2] base = all in column 1

Kelly and Swift (1983)

saying they knew about the programme of tutorials on their course attended one or more sessions.

The second common measure of attendance is the *rate of attendance at each tutorial* during a particular course presentation period, often presented as an average for the period as a whole. *Rates of tutorial attendance* measure different things from *the student user rate* — estimates of the proportion students who use tutorials – and there are important implications for the way these two indicators are used. If, for example, the 60% of students who stated they had attended one or more tutorials, only ever attended one, and that the first scheduled tutorial for the course, this would be vital information for those organising the tutorial programme — and for the tutor. The only way of checking this out is to measure attendance at each tutorial, using attendance records.

A number of such studies has been done by OU regional staff, who organise tutorial programmes annually and therefore need to monitor the extent to which a cohort of students is being 'reached' by their allocation of tutorial resources. These rates of tutorial attendance vary widely by course/faculty, by tutor and even by different years. The attendance rate also varies during the year and the first tutorial may often produce 90-100% attendance, with another peak before the examination being a common pattern. Again, the drop in attendance does vary by course, being noticeably less for example on some third level maths courses known to be very difficult. Overall averages of attendance for the whole year have been found of around 30% going up to 60%, — the higher figure taking into account dropout during course study. (Thorpe, 1983)

Apart from the need for care in specifying what has been measured, and in clarifying terminology, there is the question of the accuracy of the base on which percentages are measured. If a learner has dropped out, or is not actively pursuing a particular course, it would seem reasonable to exclude them from the total number of those doing a course and therefore considered *eligible for tutorials*. Tutorial attendance rates appear higher where the base has been adjusted in this way to account for drop-out. However it is not always easy to find out who is 'actively studying' and thus rates of attendance are best seen as approximations of more or less accuracy depending on how carefully they have been generated.

Apart from the difficulty of calculating accurate attendance rates, is the issue of how they are used as performance indicators. While they may offer an indicator of the efficiency of resource allocation, can they tell us anything at all about the educational effectiveness of tutorials or workshops? Unfortunately the existence of data on attendance can encourage an over-simple interpretation of their meaning: 'high rates of attendance justify the provision of tuition, low rates justify cutting tuition'. Tutors themselves are likely to be very wary of these kinds of response, knowing as they do how many factors affect attendance on a specific occasion — only one of which, albeit important, is the quality of tuition they provide. And, if only five out of (say) 16 students attend a tutorial, but value what they get out of it, does that adequately justify provision? And what about the 11 non-attenders? Are they happy with the situation, or would they prefer some other kind of tutorial support?

There are no hard and fast rulings here; decisions can only be taken effectively in the light of local resources and learner needs. Nor is it argued that attendance data, though difficult to interpret, are not worth having. It is now possible to see in the OU that the same tutor, on the same course, operating the same tutorial programme, can get very different attendance rates from one year to the next (Thorpe, 1983). This is one reason why surveys of the preferences of students for particular locations and times of the week for tutorials can offer misleading data for designing future programmes so as to maximise attendance rates.

However, collecting evidence of attendance over several years or several course presentations can be useful because it establishes at least the upper and lower parameters of what can be expected. A fall in attendance rates then is likely to indicate the need for further investigation. It may be that the distribution of tutorials throughout the course clashes with other demands, like the cut-off date for submission of an assignment, so that some students who would otherwise attend choose not to do so. By re-scheduling the times or locations of tutorials, it may be possible to increase attendance and thus use staff resources more efficiently.

The performance that attendance rates do not measure directly of course, is that of the tutor. This requires qualitative evidence from students or colleagues or both. On first appointment, new OU part-time tutors are usually observed during a tutorial by a member of full-time regional staff, and all those tutoring at summer school are observed, whether new or experienced. At the Social Science Foundation Course Summer School, students are asked to complete a questionnaire (anonymously) on the performance of tutors with whom they have worked during periods of 9-12 hours each tutor. Tutor competences are listed (clarity of presentation, responsiveness to questions, handling discussion, and so on) and tutors are rated on a five point scale from 'excellent' to 'very weak'. Tutors are provided with the feedback on their own performance before the end of the school, when there is some opportunity to make changes, and perhaps discuss any worrying results with the Course Director. However the main benefits are seen to be in the longer term, for the tutor, and for the student, whose evaluation is seen as important and worth taking into account. It may also help some students with strong negative reactions to express their feelings and to learn from the experience. This is also a useful mechanism for identifying weaknesses in the design of the summer school, and thus improving it for future students. (Bradshaw, 1987)

Tutor performance is one of the most difficult areas to evaluate and to develop subsequently, because the needs of learners are so varied and because the way one behaves as a tutor is so closely tied to personality factors. Any significant changes in behaviour require the tutor's voluntary commitment and a personal conviction that change is necessary. A positive step in that direction is the use by tutors themselves of some form of feedback from learners on the quality of tutorials they give, and if relevant, the helpfulness of their other functions, like assignment comments and telephone contact. Feedback forms can be handed out at the end of several sessions or when several assignments have been marked, and returned by learners anonymously. One format is to list a number of desirable characteristics of the tutoring concerned, and to ask the learner to rate the tutor against each one on a five point scale, as in figure 11. This example also includes a rating for the general importance of each item, so that the tutor can see how important a good or poor rating of one characteristic is likely to be to the learner.

It is also useful to ask learners to complete ratings of this kind *before* tuition starts, as an indication of their expectations. In this case, additional items exploring their perceptions of themselves in the group context might also be helpful: for example —

'I find it very difficult to speak out in a group'
'I prefer groups of 3 or 4 to bigger groups'
'I can speak more easily when the tutor isn't there'
'I tend to keep quiet not to show my ignorance'

— and so on.

Even if feedback forms are not used, it can still generate thought provoking comments from learners to ask them how helpful they are finding the tuition provided. Three questions which can be used in discussion to pick up most of the responses in this area are:

'What did you find most useful?'
'What did you find least useful?'
'What changes would you like to make?'

Figure 4.11: Learner ratings of tutor competences

Learners can be asked to rate the importance of particular features of tuition in general, and the effectiveness of their tutor in relation to each one.

Not applicable/ Can't decide	Not at all important	Of little importance	Neither	Important	Of great importance	Characteristic	Strongly disagree	Disagree	Neither agree nor disagree	Agree	Strongly agree	Not applicable
6	1	2	3	4	5	Characteristic	1	2	3	4	5	6
	General Importance						*Applies to your Tutor*					
6	1	2	3	4	5	a. Clarity of explanation	1	2	3	4	5	6
6	1	2	3	4	5	b. Enthusiasm for subject	1	2	3	4	5	6
6	1	2	3	4	5	c. Stimulates me to think for myself	1	2	3	4	5	6
6	1	2	3	4	5	d. Well organised	1	2	3	4	5	6
6	1	2	3	4	5	e. Stimulates good group discussion	1	2	3	4	5	6
6	1	2	3	4	5	f. Audible and easy to follow	1	2	3	4	5	6
6	1	2	3	4	5	g. Resolves specific difficulties/ questions I have	1	2	3	4	5	6
6	1	2	3	4	5	h. Prevents discussion being dominated by 1 or 2 learners	1	2	3	4	5	6
6	1	2	3	4	5	i. Encourages me to contribute to the session	1	2	3	4	5	6
6	1	2	3	4	5	j. Returns assignments quickly	1	2	3	4	5	6
6	1	2	3	4	5	k. Explains clearly where things went wrong and why	1	2	3	4	5	6
6	1	2	3	4	5	l. Leaves me feeling more encouraged to carry on	1	2	3	4	5	6
6	1	2	3	4	5	m. Accessible on the telephone	1	2	3	4	5	6

OU students have also been asked why they attend tutorials in general and, of the reasons shown in table 9, 'to meet my tutor and discuss course study matters' was chosen by 63% of all respondents. Of the reasons given for non-attendance, the 1983 survey notes the following:

> *The most common reasons respondents gave for not going to all the tutorial events for their course all related to personal factors: family, personal and work commitments. However, the second most frequent was distance/time spent getting there. Further, significant minorities did not attend because the potential value was too little relative to the time/money/ effort involved or they preferred to spend their time on the units/assignments. Student decisions were also influenced by disappointing early tutorials on their course and by past experience of unhelpful tutorials.*
>
> *Asked to assess their degree of satisfaction with the face-to-face tuition available to them on their course, 24% of respondents reported being fully satisfied, 32% satisfied but with reservations, 11% fairly dissatisfied, and 5% very dissatisfied. A further 23% had not attended any tutorials and 5% did not respond to the question.*
>
> *Insufficient tutorials to cover the course adequately stood out as the most common cause for dissatisfaction with tutorials, 24% giving this as a reason.*

(Kelly and Swift, 1983)

Table 4.9: Reasons for attending tutorials

	% for whom reason applied
To meet my tutor and discuss course/study matters	63
Help with difficult aspects of the course	51
To meet other students and discuss course/study related problems with them	50
To extend my understanding of the subject beyond the limits/scope of the units	45
Discussion and help with TMAs	44
To sustain my interest and motivation	40
Revision and preparation for exams	38
General support for studies	37
Experience of practical work/lab. sessions/computing	9*
Just because tutorials were provided	8

*These are a feature of only a small proportion of sessions.

Kelly and Swift (1983)

Conclusion

This chapter has not provided a comprehensive account of all the media through which tuition can be provided; telephone tuition is especially important, audio tape can also be used, and computer conferencing offers an exciting technology which opens up the possibility of a very much greater communication between learner and tutor (Ryan, 1987, and Kaye, 1987). However, all three can be evaluated by drawing on existing knowledge of learner perceptions and use of the core tutor functions of face to face and correspondence teaching. And some of the clearest messages in the evaluation of tuition derive from learner perceptions of the general role and value of the tutor, irrespective of the medium through which particular functions are carried out.

The effective evaluation of tuition requires, at minimum, regular monitoring of the quality of tuition offered all learners, and tutor evaluation of the quality of their own interaction with a particular group of learners. Direct tutor involvement in evaluation need not always require the tutor to invite written feedback from learners; it may take the form of meetings with learners to review their progress, or discussion with other tutors at staff development meetings. The essence of tuition should be its responsiveness to the learner, and that requires *tutor self-evaluation , as well as system evaluation.*

Further reading

Murgatroyd, S. (1980) What Actually Happens in Tutorials in *Teaching at a Distance* No 18.

Summarises models of face to face teaching and presents analysis of tutor-student interaction in tutorials at the Open University.

Teaching at a Distance: formerly published by the Open University and since 1986, replaced by *Open Learning*, published jointly with Longman. Both journals have many articles relevant to the tutor role and its evaluation. Contact Regional Academic Services, the Open University, Milton Keynes.

Estell, G.R. (1986) *Staff Development for Open Learning Tutors.*

Harrogate College of Arts and Technology co-ordinates a particularly 'open' form of open learning. 'OWTLET' accepts all enquirers irrespective of their learning goal and the period they have available for study, providing a tutor can be found, who selects any materials used and negotiates a learning programme with the individual concerned. The report takes the form of a brief summary of evaluation of the staff development needs of open learning tutors, together with the staff development units produced out of the project: unit one — the concept of open learning, unit two — the initial meeting, and unit three — a continuing dialogue.

Clarke, A., Colstello, M., Wright, T. (1984/5) *The Role of Tasks of Tutors in Open Learning Systems* Industrial Training Research Unit, Cambridge.

A very useful typology of different systems for the provision of tuition and counselling, with detailed descriptions of the tutor role in particular. Twenty-seven open learning courses were surveyed, and five very different courses studied in depth.

Rowlands, S., and N. (1986) *Into Open Learning* Open Learning Systems Ltd., 6 South Molton Street, London.

Includes some useful formats for recording workshop loading, tutor/student contact sheet, student attendance record, counselling contacts and so on.

5 Counselling and learner progress

Main themes: *What is counselling and its role in open learning? Core counselling functions. Issues in counselling evaluation: what is the need for counselling? How should it be provided? How much is it used, by whom? What are its outcomes? A framework for the evaluation of counselling. Examples of evaluation of the provider perspective and of the user perspective.*

Counselling and its role

It is more difficult in this chapter to be confident of identifying a core of common concerns because the extent to which learners are explicitly 'advised' or 'counselled' in open learning schemes varies widely. 'Counselling' is particularly difficult because there is, if anything, even less agreement about what it is than is the case with tuition. Very few open learning systems employ staff with the title of counsellor, and perhaps a number assume that any 'counselling' needs of learners will be handled by tutors. The list of tutor roles provided by Clark et al, for example, include quite a few that would be seen as educational counselling by the Open University:

— 'developing study skills in people who left school early'
— 'being prepared to make some kind of constructive response when a student comes out with a personal problem over the phone'
— 'helping students with study methods at (a) start of course and (b) near exams.'

Clarke, Costello and Wright (1985)

Similarly, those that do use the counsellor title include different functions within the role, and mean different things in practice.

The Mathematics Workshop at Bradford and Ilkley Community College for example, assigns learners to a mathematics 'counsellor', who undoubtedly counsels but whose core role in practice also includes tuition, as it has been defined in chapter 4.

Differences in terminology of these kinds mean that the evaluator needs to read this chapter together with the preceding one and to identify which topics are more relevant to the system being evaluated, whatever the occupational titles in use.

Irrespective of these differences in terminology, the position taken by many in education and training, is that 'counselling' has an essential role to play in facilitating learning.

'Counselling is not some kind of arcane pursuit but something that good educators do almost instinctively. Counselling, therefore, is relevant not just to formal educational guidance, counselling and information services, but to teaching and learning more generally.'

Woolfe (1988) p.6

Counselling is presented by the Unit for the Development of Adult Continuing Education, as one of the seven activities comprising 'guidance', the purpose of which is 'to help people make wise and well informed choices' (UDACE 1986). The seven activities are as follows:

Informing — providing information about learning opportunities and related support facilities, without any opportunity to discuss the relative merits of different options.

Advising — helping clients to interpret information and choose the most appropriate option.

Counselling — working with clients to help them to discover, clarify, assess and understand their learning needs and the various ways of meeting them.

Assessing — helping clients, by formal or informal means, to obtain an adequate understanding of their personal, educational and vocational development, in order to enable them to make sound judgements about the appropriateness of particular learning opportunities.

Enabling — supporting the client in dealing with providing agencies, or in meeting the demands of particular courses.

Advocating — negotiating directly with institutions or agencies on behalf of individuals or groups of clients.

Feeding back — gathering and collating information on unmet, or inappropriately met, learning needs and encouraging providers to respond to these.

UDACE (1986)

Woolfe however sees counselling as an interactive framework through which many of the activities of guidance are carried out — informing, giving advice or assessment. He asserts that 'Counselling, as a philosophy is relevant . . . to almost any situation in which one person seeks to help another. Indeed, people who have never read a book about counselling are using the principles of counselling simply by being good listeners or accepting people for what they are.'

The British Association for Counselling has defined the area in a way which makes clear the relevance of counselling to a wide range of functions and roles, and its applicability to many of the practitioners in open learning, whatever their title — tutor, manager, receptionist, trainer and so on.

> 'People become engaged in counselling when a person, occupying regularly or temporarily the role of counsellor, offers . . . . time, attention and respect to another person or persons temporarily in the role of client.
>
> 'The task of counselling is to give the client an opportunity to explore, discover and clarify ways of living more resourcefully and toward greater well being.'
>
> British Association for Counselling (1985)

In the context of open learning, it is possible to be more explicit about the areas in which counselling has a role to play. They can be defined in relation to the stages through which a user of open learning progresses. Although the nature of the stages differs according to different systems, and may not be so clearly demarcated in the experience of the learner, it is possible to outline a common pattern:

Stage	:	*May involve for the user:*
Pre-course	:	Enquiry, self-evaluation, vocational guidance, course choice Registration/ Enrolment
Course study	:	Learning to learn, study skills, self-evaluation, coping with pressure
Post course	:	Review of progress, course choice/ other options, vocational guidance

Each of these stages is characterized by different demands on the individual but counselling involves a number of characteristic functions which apply to a greater or lesser extent across all the stages. These are:

- listening
- reassuring
- clarifying the individual's needs and feelings

— suggesting questions and ideas the individual might use in evaluating themselves
— providing information about available systems, courses and qualifications and occupations
— referral to other specialist staff where necessary
— identifying options available to the learner
— facilitating the choice of one or more goals by the learner
— giving advice on ways of meeting/achieving the goals identified
— helping the individual decide on a course of action to meet a particular goal
— analysing problems the individual experiences in trying to achieve the goal
— reviewing progress toward goals and setting new priorities.

The quality of the counselling will take on a different emphasis with different individuals at different stages. At the enquirer stage it may often be the information giving and clarifying functions which are most demanded. Some form of pre-course advice is offered by most open learning providers, even where any other form of counselling is absent. There is a recognition of the importance of this stage and the key role of the receptionist or administrator who may be the first contact for the would-be-learner.

Once the learner has begun course work, the counselling function may become the tutor's responsibility, with no clear dividing line in practice between where counselling begins and tuition ends. The Open University emphasises this integrated role in using the title 'tutor-counsellor' for its foundation course support staff. It places great emphasis on the facilitation of learning and study skills as central to educational counselling.

On completion of a course of study, counselling also has a role to play in helping learners assess their course experience and decide whether or not further study is desirable. Throughout the process as a whole, counselling is required to help the enquirer or learner to evaluate themselves; to review what they have achieved and to decide where they want to move on to. Counselling is crucial for the kind of self evaluation introduced in chapter 3. Athabasca University refers to this as 'orientation': enabling individuals to find out information about themselves as well as information about the institution.

From this very schematic account of counselling it is clear that there is an intended association between the counselling function and the academic progress and decision making of individual learners. It is for this reason that issues of learner progress and drop-out are included in this chapter, notwithstanding the fact that they are equally as relevant to the evaluation of materials and tuition. Indeed chapters 4 and 6 do contain insights into the influence of tuition and materials on learner progress. It is not implied that counsellors or counselling bear sole responsibility for whether learners stay in or drop out, and whether they achieve their learning goals.

Issues in counselling evaluation

Counselling, like tuition, is a process, but differs from tuition in being person centred rather than course centred. This itself contributes one of the key issues in evaluating counselling, which is to ascertain the nature and the scale of need for counselling among enquirers and learners. Counselling, even more than tuition, can only be offered, not delivered; it depends upon a positive action by the learner in taking up the offer and using it. However, counselling shares with tuition other important characteristics, which is that it requires resource of various kinds, and can be organised and offered in different ways. Practitioners therefore turn to evaluation to provide clues about the need for counselling, perhaps more realistically, evidence of the demand for it, which can inform decisions about how best to provide it.

Other major themes follow on having provided counselling, in whatever form. There is first of all the issue of use; how much is counselling used and by how many learners/enquirers? Is it possible to distinguish different categories of user in relation to the frequency and nature of use of counselling? Evaluation in these areas might enable the service to be more accurately targetted, rather than provided in an identical fashion to all users. Associated with this is the means used to provide counselling, and there are issues here of staffing and communication. Should tutors also offer counselling or should there be a separate counsellor? Can part-time staff counsel as well as full-time staff and, if so, what training do they need? Is it possible to counsel 'at a distance', using telephone or written communication or both? Do these different ways of providing counselling affect its outcomes, and if so, in what ways?

Finally, there is the complex area of evaluating the outcomes of counselling. Does counselling appear to have any effect on performance indicators, for example? Are learners less likely to drop out? More likely to submit assignments? Less likely to fail the examination? Irrespective of these measures, are there other identifiable outcomes; more satisfaction among users of counselling, than non-users? Greater inclination to recommend the provider to friends? Increased take up of other opportunities for learning, subsequently? Practitioners may find themselves having to justify the allocation of resources and therefore will need evidence of the kind of outcomes counselling might be expected to produce.

Some of these themes are developed further in the examples of counselling evaluation used in the rest of this chapter. These demonstrate a diversity of approaches, but it is possible to identify a framework underlying this diversity. Figure 1 suggests that the two major perspectives are that of the user, on one hand, and on the other, the provider. Within each perspective, it is possible to focus on evidence concerning behaviour, or perceptions, or both. The rest of this chapter 'opens out' each of these perspectives in turn, and looks at examples of the different ways in which they can be explored.

Figure 5.1: A summary of the means commonly used in evaluating counselling

The perspective of:	*Focusing on:*	*Typical questions:*
THE USER (Enquirer, applicant, learner, client)	BEHAVIOUR:	How many enquirers subsequently enrol? How often do learners contact the counsellor? What proportion of learners drop out? What is the pattern of dropout during the year (or course duration). Do learners submit assignments more regularly? Get better grades? and so on . . .
	PERCEPTIONS:	Did enquirers get the information they needed, when they needed it? Was the counsellor sympathetic and helpful? Were decisions affected by the counselling process? Has counselling helped with study skills? How accessible is the counsellor? and so on . . .
THE PROVIDER	BEHAVIOUR:	What proportion of enquiries receive written information on courses, or an interview with a tutor/counsellor? Are enquirers automatically followed up? What proportion of applicants are offered an advisory counselling session? Do all tutors/counsellors follow up learners who do not submit the first assignment? Is the counsellor given information about the learner's academic progress? Are learners who have been out of touch for 2/3 weeks automatically followed up? and so on . . .
	PERCEPTIONS:	What are the advisory and counselling needs of enquirers/applicants/learners? How do these needs change at different stages of study? Are some learners more 'at risk' of drop out than others? Is the present provision of counselling adequate? and so on . . .

The provider perspective

Although some consider that the 'acid test' of counselling (or tuition for that matter) is user behaviour, performance indicators on output (number of student-initiated contacts with a counsellor, drop-out rate, attendance at examinations etc.) need to be interpreted in the light of what was offered. We need to know what the inputs into the system were before we can make sense of what users chose to do. I shall therefore take the provider perspective first, looking at behaviour, and then perceptions.

Behaviour

The evaluation of provider behaviour is concerned with two questions: 'What is meant to happen?' and 'what does (or did) happen?' The first question may be easily answered where very little advice or counselling is available, but in more complex systems the answer may be far from clear. Where there is virtually no counselling, the answer to what is meant to happen may be straightforward: 'all enquirers and their enquiry are logged, and one follow-up letter is mailed to all who have not applied for courses within an appropriate time-scale,' for example. In more complex systems it may be much more difficult to be so specific because what is meant to happen has been described in terms of *general goals* rather than *expected actions*. It may be one of the tasks of evaluation to operationalise these general goals, to restate them in terms of a set of *expected* practices, which can be compared with what *does* happen in practice.

An open learning system may declare that counselling is available through the tutor, throughout the course study period, but how is this meant to occur? Is there an opening session where the role of counselling is explained to learners? Is the tutor asked to organise workshop sessions dealing only with counselling matters? Can learners make an appointment to see the tutor individually? Should the tutor give his or her home telephone number and encourage contact out of working hours? Are learners allocated to a tutor specifically for counselling purposes? Data on how much a system is used is pretty meaningless until we can answer questions like these, and this is likely to require both desk research to check official records and briefing documents and interviews of the staff doing the counselling.

Staff contracts may contain statements about tasks, or, equally relevant, omit any mention of tasks, sticking to general role statements; similarly committee papers and briefing documents. Where there is little available policy, or significant local interpretation of policy, interviews with the relevant staff will be needed to establish their view of what is meant to happen. It may be impossible to pin this down very tightly where evaluation is being used to firm up ideas about what would be the most appropriate system — 'when we see what's happening we'll decide what model of counselling to introduce'. This is legitimate but should alert the evaluator to pursue a descriptive analysis rather than one testing the effectiveness of a specific model; 'Is there a model and who should define it?' rather than 'Is this model efficient and effective?'

Whatever the status of policy and intentions, 'what actually happens?' is the next question, and the one likely to form the most substantial part of the evaluation. The key question here is 'what does staff member X actually do?' and the answer may involve one or more of the following: analysing records, interviews, or questionnaires.

Routine records

Centralised procedures, as when a receptionist fills in an enquirer's log, or mails a batch of letters, are relatively easy to check. It becomes much more difficult when actions are meant to be taken by a dispersed body of staff, working sometimes from their homes. Such staff can be provided with a proforma for recording their contact with learners, and these can be analysed to build up a picture of what actually happens. The Open University provides its tutor-counsellors with a form on which assignments and all other contact with students can be entered and reviewed at a glance for the year. An extract for illustration is shown in figure 2.

Although data from this form has occasionally been used for evaluation by full-time staff of the University, its primary function is as an aid to the part-time staff of the University, to help them review the progress of the group of learners for whom they are responsible in that year and to initiate counselling interventions when necessary. It draws attention to the three points during the year when the University expects tutor-counsellors to initiate contact with their students-initial contact, registration for future courses and year end. Where staff know that data of this kind will be used for evaluation, routine records can be called in for analysis or reviewed with counsellors themselves, if that is more constructive (and less threatening) in the circumstances.

Figure 5.2: A sample proforma for monitoring learner contract

RECORD OF CONTACTS MADE

CODE								Indicate by circling that adequate contact has been made with each student at the listed 'critical' points		
LETTER SENT... L										
LETTER RECEIVED................................... Ⓛ		1	2	3	4	5	6			
TELEPHONE BY TUTOR/COUNSELLOR... T										
TELEPHONE FROM STUDENT.................. Ⓣ										
PERSONAL VISIT...................................... P	WEEK BEGINNING							INITIAL CONTACT	REGISTRATION FOR FUTURE COURSES	YEAR END
STUDY CENTRE CONTACT...................... S										
STUDENTS										
_____	A							A		
_____	B							B		
_____	C							C		
_____	D							D		
_____	E							E		

Extract Adapted from form (PT4) Part-Time Staff record for assignments marked and contacts made, The Open University, Milton Keynes

Log and diary exercises are a similar form of regular reporting but allow for open-ended and varied responses. They may be necessary if so little is known about the kind of contact to expect that a pre-coded form of the kind shown in figure 2 would not be workable. A log can provide much more detailed information about the content of contact, and can be used to develop case-studies of the counsellor role for staff development as well as for evaluation. It is quite demanding on the log keeper though, and not often used for that reason.

Interviews

Interviews have been used characteristically to elicit perceptions about learners' counselling needs, and it would be a missed opportunity to use an interview only to establish factual detail about what a counsellor did and when. Nonetheless an interview can be used to get this information if the counsellor has kept some form of continuing record of his or her actions. Where only a small number of staff are involved, it may be an economical way of collecting quantitative and qualitative data at the same time, the one helping to make sense of the other.

During the 1970s, a number of evaluations based on interviewing were undertaken by Open University tutorial and counselling staff to explore the amount and kind of counselling received by students on post-foundation courses (Fotheringham, 1976 and Simpson, 1977). As counsellors themselves, both evaluators knew what being a counsellor entailed, and therefore what questions to ask their colleagues which would reveal what they did and their approach to the job. Studies of this kind, however informal, have helped the University develop a much more detailed grasp of what the counsellor ought to be doing at different stages, and what the demands from students are likely to be.

One study in particular contributed a very useful distinction to the debate, in identifying contrasting approaches to counselling for students studying post-foundation courses: the 'General Practitioner' versus 'the Interventionist' type of counsellor. (Simpson, 1976) The GP makes an initial contact and thereafter operates a 'surgery', i.e. waits for the student to make contact and then handles the problem. The Interventionist initiates more than just the first contact, following up evidence of missed assignments, fail grades or problems with course choice. Simpson notes that 'the distinction is quite clear from an examination of student records', and provides figures of the number of contacts per student initiated by the counsellor-GP counsellors average one contact in each of the first two months of the year and 'Interventionists' two to three contacts per student per month.

Questionnaires

A survey is not likely to produce a comprehensive picture of what the counsellor has done, as is possible through the analysis of a continuous record of action. It can be used however to gain a snapshot of what happens, particularly if the amount of counselling work is not large and therefore the demands on memory not unreasonable. The type of questions that might be developed to provide an overview of the amount and type of contact are shown in figure 3.

Figure 5.3: Gaining an impression of counsellor/learner contract

The type of questions that might be used:

1. How many learners are allocated to you?

2. How often have you been in contact with each of them during the course?

	Number of contacts			
	0	1-2	3-4	5 or more
Number of learners				

3. How many learners have needed your help in each of these areas?

	No of learners
Course choice	
Study skills	
Getting behind with course work	
Problems in understanding the course	
Feedback on assignments	
Exam preparation	
Domestic/work commitments	
Other (please explain)	

Questionnaires can also be used effectively to canvas general views about counselling and more examples are given in the next section on perceptions of the providers.

Perceptions

The perceptions staff have about the value of counselling to learners clearly affect the action they take. In systems which rely at least somewhat on the judgement of counsellors themselves, it is particularly important to elicit their views. Semi-structured interviews can generate very detailed information on counsellor perceptions and these can also contribute usefully to the design of questionnaires, if a larger sample is necessary.

The kinds of questions which might be incorporated into an interview schedule will obviously depend on the subject matter of the evaluation. The list of questions in figure 4 illustrates just one example of an approach towards eliciting counsellor perceptions — in this case about the value of early contact with applicants, those who are potential learners but have not yet enrolled or started course work. Naturally the counsellor's response would prompt the interviewer to ask follow-up questions, and the order of questions would reflect the sequence of topics as they arose during the interview — not necessarily therefore the order shown here.

Figure 5.4: Sample questions forming part of an interview schedule with counsellors

(a) Do applicants seem surprised to be contacted by someone from . . . . . ? (the college or other institution)

(b) Do you feel they welcome such contact or feel it's unnecessary? (Does it matter whether contact is by letter, phone or face to face?)

(c) Do you generally describe your role as counsellor? If so, what phrases or terms do you use?

(d) What topics come up most often in these counselling sessions?

(e) Is it useful to contact *all* applicants? (How would you decide which people to contact?)

(f) Do you feel there are drawbacks in providing early contact?

(g) Do you feel there are benefits? (More information about course, method of study, review of reasons for study, etc.)

(h) What are you trying to achieve as a counsellor?

Another technique which can be used to explore counsellor perceptions of their role and the ways in which they carry it out, is to use critical incidents; a scenario of a not untypical counselling event is described briefly, and the counsellor asked what they would do in a similar situation. Scenarios might consist of examples like these:

the learner who

(a) phones up during the first week of a course and says they want to drop out

(b) never asks for clarification/advice in workshop sessions and gets low assignment grades

(c) attends workshop sessions sporadically and has submitted only two out of five assignments.

Counsellors can be asked during interview what action if any they would take in each of these instances (or comparable situations), and their reasoning explored. This can also be done in a group setting and, if so, provides a useful opportunity for staff development as well.

Table 5.1: A selection of attitude ratings indicating preference for the joint tutor-counsellor role

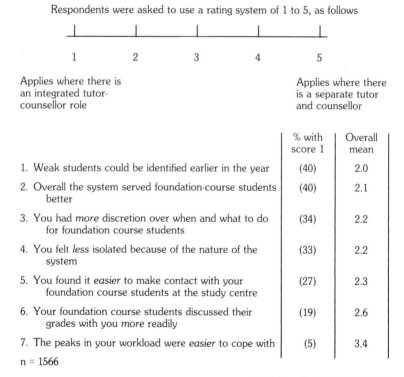

Respondents were asked to use a rating system of 1 to 5, as follows

| 1 | 2 | 3 | 4 | 5 |

Applies where there is an integrated tutor-counsellor role

Applies where there is a separate tutor and counsellor

	% with score 1	Overall mean
1. Weak students could be identified earlier in the year	(40)	2.0
2. Overall the system served foundation-course students better	(40)	2.1
3. You had *more* discretion over when and what to do for foundation course students	(34)	2.2
4. You felt *less* isolated because of the nature of the system	(33)	2.2
5. You found it *easier* to make contact with your foundation course students at the study centre	(27)	2.3
6. Your foundation course students discussed their grades with you *more* readily	(19)	2.6
7. The peaks in your workload were *easier* to cope with	(5)	3.4

n = 1566

extract from Field (1979) table 4

Table 5.2: Preference for the integration of tuition and counselling

Respondents were asked:

On the basis of your experience tuition and counselling should not both be the responsibility of the same person		Some truth in both views		Tuition and counselling are inter-dependent and should be the responsibility of the same person	Can't say
1	2	3	4	5	6

Old System   New System

Tutor counsellors	% preferring items 1 & 2 above	No preference	% preferring items 4 & 5 above	No opinion
Formerly tutors	14	4	81	1
Formerly counsellors	16	4	77	3

Field (1979) p.1

Although questionnaires cannot give as rounded a picture of the counsellor's orientation and behaviour, they can be used to gauge the strength of particular attitudes and might be useful where a large number of staff is involved and the issues are very specific. This was the case when the Open University changed its support system from a separate tutor and counsellor to the integrated tutor-counsellor role for foundation students, with a separate tutor and counsellor for post-foundation students. Although an extensive programme of interviews was undertaken to evaluate the changes between old and new system, there was also a survey of all those who become tutor-counsellors as a result of the change. It was possible to ask respondents whether or not they had a preference for either the old or the new system in relation to their effect on a number of factors, such as the counsellor's ability to identify weak students, make contact with students regularly, counsellor workload and contact with other staff. Tutor-counsellor responses to a selection of these items is shown in table 1. All except the last two items in table 1 were seen to describe the new system rather than the old and, as table 2 shows, most part-time staff preferred the new tutor-counsellor role, where the functions of tuition and counselling are integrated.

The questioning approaches used to generate tables 1 and 2 could be applied to different issues or to attitudes which are relevant across different systems, as in figure 5:

Figure 5.5: Attitude ratings for counselling

(a) When you are under time pressure in a session, on which side do you put the greater emphasis:

Not falling behind the course schedule		Equal emphasis on both		Attending to learner needs	Can't say
1	2	3	4	5	6

|_____|_____|_____|_____|

(b) When deciding assignment grades is difficult, do you have a bias towards:

The particular needs of the individual learner		No bias		Sticking to the marking system	Can't say
1	2	3	4	5	6

|_____|_____|_____|_____|

(c) Do you think you have a bias towards:

Initiating contact with learners who may have a problem		No bias		Waiting till learners contact you	Can't say
1	2	3	4	5	6

|_____|_____|_____|_____|

The perspective of the user — enquirer, applicant, learner or client

Behaviour

Often one of the most important tasks of evaluation is to find out how often counselling is used, and by which students. A questionnaire can be used to provide an impression or estimate of usage, and indications of the degree of user satisfaction. Table 3 shows the results of a 1979 Open University survey of a large sample of students studying a total of 91 undergraduate courses. This suggests that counselling is used by about one in three undergraduate foundation level students, by one in six post-foundation students and by one in five assoicate students (those not registered for a degree, studying courses one-off). There is a high level of satisfaction with the service, and when levels of satisfaction and helpfulness across all course components are compared (table 4), it is clear that level of satisfaction equals that of correspondence texts, and though the helpfulness rating is lower than the mean for all course components, it is similar to that for television broadcasts.

Table 5.3: Student use and appreciation of counselling

	USE %	SATISFACTION %	HELPFUL-NESS	STUDENTS FINDING ACCESS TOO DIFFICULT %
FOUNDATION LEVEL COURSES	36	87	3.62	4
POST FOUNDATION LEVEL COURSES	16	87	3.5	7
ASSOCIATE STUDENT COURSES	22	85	3.48	5

Source: Grundin, H.U. (1980)

Table 5.4: Student use and helpfulness ratings for major course components

	CORRESPONDENCE TEXTS	SET BOOKS	TV BROADCASTS	RADIO	CORRESPONDENCE	CASSETTES RECORDS	COUNSELLING	FACE-TO-FACE TUTORIALS	TELEPHONE TUTORIALS
USE %	98	90	77	63	63	90	17	59	15
SATISFACTION %	87	81	73	71	80	83	87	74	81
HELPFULNESS (1-5 Scale)	4.67	4.11	3.55	3.42	3.56	3.76	3.54	3.85	3.52

Satisfaction index: Grand Mean for all courses and all (14) components = 80%
Helpfulness Index: Grand Mean for all courses and all (14) components = 3.80
Source: Grundin, H.U. (1980)

However, a more accurate and reliable measure of counselling can be derived from the kind of record keeping (cf. figure 2) and reporting by the provider described above. This can be used to calculate the percentage of a particular cohort which is 'reached' by an advisory or counselling service. Judgement as to whether this represents a satisfactory result will depend on a host of local factors, including other performance indicators. Suppose for example that, out of 500 enquirers, 100 finally register on a variety of learning programmes – a 20% 'conversion rate'. Routine records are analysed and show that the great majority of enquirers used the telephone and received only preliminary information (from a receptionist) and a prospectus through the post. Most of those who did drop in to the centre or workshop however, had a chat with an advisor/counsellor and many subsequently enrolled. In the context of this kind of scenario, it may look desirable to include more self counselling information in the prospectus, and to encourage enquirers to come in to the centre for advice and counselling, with a view to increasing the number who enrol. If in the event let us say that 350 enquirers were more effectively advised and the total enrolling increased to 200, we may feel that the experiment 'worked', assuming of course that:

(a)   the cost of providing advise/counselling was not greater than the fee income;

(b)   course provision remained more or less the same;

(c)   those who enrolled were satisfied with their course and progress;

(d)   there was no very obvious change in the characteristics of enquirers.

Although this example is deliberately simplified, it does illustrate some important considerations in the evaluation of counselling. First of all it is very difficult to find a direct measure of the effect of counselling and so we are often forced to rely on indicators of the *possible* effects of counselling *in combination with a number of other factors*, such as the effects of tuition, learner characteristics, economic or social changes in the catchment area.

Second, counselling is about the client's needs, and if these, when fully appreciated, suggest that enrolling for a particular course would be undesirable, then success ought to be defined by the non-enrolment of the enquirer, or perhaps even by their enrolment for a different course in a different institution. The criteria for judging the success or effectiveness of counselling are difficult to operationalise, though it is possible to pin down some of the general goals by describing events or indicators which would be some evidence of goal achievement. Take the goal of providing an effective advisory service; it might be possible to specify a definition not so much of the ideal we aim for in being effective but of *the minimum condition we would expect to see fulfilled* by a service which was effective. This might be phrased rather like a behavioural objective, as follows:

'At enrolment all learners will know how many hours of study their course is expected to take on average, how it will be assessed and when they can contact tutorial and counselling staff.'

Similarly it might be possible to convert a statement like this:

'the role of advisory counselling is to set up a good working relationship with the learner.'

into a statement about expected outcomes:

'the majority of learners will contact their counsellor at least once and most learner/counsellor contacts after the second assignment will be initiated by the learners.'

The second statement has defined 'a good working relationship' as one where the learner feels able to contact the counsellor when necessary, and assumes that this is likely to happen on at least one occasion, for most learners.

Although these definitions of what we might reasonably expect counselling to achieve make no mention of other issues which should also be explored, such as how satisfied learners are with the counselling they receive, they do offer a number of benchmarks of performance which can be observed and probably quantified in some way. We can find out how many who enrol know the key items of information we have specified; we can monitor learner/counsellor contact and check out what proportion is initiated by the learner. This does not tell the whole story by any means, but it does provide some general measures of what is happening against which to provide more qualitative judgements by individuals.

In 1978/9 a number of Open University regions used a form similar to that in figure 6, for recording all contacts between counsellors and applicants. Counsellors completed one form for each applicant and these provided a 'case record' of the individual and any action taken by the counsellor. The forms thus had two purposes; to provide applicant records for the regional centre, and data about the use made of the counselling service offered. An analysis of the forms from five counsellors covering 136 applicants in one region provided a useful overview of the applicant counselling service. Sixty-eight per cent of applicants had had at least one contact with a counsellor during the advisory period, most lasting for 20 minutes or less; 28% had had two or more contacts, and of these 28%, three-quarters were initiated by the applicant. Three-quarters of all contacts were counsellor-initiated, usually by telephone, and very few (7.3%) of all applicants responded to the offers of counselling in the literature they received by making the first contact themselves. (Kelly 1979)

Figure 5.6: Counselling contact record form

(1) Name of Counsellor (block capitals) ———————— Staff Number ————————

(2)

1	2	3	4	5
User Name	Serial No.	Course(s) Applied for	Date of Contact	Length of Contact

(3) Form of Contact (please tick)

Letter sent..................... ☐

Letter received.............. ☐

Telephone by Counsellor........... ☐

Telephone from Applicant............ ☐

Personal visit.................... ☐

Study Centre/Workshop contact.... ☐

(4) Type of Contact (please tick)

Individual................ ☐

Group ☐

(5) Topics covered during the session (please tick)

1. Educational preparedness for course(s) to be undertaken ☐

2. Appropriateness of course for user aspirations ☐

3. Referral to specialist course adviser ☐

4. Preparatory study ☐

5. Home study conditions and time

6. Other factors affecting study disadvantage/ disabled ☐

7. Guidance Services available e.g. frequency of tutorials, workshops, tutor contact etc. ☐

8. Finance ☐

9. Referral to other agencies/ vocational guidance ☐

(6) Please describe the advice you offered the user, or other relevant comments.

(7) Record of contacts made after the initial meeting

Date	Form	Duration	Please comment on purpose and content of contact

Drop-out

Counselling is about helping the learner define and achieve his or her objectives. This often involves helping the learner resolve problems encountered before, during or at the end of study. Some problems are not resolved, or resolvable, and the learner decides to drop out. Drop-out does not *always* imply a negative situation of course. In open learning especially there are many who enrol for courses without a commitment from the beginning to complete the course as planned. They know they are free to stop when they choose, and a number do so for positive rather than negative reasons i.e. they have learned as much as they want to, or they do not want to be assessed, only to read course materials in their own time, or they have moved on to something else which interests them more.

Notwithstanding, drop-out is generally associated with problems the learner cannot resolve while continuing with the course, and this is where the link with advice and counselling occurs. Since counselling is one of the means (perhaps the key means) through which providers can help the learner resolve problems, evaluating drop-out provides a measure of the scale of difficulties learners are experiencing and the sorts of problems commonly experienced to which counselling ought to be addressed.

'Drop-out' may seem like a straightforward issue but needs careful definition and interpretation of the various measures in use, particularly the base used to calculate percentages. Some institutions provide data on the basis of those who complete the first assignment, presumably because (in distance learning institutions in particular) this indicates that the learner had effectively started the course. (See Woodley and Parlett, 1983, p.3) The measures used by the Open University are shown in table 3 which suggests the major stages or 'milestones' at which drop-out and course progress can be measured — payment of final registration fee (applicable only to new students who make two part payments), at examination and at the course result stage. (Course progress is also measurable at each assignment but some who do not complete a particular assignment *will* continue with the course, so drop-out and course progress measures are not synonymous.) Different systems produce different 'milestones' and this sometimes makes direct comparison of rates between institutions impossible.

Table 5.5: Open University undergraduate performance in 1982 (student based)

		TOTAL	NEW STUDENTS	CONTINUING STUDENTS
			(%)	(%)
i	Non-completion of final registration (Base all provisionally registered)	N/A	28	N/A
ii	Withdrawal/Drop-out rate (Base = all finally registered)	24	17	27
iii	Failure rate (Base = all who sat the exam)	6	6	7
iv	Overall wastage rate (Base = all finally registered) includes failure rate and withdrawal	29	22	32

adapted from Woodley (1987) p.56

One of the features which Table 5 highlights and which *has* influenced the orientation of counselling at the Open University is the concentration of drop-out by new students in the February to April period. New undergraduate students can signal their decision not to continue the course by not paying the final registration fee. Although there is not a comparable quantitative measure for continuing students, tutors tend to expect the period up to and including the first assignment to be a sensitive time for drop-out for all students, a period during which students are to some extent trying out the course, and gauging their own likely performance.

This has led the University to emphasise the period up to and including the first assignment as a time during which many students might value counselling, *whether they stay in or drop out*. Part of the rationale for this emphasis relates to resource issues. Where counselling resources are limited, it makes sense to alert counsellers to the possibility that learners might be more at risk of dropping out, or being in difficulty, during particular periods. Equally important is that counsellors are aware of the factors which play a part in drop out, and evaluations using interview and survey methods have identified time and again a list of factors which, in aggregate, represent the reasons learners give for why they have dropped out (see figure 7).

Earlier research at the Open University also suggests that between two-thirds and three-quarters of all the reasons learners give for drop-out are related to work and domestic factors, most of the remainder relating to the course and associated study problems. (Woodley, 1987) Although this might suggest that providers can do little to ameliorate the circumstances which lead to drop-out, it would be misleading to jump to such a conclusion.

Figure 5.7: Factors associated with learner drop-out

A COURSE FACTORS

Examples: • Course either too difficult or not sufficiently advanced
• Content not as expected, uninteresting, etc.
• Course overloaded – too much material to work through in the time allowed

B INSTITUTIONAL FACTORS

Examples: • Not enough tuition/counselling available
• Problems with individual tutor
• Poor administration – schedules disorganised, inadequate facilities, etc.

C LEARNING ENVIRONMENT

(i) Unforseen changes

Examples: • Illness/accident
• Job/responsibility changes
• Unemployment

(i) General conditions

Examples: • Lack of encouragement from family/employer
• Lack of money
• Clash with other domestic/leisure/work commitments

D LEARNER'S APPROACH TO LEARNING

Examples: • Perceives self as 'not clever enough', 'too old to learn' etc.
• Low level of skill in learning – difficulties with using texts, writing assignments, problem solving, etc.
• Lacks confidence in own ability to learn, pass the examination, etc.

E MOTIVATIONAL FACTORS

Examples: • Course work associated with achieving a goal which is no longer desirable, or has been achieved another way
• More appropriate learning opportunities offered elsewhere
• Another goal takes priority, e.g. learner decides to spend more time on a hobby, trade union work, with family, etc.

adapted from Woodley (1987) p.61-62

First, it is often difficult to get learners who have dropped out to reply to surveys, and response rates may be 50% or lower. This means that results are vulnerable to bias because no information exists for a large proportion of the target group — perhaps many of those who did not respond felt a greater sense of failure, or were more disappointed with course work.

Second, (and related to the last point) learners may need to rationalise dropping out by finding 'reasons' which minimize their sense of failure and embarrassment. It may be much easier to say that 'work pressures' led to drop-out than that the course was more difficult than expected or that assignment grades were disappointing. Survey results alone may be misleading and should certainly be compared with data on the rates of dropout overall and within particular categories, defined by age, educational qualifications, level of study and so on.

When this was done at the Open University during the first five years of its operation, it was clear that the drop-out rate among new undergraduate students was highest among those with no, and with low, formal educational qualifications. Various positive discrimination approaches were tried, culminating in 1977 in a national scheme whereby all 13 regions allocated a significant proportion of their funds for use by tutor-counsellors on special sessions for their new foundation course students, especially in the period just before and at the start of course work. A special session was defined as any form of contact of at least half an hour, over and above the number of hours tuition allocated in advance for each course. Tutor-counsellors were allocated an initial two hours for special sessions, and more 'hours' were available on request. Earlier efforts had specified particular categories of student as 'at risk' — not only according to educational category, but to workload (i.e. attempting two foundation courses at once, rather than one), disability, inability to attend regular study centre sessions, and so on.

Evaluation of this approach identified a number of problems, chief among which were the difficulties for tutor-counsellors in applying these 'at risk' categories to their own students. Some of those falling within 'at risk' categories were clearly successful students, and many of those who subsequently dropped out did not fall within the 'at risk' categories, and could not have been predicted beforehand. This experience led to an approach in 1977 based not on 'at risk' categories as identified by aggregate statistical data, but on the discretion of tutor-counsellors themselves. The goal was not limited to giving additional help to prevent drop-out, but to giving additional help for the progress of all new undergraduate students throughout their first year of study with the University. (Thorpe 1979)

The results of this exercise were startling, although not easy to interpret. As table 6 shows, the drop-out rate over the whole of each foundation course was much lower among those students who had received special support; their dropout rate was less than half that of all other provisionally registered students. The fall in drop-out is most marked however among the group with no or low formal qualifications (table 7). The drop-out rate for students in this category who had not received special support, was 51.0%, whereas for those who had, drop-out was 17.6%. Drop-out rates for all other categories are similarly more than halved in most cases.

It would be mistaken however to conclude that special support is causing these dramatic reductions in drop-out. Three-quarters of the support students received one extra session, and fewer than 10% participated in three or more sessions. This represented a very small proportion of the total 'input' of a tutor-counsellor's scheduled contact time of 40 hours in face to face tutorials, and correspondence teaching on eight assignments. it seems improbable that 'special support' alone could halve dropout rates. What can be concluded however is that support students have made an effective, early contact with their tutor-counsellor; we know that such contact has taken place because it was recorded as part of the evaluation. Although students who did not participate in special support could attend subsequent study centre sessions, we do not know whether they attended, and they include those new students who, every year, fail to contact their tutor-counsellor at all, and subsequently drop out. It seems likely therefore that the reduction in drop-out among support students reflects two

Table 5.6: Support students compared with all other provisionally registered new undergraduates: by course result

STUDENTS BY COURSE	Pass 1*	Pass 4*	Fail	Drop-out	Total
A100 Arts Foundation Course					
Support students	1.6	68.5	16.2	13.7	100.0
Provisionally registered students minus support students	2.0	58.0	9.1	30.9	100.0
D101 Social Science Foundation Course					
Support students	4.3	62.2	15.8	17.7	100.0
Provisionally registered students minus support students	4.0	51.4	9.9	34.7	100.0
M100 Maths Foundation Course					
Support students	13.4	48.0	19.7	18.9	100.0
Provisionally registered students minus support students	12.4	36.6	9.7	41.2	100.0
S100 Science Foundation Course					
Support students	15.9	50.6	14.4	19.1	100.0
Provisionally registered students minus support students	15.5	31.6	10.3	42.6	100.0
T100 Technology Foundation Course					
Support students	2.4	60.6	17.3	19.7	100.0
Provisionally registered students minus support students	2.4	47.2	12.1	38.3	100.0

Source: Thorpe (1979)
* Only 3 categories are used for foundation course result: Pass 1, Pass 4 or Fail

factors; qualities in the student which prompt them to take up
the offer of contact with their tutor-counsellor, and the effects
of contact (face to face in most cases) with a tutor-counsellor
early enough to forestall loss of confidence, and to establish a
good working relationship for the rest of the year.

Although support students did include many students who were
not in any case at risk of dropping out, it appears that tutor-
counsellors were successful to some extent in discriminating in
favour of students who were academically borderline. A much
higher proportion of support students completed the assessment
requirements for their courses, but a higher proportion of these
failed their course, by comparison with all other provisionally
registered undergraduates. (Table 7)

Table 5.7: Support students compared with all other
provisionally registered new undergraduates: by level
of highest educational qualifications and rate of drop-
out

Level of highest educational qualification	Support students			All provisionally registered minus support students		
	Provisional Registration	June 1977	% Drop-out	Provisional Registration	June 1977	% Drop-out
No formal	703	579	17.6	1189	583	51.0
CSE/RSA	236	196	16.9	455	238	47.7
1-4 'O' levels	498	422	15.3	1478	896	39.4
5+ 'O' levels	635	537	15.4	1674	1102	34.2
1 'A' level	266	214	19.5	739	507	31.4
2+ 'A' levels	600	527	12.2	1762	1238	29.7
ONC/OND	245	220	10.2	605	408	32.6
HNC/HND	424	370	12.7	1116	872	21.9
Teaching Certificate	1184	1073	9.4	3818	3014	21.1
University diploma	392	347	11.5	1251	949	24.1
University degree	148	134	9.5	582	463	20.4
Total	5331	4619	13.4	14669	10270	30.00
No information	136			173	67	

Source: Thorpe (1979)

The attempt to identify and give special help to particular individuals in a group is notoriously difficult; many tutor-counsellors in 1977 found that the most supportive and least threatening approach was not to single out individuals, but to include their needs in particular in sessions offered to all students in the group. Some of the problems and opportunities in operating a positive discrimination role are highlighted by these reports from four different tutor-counsellors.:

'I see the key times for support as —

1)   initial weeks when student is either a) overawed by the calibre of some students in study centre sessions, or b) having difficulty in disciplining himself/herself to examining course material rigorously.

2)   the period between the first and second assignment, if there has been poor performance on the first.

I would prefer to identify weakness within the context of the course and act accordingly. Any suggestion of 'general' weakness before the course begins could be demoralising to the insecure student.'

Tutor-counsellor Report

'As a result of being able to arrange a meeting before Christmas, I was able for the first time to meet all my students face-to-face. In previous years students have dropped out without my ever being able to make contact.

I do not think that this contact prevented drop-out, but I do now know why students dropped out. (One student's wife had 'turns' in January, another left the country for a year on business, another went into hospital.)

The problems which the drop-out students encountered seem to beset all students at one time or another, but whereas a student who has embarked on a course will attempt to cope with the crisis and carry on with the course, a student who is about to embark on the course will decide not to add to his/her troubles by taking on what is to him/her an unknown commitment in time and effort and will drop out.

The ability to give early tutorials was very useful for establishing self-help groups, and was also a good opportunity to familiarise maths foundation course students with the computing element of the course before they get embroiled in the maths proper.'

Tutor-counsellor Report

'Mr E's mathematics consist only of (very) basic arithmetic. He attended a group maths tutorial on Jan. 14th but found it a bit beyond him, so I gave him an individual tutorial on Jan. 28th.

He is going to need further individual help in the early months of the Technology Foundation course, so I should like to request authorisation for this. I think about four hours would be needed to get him to the level of the weakest of the other students, but even one or two would be very useful.'

Tutor-counsellor Report

'This student asked for a special session because he hadn't been able to attend the induction meeting. He was anxious for a face to face interview (I had offered to discuss matters on the phone). The interview was informal with me answering the student's questions and giving suggestions for background reading and discussing course content, especially the art, logic and philosophy. Before the interview I felt that this student didn't really need a session (special) but I now feel it was a good idea as he is going to have trouble getting to the centre regularly because of personal commitments. I don't envisage having to give him any special support sessions but do intend to keep in touch by telephone . . . . . .

It seems to me it isn't always the students who apparently need help who ask for it!'

Tutor-counsellor Report

Perceptions of counselling

For some practitioners, what the user thinks about the counselling they receive may be more important than any other considerations, and the problem here may not be interpreting the users' response, so much as separating counselling out from all the other ways in which the user has been affected by the institution. Learners do not always remember whether they were counselled before enrolling, or may not realise that they *have* been counselled: some of the best counselling is 'invisible' in this sense. A number of instances of this were found during an evaluation of counselling for Open University Associate Students, where some interviewees who said they had not received any counselling had definitely been interviewed by a counsellor during their application. They had either forgotten the interview or not perceived it at the time as a counselling session.

When interviewing users, the interviewer needs to be prepared with 'probing' questions which do not use the term 'counselling' or depend on a common interpretation of 'what counselling is', e.g. 'did you discuss your choice of course with *any* member of staff from the workshop?' 'Did you receive any other information or advice, whether from staff in the workshop or outside?' 'Would you have liked the opportunity to discuss your decision?' It may be most productive to avoid using the term 'counselling' at all, if there is reason to believe that interviewees are likely to associate it with personal crises like divorce and bereavement, or with people who cannot manage their own lives. Negative perceptions of this kind have certainly been found among applicants and students in the Open University (Kelly, 1978).

Before interviewing users, it is essential to decide on specific aspects of the user's behaviour or experience where one might expect counselling to have an effect or a role to play. These can be derived from statements of the kind discussed earlier, outlining the kinds of outcome we might reasonably expect counselling to have. These may legitimately refer to value judgements and feelings, as well as behaviour, since the interviews will be used to explore user perceptions. It might be possible to formulate a number of tentative hypotheses like the following:

— Learners who discuss their decision with a counsellor before enrolment

(i) will feel satisfied with the information and advice they received before study

(ii) will feel better able to complete the assessment for the course

(iii) will have selected courses appropriate to their goals

(iv) would be prepared to recommend the course/the institution to other interested people.

These and other hypotheses can be used as the basis for questions in an interview schedule which moves from the more general open-ended question to the more specific. In this way the user's experience of counselling and their evaluation of it should develop bit by bit during the interview. This is likely to be a better approach than asking directly about how effective counselling has been, or whether the learner has had any problems, especially at the beginning of an interview.

The effectiveness of a counselling service can also be evaluated by a questionnaire to users, assuming that enough qualitatitive understanding exists to formulate questions and pre-code answers. Figure 8 shows the kind of questions which can be developed to explore user perceptions of pre-course counselling, whatever form that takes.

Figure 5.8: User perceptions of pre-course counselling

(Examples of questioning style, *not* including all elements that would be needed in a full questionnaire, analysed by computer)

(a) Were you aware that you could contact someone to discuss your decision and course choice before enrolling?

Yes ....
No ....

(b) Did you actually receive any advice or counselling of this kind?

Yes ....
No ....

If YES

(1) Who initiated the contract?
Myself.......................
Receptionist ....
Counsellor
Other (please specify) ....

(2) How did it help you?
(ring all that apply)

– Clarification of my own needs
  and objectives
– More information on the
  course(s)/method of study ....
– More prepared for the realities
  (workload, attendance, etc.) ...
– Advice on preparatory work...
  sources of financial help.
  occupational/career
  applications ....
– Non of these ....
– Other ....

(3) Did the help provided lead to any
of these decisions?

Do a different course?
Do fewer courses?
Do a course elsewhere?
Enrol at later stage?
Do some preparatory work?
Discuss with employer?
Apply for financial support?
Other ....
....

If NO

(1) Would you have welcomed such
contact?
Yes............................
No ....
Unsure ....

(2) How might it have helped you?
(ring all that apply)

– Clarification of my own needs
  and objectives
– More information on the
  course(s)/method of study........
  More prepared for the realities
  (workload, attendance, etc.) .....
– Advice on preparatory work.....
  souces of financial help.
  occupational/career
  applications ....
– None of these...........................
– Other...

(3) Might more help then have led to
any of these decisions?

Do a different course?
Do fewer courses?
Do a course elsewhere?
Enrol at later stage?
Do some preparatory work?
Discuss with employer?
Apply for financial support?
Other...
....

Adapted from the Open University questionnaire to Associate Students, 1979, Betty Swift.

Questions in figure 8 explore a specific period during which counselling might occur, but questionnaires can also be used to explore the learner's general impressions and preferences concerning counselling, as the items in figure 9 indicate.

Figure 5.9: Questions probing learner perceptions of counselling

Looking at each item below, to what extent does it apply to your work with x (a counsellor) on the course you have just completed? (Circle one of the numbers for each item.)

	Very much Applies		Neutral		Does not apply at all	Can't say
	1	2	3	4	5	6
I felt I was known to someone in the system and not just a name/number	1	2	3	4	5	6
I felt encouraged to keep studying	1	2	3	4	5	6
Without his/her help I would probably have dropped out	1	2	3	4	5	6
I felt there was someone I could turn to when problems arose	1	2	3	4	5	6
I felt he/she listened to my view on things	1	2	3	4	5	6

In concluding this section, it is worth emphasising that expressions of satisfaction/dissatisfaction among users of counselling may not be matched by a commensurate improvement of success in output measures like drop-out and course credit achievement. Counselling may contribute to the improvement of both the efficiency and effectiveness of an institution by helping enquirers choose appropriate courses, improving learning skills, listening to problems, and so on. But so many other factors also influence drop-out and course progress that aggregate data on outcomes can rarely if ever be used to single out the effects of counselling specifically.

Conclusion

It is particularly important to identify the goals of a counselling system at an early stage in its evaluation so that appropriate data can be identified and collected. It is difficult in system where counselling has more than a merely instrumental function, to identify measureable outcomes of its effects. Counselling may be oriented towards helping the learner make more informed decisions, for example, and it is extremely difficult to find measures of goals of this kind, which are at all adequate or useful.

Whatever the goals of a counselling system, however, quantitative data are likely to be useful for a portrayal of what is happening overall: to provide evidence of how often counselling takes place, the inputs of different counsellors, user take up and problem areas covered. One of the most important tasks for evaluation is *to document the counselling process* and thus to help develop an understanding of what counselling is about, among practitioners generally. It is very often the case that only a minority of learners uses the counsellor frequently, in any one year or course period, and that the majority of learners use the counsellor only once or twice. it may be tempting for some therefore to see the counselling interaction as a minority concern for 'problem' learners, or a peripheral issue. Counselling is much less likely to be viewed in this light where there is an understanding of what the counselling process involves and of the significance of its outcomes for individual learners. This requires qualitative as well as quantitative data, and the preparation of case studies which provide insights into individual needs and experience.

Further reading

Bailey, D. (1987) *Guidance in Open Learning : A Manual of Practice* National Institute for Careers Education and Counselling, with the Manpower Services Commission.

Produced as part of the NICEC project on guidance in the Open Tech Programme, funded by MSC. Provides state-of-the-art descriptions of open learning and guidance, with detailed examples of how schemes can provide information, advice, counselling, coaching, assessment, advocacy and feedback. There is also an excellent section on evaluation and development, which offers checklists of qualitative and quantitative measures of effective guidance, from which providers can select those which are appropriate.

6 Course and learning materials

Main themes: *What is a course? How is evaluation affected by the different ways in which course production and course delivery or presentation take place? What are the main ways in which materials can be evaluated? What approaches have been used in each of these areas: learner performance, learner feedback and peer/tutor feedback.*

The extent to which open learning providers monitor and evaluate materials tends to depend on how much control they have over their content and future production. However, even where providers have no control over materials production, there is good reason at least to monitor learner reaction to them. Learner feedback may offer useful advice to future learners; deliverers of open learning may as a result be able to provide better advice to enquirers and better support to those actually using the materials. It may be possible, for example, to produce a study guide or additional material which will help future learners use an existing course or pack. Furthermore, those who do produce the course materials ought to know about their strengths and weaknesses, and organisations delivering open learning perhaps have a responsibility to pass on whatever feedback they can get from learners. This is certainly one of the ten items in the Training Commission's Code of Practice, which stipulates that Deliverers of open learning should evaluate programmes both to improve their own service, and 'to give feedback to Producers about the effectiveness of their learning materials and any unexpected problems (or opportunities) that may have become apparent while using them'. (Training Commission 1987, p. B.4.)

What is a course?

Before working through the main ways course materials can be evaluated, two general points need making. The first concerns how we define the course which is the subject of evaluation. This chapter is focused mainly on the materials provided to learners, because preceding chapters cover tuition and counselling in greater depth. However it would be wrong to assume that we can evaluate a course adequately merely by evaluating its materials.

This may be enough if all the learner does is to work through what is provided without any other form of contact, but such additional opportunities for learning often are provided, whether in the form of assignments and correspondence tuition, workshop sessions, counsellor support, group meetings, or whatever. All of these things constitute 'the course', if they are provided, because whether successful or not, they are aspects of the learner's experience in setting out to study a particular course or to meet a learning goal. In this context, materials evaluation is *not* synonymous with course evaluation.

The alternative starting point suggested here, is that 'a course' is not so much a product, as a process of interaction between the learner and any materials, staff or facilities associated with the achievement of the course or learning goals decided on. Certainly a product (the learning materials) is involved very often, and the quality of that product is likely to be a very important (sometimes the most important) factor in the success of the course from the learner's point of view. It is unlikely to be the whole story however, and the reader should review each of the other chapters in this part for topics which may be necessary for the evaluation of their course provision. Learner evaluation of the tutor's role, or the examination of tutor reliability in assignment grading for example, both reveal important aspects of the learner's experience of a course, and are covered in chapter 4.

The course context

The second general issue is the importance of the context for evaluation. Can course materials for example be changed promptly in response to feedback, or must they wait for some date in the future, perhaps several years ahead? Perhaps course materials have not yet been written and evaluation is required to explore the local needs for a course and the areas it should seek to cover. Rowntree comments,

> 'Even before the course is put on, administrators will be asking whether there is a sufficient demand for the course, what its 'competitors' are, and whether the cost of putting it on

will be justified, and so on. Such 'market research' and
budgeting questions are, in essence, evaluative.'
Rowntree, (1981) p.244

Then there is the question of the division of labour in presenting courses: are the course tutors also authors of the material or not? Is the course provided by a different organisation from that which enrols learners? Factors like these affect the amount and kinds of effort put into evaluating materials and should certainly be taken into account in deciding what to evaluate and when. Two contrasting examples here can be used to make the point.

In the Bradford and Ingley Community College (BICC) Maths Workshop, the counsellors (FE Lecturers) to whom learners are allocated also write and revise the GCSE course units used by the College and provided to learners. They are able therefore to find out how effective these materials are (at least to some extent) through their contact with learners when they attend the workshop. Counsellors often work through the course material with learners and in this way find out any stumbling blocks for the learner, and improved ways of presenting ideas. The counsellor is able to use this experience directly in revising the appropriate unit texts, which are held on disc and can be (fairly continuously) re-written and updated. Although materials are not systematically evaluated, all the feedback that is gathered through regular counselling can be used, because there is frequent revision and re-printing in-house (i.e. in the college).

By contrast, the Open University Undergraduate programme has a lead-in time of around two to three years for the production of a course, and a presentation period for each course of about eight years, during which time the assignments and examination are changed every year, but most other materials remain constant. A number of units or other components may be revised but the course materials as a whole are relatively fixed during the presentation period. Although there are exceptions to the model, shown in figure 1, and desk top publishing may eventually relegate its status to 'the way we used to do things', it offers an example of a course model based on relatively clearly defined stages of production, presentation and possibly re-make. Figure 1 illustrates differences in the purpose of evaluation at different stages in that process and some of the methods appropriate to each. This is not meant to be an exhaustive map, and concentrates particularly on evaluation to improve the course for future learners. This is one of the most common purposes for evaluation because it is often difficult to collect data and make improvements sufficiently quickly to affect current learners.

Figure 6.1: The context for course evaluation
An example based on OU course production and development

Stages in Course Devevelopment	Main goals at this stage	Main User(s)	Possible Evaluation Methods
COURSE PRODUCTION			
1. Course Design in Outline	deciding on overall aims, content and strategy	Course Team or Authors	Comments from peers/experts, sponsors/clients
2. Materials in final draft form	to pilot the course by trying out on potential students	Course teams providers of tuition and counselling	developmental testing [Dry run of the course with potential students and structrued feedback]
COURSE PRESENTATION			
4. Course studied annually by a new cohort of students. Course units remain largely unchanged, study guides, broadcast and audio cassette notes, summer school, assignments and examination papers are often changed each year. Tutorial strategy and study guide can also be revised annually. Sometimes parts of the course may be revised or updated.	To develop the assessment strategy. Identify any *major* difficulties for students which need revision of limited parts of the course, or changes to study guide for students. Refine the amount and kind of tutorial support students require, including summer school, if relevant.	Presentation Course Team, tutors and Regional Academic Staff	Student feedback, tutor feedback, student progress statistics
COURSE RE-MAKE			
5. 'Old' course in use: 'new' course in design	To decide on the scale and nature of changes required: e.g. updating, partial re-make, complete re-make, etc	course team	Review of evaluation data on the 'old' course – new survey of tutor and student perceptions of the needs for change

The model of course production and presentation outlined in figure 1 does not apply uniformly to all OU courses, and it now seems much more likely that new technology will enable more regular revisions during the 'life' of a course. The model is useful however as an instance of the constraints — and opportunities — created for evaluation by the production to a very high standard of design and quality, of 'state of the art' courses. These require very large amounts of human and financial resources during production with the concomitant expectation that they will be of sufficiently high quality to last for several years at least. Large amounts of resource (certainly by comparison with the BICC example) are put into evaluation, but this is concentrated in the production stage and the first year of presentation. If the course is to be re-made, there is also likely to be renewed evaluation in its final year to provide directions for the new course team.

Evaluation is concentrated in these periods because there are opportunities to make important use of the findings at each point. During course production, it is possible to re-write completely whole sections of the course, so that it is worth eliciting detailed feedback from students on a page by page basis. During the first year, the course team needs to check out whether it has 'got it right', and whether guidance to students and tutors needs revising. There is likely to be particular interest in the assignments because these are changed annually and on the amount of tuition students need. Consequently learner and tutor feedback is focused on experience in using the course components, with only general reactions on course content. If there is evaluation at the end of the course, this is likely to be most useful if focused on *alternatives* to the old course, rather than a detailed critique of it.

This schematic outline makes clear that the evaluator needs to keep to the fore a clear idea of who wants the evaluation and for what purposes.

First, it should be clear what counts as 'the course' for the learners concerned. Second, the context for materials evaluation needs to be analysed *to show the chronology of materials production and presentation*, the goals of action at key stages and the staff who will use the findings. The content and design of materials evaluation needs to be derived from a 'mapping' of all of these factors.

Once this has been done, the evaluator can set up procedures for collecting the kinds of feedback or data required. There are three kinds of information which are most commonly used in materials evaluation: performance data for learners who have used the materials, whether derived from assignments, examination or performance 'on the job'; second there is feedback from learners about their experience in using the materials; and third, there is feedback from peers or sponsors, whether tutors on the course concerned or anyone with expertise in the relevant area. The rest of this chapter examines each of these areas in turn.

Learner performance

The relevance of learner performance data is most clear on courses which are assessed or which are closely tied to job performance. Even where courses are not assessed or job related, it may be possible to specify particular outcomes or competences which are the goal of the course, and to ask learners the extent to which they feel they have achieved them. Many of the Open University's Community Education courses are not assessed, but are oriented towards changes in the behaviour of learners, as well as attitudes and knowledge. Extensive evaluation of these courses has provided positive evidence of changes in all these areas. Over 50 per cent of learners on courses about parenting reported changes in the things they do with their children, and those studying the course 'Healthy Eating' reported changing their eating habits to follow national guidelines. Around two-thirds of the learners on the parenting courses in the late 1970s reported some attitude change in themselves, and increased self-confidence was reported a major benefit by about one fifth. (Ballard, 1987).

In other circumstances however, a more rigorous test than self-report is required, and it may also be important to distinguish between the assessment of learning and job performance. High marks on tests which measure learning of course materials do not guarantee a commensurate improvement in the job performance to which the training materials relate. The disjunction between course learning and job performance means that training managers in industry probably have to undertake both, and certainly cannot rely on the former alone.

Job performance

Where courses are provided or commissioned by a corporate sponsor, job performance and any improvements which the course appears to have brought, is likely to be the focus of an evaluation. Large companies like W.H. Smith and B & Q which provide their own open learning packages, are developing ways of using supervisors and training staff to monitor job performance following course completion. B & Q for example use Regional Training Officers (RTO) to report regularly on the progress of staff who have been trained. Each RTO covers 25 stores, each of which is visited for half a day every four to six weeks, and a report is completed with copies for the store, head office and the RTO.

In evaluating the use of open learning for over 10,000 of its staff involved in stocktaking, B & Q are comparing the stocktake in July 1987 with that in July 1986, using three sources of information: reports of RTO visits, head office observer reports and a representative sample of stocktake sheets from both stocktakes. (MSC, 1987.)

The demands of this kind of evaluation may lead to refinements in the quality of on the job supervision. Supervisors may be given for the first time, a list of specific behaviours or competences to be observed. For example, after staff from Heathrow airport had attended a three-day Customer Contact Skills training course, not only were they interviewed on course effectiveness, but their supervisors and other staff who had not attended the course were asked about changes in their behaviour following course completion.

Trainees were asked about the relevance of the training to their job and whether their work behaviour had changed in the areas covered by the course (see figure 2). Of the six behaviours listed, four were used more often by around half the staff interviewed, and results were most positive for 'asking questions to establish the passenger's need' and 'checking understanding'.

Figure 6.2: Checking learner behaviour after course completion

Do you use any of the following behaviours:

a) more often
b) more skilfully as a result of the training?

	More often		More skilfully	
	Yes	No	Yes	No
Greeting the passenger	28	33	25	36
Establishing eye contact	28	33	23	38
Using the passenger's name	15	46	14	47
Asking questions to establish the passenger's need	30	31	31	30
Checking understanding	39	22	29	32
Closing the conversation	15	46	17	44

Total number of staff interviewed: 61

Although the supervisor interviews were not covered in the report, the findings from 37 staff who had not received training were. Nine had noticed changes in the behaviour of colleagues who had been trained and about half said that they would like to attend a similar course. (Nixon et al, 1975)

Assessment

Assignments submitted by a learner are a very important indicator of two things: how many learners are still actively studying, and how effectively. Assignment monitoring is one of the key means therefore of finding out how learners are progressing at a stage early enough to take action to help them, as well as to suggest changes that might be made for future learners. It is important therefore to keep records which enable the tutor or manager to see at a glance, who has submitted assignments and their grade, and those who have not submitted assignments.

The submission rate of assignments can indicate that things are going wrong on a course but not the reason why; if those who submit get reasonable grades, there may be individual difficulties rather than course difficulties associated with the non-submission by other learners. Further investigation would be needed, to find out. However if grades are generally disappointing, this may be evidence that the assignment is poorly designed, or that the materials it draws on need improvement. We would have to get feedback directly from learners to find this out, and this is covered in the next section.

Examination performance is similarly an indicator which does not directly measure the success of course materials, but which provides a signal which we can interpret as either 'no need for change', or 'not good enough, lets find out more'. A high failure rate on an undergraduate level mathematics course for example may not mean a poor course but subject matter which even competent mathematicians find difficult.

Care is also needed in comparing pass rates between candidates taking the same exam but studying by different methods. Are the two groups of learners comparable, for example? Those studying by open learning may include a higher proportion of candidates with low or no formal qualifications. They will usually be studying part-time, whereas other groups may be enrolled in full-time course work.

Another caveat arises from the process by which candidates put themselves forward for an examination. In conventional provision, it may be the decision of a lecturer/trainer, on the basis of his/her judgement as to which candidates are likely to pass. Open learners are usually free to put themselves forward for examination, and may choose to do so, even against the advice of a tutor/counsellor. This may lead to a lower pass rate overall on the open learning course, but this would not reflect the comparative quality of the course, so much as the examination procedures in both cases.

Equally learners may choose not to take an examination, even though they have submitted assignments and worked through the course. A proportion of OU students eligible to sit the end of course examination, for example, always fails to turn up on the day. This phenomenon, revealed by the student progress statistics for the course, does not suggest there is anything wrong with course materials but does suggest other improvements: better information about the examination paper, specimen examples to work through, tutor/counsellor reassurance, and so on.

Though they need careful interpretation, assessment results ought to be monitored regularly. Course materials may not be 'causing' low pass rates, but providers need to know more about what is doing so. It may be unsatisfactory tuition, or a lack of practice in doing the kind of work required in the examination for example. There is likely to be a combination of factors influencing results, and some at least might be influenced by improvements in the service of a provider, as well as by changes to materials.

Learner feedback

Many open learning providers will feel that their view of the courses they offer is based at least in part on learner feedback gathered from teaching, conversation and general impression. This is the bedrock on which we all rely in forming opinions, and it is not going to be supplanted by the results of evaluation. On its own however, it is not enough. Seventeen years of student feedback to Open University course teams, for example, has shown that learners can always surprise 'the experts'. Material 'we' thought they might find difficult presents few problems, and vice versa; the order of topics/subject matter which 'we' take for granted turns out to be a barrier for some learners; the amount of choice which we offer in assignments is seen by learners as confusing, or too difficult, and so on.

As a result the evidence which tutors and others gain through *informal* contact with learners can be used most productively when moderated by evidence of *what learners themselves say*, particularly those learners (probably the majority) with whom tutors have had no direct contact themselves. As tutors/administrators, our views may often be based on a very small sample of the total population of learners, and likely therefore to be a partial reflection of learner response.

Having presented an argument for eliciting structured learner feedback, the next stage is to look at how such feedback can be generated. The methods we use will obviously reflect practical constraints, like staffing and costs, but should also reflect whether it is the experience of existing or future learners that we want to improve. A well designed evaluation should also take into account the nature of the change that is possible, using evaluation data. If it is only possible to change the assignments it is pointless to collect information on changes that might be made to the course materials, however tempting it might be to find out what learners think.

Melton and Scanlon have distinguished between content related and strategy related data. The former, as its name suggests, is about the concepts and ideas in the course, the latter is about how students use the course materials — time spent studying, whether they use in-text questions, radio and television, and so on. In some circumstances it may be more useful to concentrate on one kind of data rather than both kinds. For example, it is likely to be more productive to generate strategy related findings when about to make changes in the materials being developed for a revised course, if the content of the old course is being changed very substantially.

This was the case in the replacement of the first OU science foundation course, on which content-related data had been collected between 1971 and 1976. In the event the new course was to be substantially different from the old and at least 20% of the content findings were irrelevant 'simply because about 20% of the concepts in the old course were not covered by the remake'. (Melton and Scanlon, 1983.) Those that were in the new course as well as the old were often presented in such a different manner that content related findings were little help. The strategy-related data were easier to use because they related to features which would be used in the new course as well as the old, and because it was easier to suggest solutions to problems identified. For example the home experiment kit was redesigned for easier handling and the experiments were timed realistically and built into the assessment structure.

Piloting course materials during production

Course materials can be tried out on 'guinea pig' learners, with some attempt to replicate the actual learners' experience as they work through a real course. Rowntree gives a good introduction to this, which applies to the open learning context as much as to any other (Rowntree, 1981). He suggests that, where the reader is working independently with materials, some means of recording time spent studying and reactions to the materials is provided for their use. Figure 3 is the format he suggests which has been used successfully.

Figure 6.3: A proforma of a log for recording study times and comment

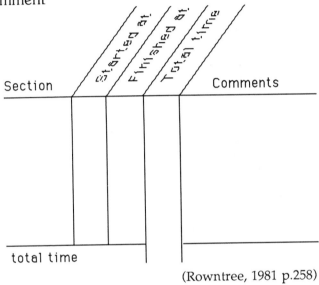

(Rowntree, 1981 p.258)

Testers can also be asked to review their experience at the end and provide some summative comments. At this level of generality, the sort of questions which have often been used and seem to allow the respondent to say what is important to them are these:

- What was most successful about this module/unit?

or
- What did you like best about....?
- What was least successful about this module/unit?

or
- What did you dislike about it?
- Which aspects/parts did you find difficult and why?
- What changes would you suggest?
- Should any additional material be included?
- Would you be interested in taking this course? (Please suggest reasons for your answer.)

It may be adequate to try out materials on only a handful of people who agree to help; this is certainly better than no feedback at all, and the experience of eventual learners can be significantly improved by even small changes, as in the study guidance provided at the beginning. However there can be drawbacks which make this approach unsatisfactory for very big courses with expensive materials (both to produce and for the eventual consumer) which need to last for years and be used by large numbers of learners. The problems with piloting in these circumstances are often these:

• the testers are not comparable with eventual learners — in age, sex, qualifications or motivation. This latter is very important, because it leads to the next problem;
• the testers do not use the materials, and try to learn from them as 'real learners' would;
• a high proportion of testers drops out;
• there is lack of consistency in feedback. The amount and kind of feedback from testers varies and also tends to drop off;
• There is an absence of measures of learner performance. Asking testers their reactions to materials tells us nothing about how well they would perform in assignments or examinations. Testers themselves may not really know how much they have learned without being assessed.

Ways can be found round some or all of these problems and one particular model for doing so — developmental testing for credit — is worth looking at. It might be possible to use some if not all features of the model in circumstances very different from the Open University where it was developed. It is also an approach which could be used in the initial presentation of a course if the possibility of changing materials has been allowed for. This is an important consideration since course materials are often not ready long enough in advance of their use by learners to allow the full developmental testing model to go ahead.

Developmental testing

In the developmental testing for credit model, testing was designed so as to achieve as near a 'dry run' of the eventual course context as possible. Testers were chosen from a sample of people in the London region who had applied unsuccessfully to study the Arts Foundation Course. The course they were to test (A241 The Elements of Music) was to be studied with all the components of the eventual course over a full Open University year, with a tutor, assignments, tutorials and end of course examination. Those who passed the course were to be awarded a credit, and all who completed the assignments and 75% of the feedback activities were guaranteed a place on the Arts Foundation Course in the following year. It seemed reasonable to assume that these testers were going to work through the draft course with motivation similar to that of the eventual students. Although the exercise as a whole worked, it is worth noting that half of the 28 testers who started did drop out; 14 took the examination. This is still much better than earlier efforts where testers were paid (around £5 per unit in the mid 1970s) but mostly dropped out before completing the work, (Nathenson and Henderson, 1976).

The last two problem areas noted above were resolved in this model by using assignment performance data and including detailed questions at a number of key points throughout every unit. The tester or learner was thus directed to respond at points chosen for their significance by the course designer, rather than left to comment on what struck them. The feedback questions combined items which tested for effective learning (performance) as well as calling for open-ended comment on the learning experience. The evaluators combined this with assignment data as a basis for suggesting changes to the course team. The feedback questions typically indicated 'process' problems, or learning problems as experienced by the testers, and these were also used on their own to suggest changes, if no performance indicators were available. (See figure 4)

The value of this model may often be greater during course presentation than course development, which is often so pressured that extensive testing cannot be managed as well as writing the materials in the first place. The use of a regular review of learning (as suggested in chapter 3) is also a very helpful learning strategy in itself and a way of getting learners to identify their own problems as well as any weaknesses in the course. Feedback questions with tutorial support could be used to improve the learning of an existing group of learners as well as to make changes for the benefit of future learners.

Materials evaluation during presentation or delivery

Quantitative data

The last section suggested that feedback questions for both content and strategy related data could be applied to courses during presentation, as well as at draft stage. There are also other options, not necessarily so demanding on the learner, and some designed to elicit more impressionistic feedback on the course experience as a whole. Learners can be asked to complete a questionnaire

Figure 6.4: The use of performance indicators and feedback questions in developmental testing

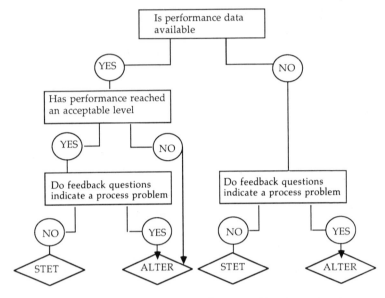

Source: Nathenson and Henderson (1976)

at the end of a course with a view to suggesting changes which will affect succeeding learners. Surveys of this kind can give good feedback on strategy related issues, but probably less good feedback on content, unless surveys are taken several times during the course of study.

At the Open University all new courses are generally surveyed after the end of course examination but before students have had the results, using a format which has been kept more or less constant for several years. This allows comparisons across all new courses each year, and across different years. There are two sections; one using questions common to all courses, the other differing according to the needs of each course.

Questions common to all courses typically cover strategy related issues: degree of use of course materials, helpfulness, interest and difficulty ratings, media comparisons and time spent studying. With a population size of thousands, the questionnaires must be pre-coded and designed for computer analysis. Figure 5 shows an example of one of these questions eliciting student ratings on degree of use of various components. The format used is similar for ratings

Figure 6.5: An example of a question asking for ratings of course components

Most materials/services in OU courses are used to varying degrees – or not used at all – by different students. Please indicate *your* use of the following in (the course being surveyed) or, where appropriate, indicate that the item was not included in this course.

Note: The top category in the 5-point usage scale, 'fully' means that you used the available materials/service as much as was reasonably possible in this particular course; for example, attending all or nearly all the tutorials, or reading nearly all of the set books.

	Not included in Course	Not at all	Degree of Use			Fully
Text units	0	1	2	3	4	5
Course Guide/Handbook	0	1	2	3	4	5
Course Reader(s)	0	1	2	3	4	5
Set Book(s)/other prescribed reading	0	1	2	3	4	5
Study Guide(s)/Commentaries/Notes	0	1	2	3	4	5
Broadcast Notes	0	1	2	3	4	5
Audiocassette Notes and/or visuals	0	1	2	3	4	5
Videocassette Notes	0	1	2	3	4	5
Other supplementary printed materials	0	1	2	3	4	5
Television broadcasts	0	1	2	3	4	5
OU video recordings of TV broadcasts	0	1	2	3	4	5
Videocassette material – non broadcast	0	1	2	3	4	5
Radio broadcasts	0	1	2	3	4	5
Audiocassettes/records/sound discs	0	1	2	3	4	5
Home experiment kit	0	1	2	3	4	5
Computer practical/software	0	1	2	3	4	5
TMAs as conslidation of learning	0	1	2	3	4	5
Tutor comments on TMAs	0	1	2	3	4	5
CMAs as consolidation of learning	0	1	2	3	4	5
Tutorials at study centre	0	1	2	3	4	5
Group telephone tutorials	0	1	2	3	4	5
Individual phone contact with tutor for advice	0	1	2	3	4	5
Counselling	0	1	2	3	4	5
Self-help study groups	0	1	2	3	4	5
Half-day school(s)	0	1	2	3	4	5
Day school(s)	0	1	2	3	4	5
Residential school (Summer/Easter)	0	1	2	3	4	5

Source: Lawless (1988)

on helpfulness and media comparisons. Figure 6 shows two questions from the course specific section where course teams can ask questions relevant to their students only. (The annual survey of new courses in 1985 went to 9,544 students covering 15 courses, with a response rate overall of 78%; in 1986, 4,262 students were surveyed on 20 courses and the response rate was 80%.)

Figure 6.6: Two examples of course-related question formats

Example a

Ring the corresponding code if you agree with any of these statements relating to (Course being surveyed)

(a) The intellectual level of the course was as I expected 1
(b) The topics covered in the course I found interesting and informative 1
(c) I would have preferred a course more biased towards environmental problems 1
(d) Of all the OU biology courses I have undertaken, this was the most enjoyable 1
(e) The amount of study time demanded by the course was excessive for a third-level half-credit 1
(f) The examination paper was a fair test of my appreciation of the course material 1

Example b

Which of the following sources of help did you use during your project work? Rate each source according to the amount of help obtained. (5 = invaluable help, 1 = marginal help, 0 = not used.)

Your own tutor	1	2	3	4	5 0
Another tutor	1	2	3	4	5 0
Residential school	1	2	3	4	5 0
Project Guide	1	2	3	4	5 0
Other (please specify)	1	2	3	4	5 0

(Extract taken from Lawless, 1987)

The results of this kind of questionnaire — especially the general ratings on use, helpfulness and media components — need careful interpretation and comparison with other similar courses, and with other data, particularly course assessment and examination performance. A low rating on one characteristic does not necessarily mean that the materials need changing, and should not be considered in isolation from other measures. Table 1, for example, shows that the course U205 *Health and Disease* had low helpfulness ratings for its components overall but a high pass rate (79.2%). The texts and course handbook were rated above average for helpfulness but lower ratings were given for the assignments and tutor comments, so that further exploration of those items looked desirable.

Table 6.1: Course helpfulness ratings by pass rate

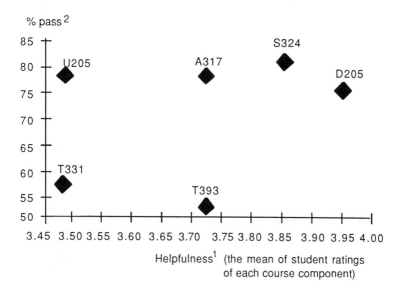

% pass [2]

Helpfulness[1] (the mean of student ratings of each course component)

1 The scale is from 1 'Not at all helpful', through to 5 'Very helpful'.

2 The pass rate for finally registered students, based on continuous assessment and examination performance

Course Codes

A317 Themes in British and American History: A Comparative Approach
D305 Changing Britain Changing World. Geographical Perspectives
S324 Animal Psychology
T331 Engineering Mechanics, Solids and Fuels
T393 Electronic Materials and Devices
U205 Health and Disease

The course with the highest pass rate of finally registered students was S324 Animal Psychology but although its components were given good ratings by students, it was not as well received as D205 *Changing Britain, Changing World: Geographical Perspectives*, which appears to have been the best received of all new 1985 courses on the basis of helpfulness ratings. Another course, T393 *Electronic Materials and Devices*, shows that although students gave average, (not poor) ratings, the pass rate (51.6%) was lower than other courses and students found the course difficult. In T331 *Engineering Mechanics, Solids and Fluids*, the pass rate was higher, though still low at 59% but the course components were given the lowest overall helpfulness rating of new courses in 1985. (Lawless and Crooks, 1985)

However, the helpfulness ratings in table 1 are the mean of each of the separate ratings for the various components on each course. Not all courses have the same number of components, and one component (audio cassettes for example, or tutorials) may be used to a greater or lesser extent on different courses, and for very different educational purposes. The one component which all undergraduate courses have, and which has a central teaching

Table 6.2: Relationship between helpfulness of text/units and pass rate

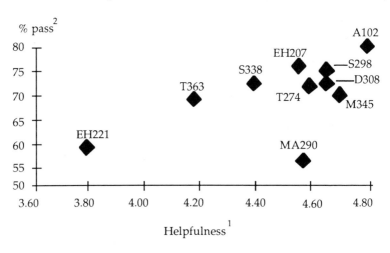

1. The scale is from 1 - 'Not at all helpful', through to 5 - 'Very helpful'
2. The pass rate for finally registered students, based on continuous assessment and examination performance.

Course Codes:

A102	-	*An Arts Foundation Course*
D308	-	*Democratic Government and Politics*
EH207	-	*Communication and Education*
EH221	-	*Educational Computing*
M345	-	*Statistical Methods*
MA290	-	*Topics in History of Mathematics*
S298	-	*Genetics*
S338	-	*Sedimentary Processes and Basin Analysis*
T274	-	*Food Production Systems*
T363	-	*Computer Aided Design.*

role in all cases, is the course text/units, and when helpfulness ratings for the text component are cross tabulated with pass rate, a much clearer relationship between the two variables emerges (table 2). Table 2 shows that the helpfulness of course text/units is positively associated with pass rate. Although the correlation co-efficient is not statistically significant in this case, this reflects the very small number of courses surveyed in 1987 from which the data were drawn. The results of the same cross tabulation using data from 15 courses surveyed in 1986 did produce a significant correlation of .59, p<.05. (Lawless, 1987 and 1988)

Questionnaires can of course be used to ask more focussed questions on course content rather than the 'how helpful did you find this' type. Where there are particular items in the package or learning environment that the author/course team wants feedback on, more content-oriented data can be elicited. The Open University surveys a proportion of each year's new courses several times a year, and these questionnaires canvass student reaction in some detail to the materials they should have studied in the preceding period. These surveys are used to evaluate assignments and tuition as well as other materials, summer school (where relevant) and workload.

Workload may appear to be one of the most straightforward items to measure, but it is not. The Open University has used a variety of approaches — hours of study, perceived difficulty and perceived amount of work set. (Field, 1983) Figure 7 shows some examples of this kind of question. If students are asked how many hours they spent, are they guessing or have they kept accurate records? If they feel the amount of time they spent on each block was 'much too much', does that mean it took them twice as long as the expected 10 to 12 hours per unit? Clearly we cannot say, but the value of questions like the latter is that they tap general feelings about the course, whether of satisfaction or resentment, rather than pinpointing problems and their causes precisely.

Workload is an important area for course feedback in open and distance learning because course materials are designed on the basis of certain assumptions about how long it will take to study them. If these assumptions are very far from the learners' experience they are justified in complaining. More often than not students just drop out or muddle through with not very satisfactory results for themselves or the providers.

Although the number of hours people spend studying may look less important than their reactions to the content of the course, it is an important issue for the part-time learner particularly, and in any case associated with perceptions of course difficulty. Figure 8 shows four measures of workload on one course (A381 *Science and Belief*) and, (in Part 2 of the table) measures of correlation,

Figure 6.7: Examples of different question formats for 'workload'

Example 1

(a) How did you find the units in these blocks in terms of *amount of work* required?

	Very light	Fairly light	About right	Fairly heavy	Very heavy
Block 6					
Units18/19	1	2	3	4	5
Unit 20	1	2	3	4	5
Unit 21	1	2	3	4	5

(b) Please specify here any components you found unduly time-consuming (this may include course texts, activities, set reading, TV and audio notes).

Example 2

		BLOCKS						
		1	2	3	4	5	6	7
a) How difficult did you find each Block	Very	1	1	1	1	1	1	1
	Fairly	2	2	2	2	2	2	2
	Not very	3	3	3	3	3	3	3
	Not at all	4	4	4	4	4	4	4
b) How did you feel about the amount of time you had to spend on each Block? (Everything to do with each Block except assignment work)	Much too much	1	1	1	1	1	1	1
	Rather too much	2	2	2	2	2	2	2
	About right	3	3	3	3	3	3	3
	Rather too little	4	4	4	4	4	4	4
	Much too little	5	5	5	5	5	5	5

(Example 1)   Womphrey EH207
(Example 2)   Womphrey S326

where 'p' stands for probability: the lower the figure, the less likely the association could happen by chance. The strongest correlation is clearly between 'perceived workload' and 'perceived difficulty'.

We can see from the table that the relationship between hours spent, perceived workload and number of pages per unit is not a simple one. Unit 6 with 49 pages took a median of 9.7 hours to study, for example, whereas unit 1 took 10.3 hours but had five fewer pages; however it was also perceived to be more difficult and to have a heavier workload. And unit 2, with 23 pages (less than half that of unit 6) got virtually the same ratings as Unit 6 — 9.6 hours, 2.5 (perceived workload) and 2.0 (perceived difficulty).

The correlations between each of these measures suggest that they are generally associated with each other (Field, 1983), as one would expect, but that there are other factors influencing learners

Figure 6.8: Measures of workload compared

Unit No in the course	Hours spent (median)	Student ratings for		No. of pages per unit
		Perceived workload (mean)	Perceived difficulty (mean)	
1	10.3	2.7	2.4	44
2	9.6	2.5	2.0	23
3	8.3	2.3	1.7	12
4	9.0	2.2	1.6	35
5	8.8	2.3	1.8	35
6	9.7	2.5	2.0	49
7	9.6	2.4	2.0	42
8	9.1	2.2	1.8	31
9	6.3	2.1	1.5	14
10	7.0	2.0	1.4	24
11	7.9	2.0	1.5	26
12	9.7	2.1	1.3	28
13	9.5	2.3	1.7	28
14	9.0	2.6	2.2	38
15	9.7	2.5	1.8	58
Means	8.90	2.31	1.78	32.47
Standard Deviation	1.10	0.22	0.30	12.53
Range	6.3-10.3	2.0-2.7	1.2-2.4	12-58

Part 2: Correlations

	Perceived difficulty	Perceived workload	Hours spent on unit
No. of pages per unit	+0.52 ($p < 0.05$)	+0.58 ($p < 0.002$)	+0.66 ($p < 0.01$)
Hours spent on unit	+0.59 ($p < 0.02$)	+0.69 ($p < 0.01$)	
Perceived workload	+0.93 ($p < 0.001$)		

when they decide on ratings. The implications of high workload are probably more negative than those of 'difficulty'. Unguided projects on OU courses for example have been rated more difficult than more structured projects on other courses, but they are also rated more highly on 'interest' scales than are the more structured projects. (Henry, 1978)

As Field notes: *'In general, the quantitative approach is not, on its own, either sharply focussed enough or insightful enough to indicate clearly the nature of any underlying problem. Response measurements are therefore best combined with qualitative comments in the student's own words, tied to a defined stimulus (e.g. an argument in the text; a location in the unit). The loss of precision in aggregating global scaled responses is then balanced by the precision of individual comments.'*

(Field, 1983)

Qualitative data

Although interviews provide the richest source of qualitative data, questionnaires can also be used to generate open-ended responses. Figure 9 shows a useful format, which prompts the learner initially with a number of attitudinal statements based on existing evidence of reactions to similar material. It then invites the learner to expand on their choice and to make any other comment.

Figure 6.9: Eliciting learner reactions: 1

Example combining closed-ended responses plus open-ended comment.

Have you any particular reactions to this chapter/unit/module?
Please ring one or more codes below:

No strong feelings	1	Some parts extremely difficult	6
Quite interesting	2	Awful	7
Very much what I wanted	3	Very good	8
Boring	4	Frightening	9
Some parts quite difficult	5	None of these	10
		Did not read	11

Please explain your response in a little more detail, giving page/section references where possible or relevant. _____

Adapted from Questionnaire Design for the Arts Foundation Course by Bob Womphrey, OU.

Learners can of course be asked to comment on any particular part or component of a course, without suggesting what their attitude might be, or with only very general indications of the kind of comment required, as in the examples in figure 10. In the first example, the learner is asked to comment on one aspect, presumably that which was the most important aspect of the audio-cassette, i.e. its helpfulness to the learner in completing the assignment. This is a question more related to the strategic use of the cassette, rather than its content, though we might expect comments to refer to the content of the cassette, to explain why it was or was not found helpful.

The second example in figure 10 asks the learner to concentrate on the main aims of the item, though it leaves the learner free to comment in any way they may want.

A third type of approach is one which does not direct the respondent to any particular part of the course or materials, but asks them to pick out good and bad points, as in figure 11. This can be used in tutor commenting (see the next section) as well as learner commenting.

Figure 6.10: Eliciting learner reactions: 2

Some examples of questions for open-ended comment.

Example 1: Did you work through audio-cassette 1   Yes/No
If yes, did you find it helpful in answering the assignment?

Example 2: Having completed the work for unit x, how well do you think it explains:

    i)   different meanings for the diffusion of innovations?

    ii) specific problems in implementing changes in information technology?

    iii) the difference between technological and social issues?

Figure 6.11: Eliciting learner reactions: 3

An example of non-specific 'over-view' type questions.

Thinking back now over the whole course/Block 1/the 1st module etc.

a) What for you have been the best aspects?

b) What for you have been the worst/less good aspects?

What changes would you recommend? (Please indicate page references or identify the parts you are referring to.)

Interviews offer the best opportunity for getting detailed and focused information about the quality of learner response — not simply 'this was good/bad', but why, and which of a variety of different reactions is the dominant one. Having generated a large amount of feedback through a mailed questionnaire, it can be difficult to know the priorities learners would make, and therefore which of a number of possible actions to take. Moreover a survey of learners is more likely to be helpful, if we already know something about the *kinds of response* individuals have had and can use this to frame the questionnaire items accordingly. The interview can also be a way of developing vignettes of different kinds of learners and the ways they use the course materials, which can be very useful to course authors. There are circumstances in which it is important to know not only how a course is rated overall, but how particular learners reacted to it.

Exploring learning from the learner's perspective

Researchers at the Open University followed a group of 29 students through their first year of Open University study on the Social Science Foundation Course. The group was interviewed before, during and after the course, by which stage drop out had reduced the group to 18. The final interview was focused on students' perceptions of gains from studying, elicited by a number of key questions:

1. First of all, tell me in general how the course has gone since I saw you last?
2. Tell me what you feel like now it's over?
3. If you hadn't done the Social Science Foundation Course this year, what do you think you would have missed?
4. Was the course as you expected it to be?
5. What were the best parts/worst parts of the course?
6. What do you think you have learnt from the course?
                            (taken from Taylor, Morgan and Gibbs, 1982)

These were semi-structured interviews where the interviewer used the same framework of questions for each interview but was free to ask questions relevant to each interviewee, in response to the dialogue as it developed. This seems the most productive approach to use for exploring learning from the learner's perspective. The value of repeating a core of questions in each interview is that we can then compare the responses and identify a range of different positions along the same dimension. If we ask completely different questions in each interview it becomes difficult at the analysis stage to do more than present a set of unique learner case studies.

However the interviewer need not be restricted by the list of core questions from asking about areas which arise during the interview and may only be relevant to the particular learner. The core questions in general are meant to be a starting point for discussion and the good interviewer uses prompts like 'can you tell me more about that', or 'what made you feel that way', which do not pre-empt the reply but encourage the learner to talk freely about things from their own point of view.

Peer and tutor feedback

Feedback from those who already know the area covered by course material (because they are tutors, or experts in the field) should ideally be seen as *complementary* to learner feedback rather than as an alternative to it. It is so easy for the expert to miss important learner reactions or difficulties precisely because they do already know what the course is teaching. Even so, there are also good reasons to elicit feedback from peers, whether or not there is also learner feedback.

First, learners may only be able to say that they find something difficult, not explain why. An experienced teacher may be able to provide reasons for learner feedback and, even more, to suggest alternative approaches which would be an improvement. On its own, learner feedback can leave us knowing there is a lot wrong with a course, but without a coherent idea of how to put it right. And unfortunately, it is always possible to change a course and make it worse, rather than better.

Second, in systems which employ a lot of tutors, it is important to elicit their views on the course they are teaching because their attitudes may be passed on in various ways to learners. The Open University for example relies heavily on conscientious tutoring, and course teams recognise that tutors are not likely to be enthusiastic if they dislike the course materials generally. As a result systematic tutor feedback was collected for a number of years for all new courses, and still occurs on some course teams where there are resources available to do so.

Third, if tuition is provided for a course, it is important to document this course component by getting feedback on what tutors actually did. Tutors have a particularly important role in feedback on assignments, since they are the only ones in a position to comment on the difficulties which learners as a whole experienced in completing assignments, any problems in the assignment design, and its validity as a tool for assessing student learning at that stage in the course.

Fourth, it may be quicker and cheaper to elicit peer feedback than learner feedback, and if learner feedback is impossible, comments on materials from peers is better than no feedback at all.

In summary therefore, feedback from peers, whether colleagues, experts in the field, or tutors teaching the course can provide information in a range of areas:

— the appropriateness of the overall aims and structure of the course, (especially helpful during the design stage);
— strengths and weaknesses in the detailed content of the materials;
— suggestions for alternative ways of doing things;
— exploration of the tutor role and documentation of tasks undertaken by the tutor;
— review of learners' performance on assignments;
— review of any difficulties in grading/commenting on assignments;
— validity and reliability of assessment;
— relationship to other relevant courses in the field.

Although peer commenting may be quicker to set up than learner feedback, it does require preparation. Here again, the distinction between materials production and delivery or presentation is an important one for the different approaches used.

Peer commenting during materials production

It is not easy to comment in detail on what might be done at this stage, because so much depends on the time scale, subject area and level, and the preferences of the authors. There are two points during the preparation of materials however, when constructive comments from a peer can be helpful; at the very earliest stage when general aims and overall structure are in outline, and at the stage when a complete version of the material exists but there is still time to make changes which will improve it for the learner. (Stages 1 and 2 in figure 1 at the beginning of this chapter).

The design stage

The first consideration is to find someone appropriate for the job. It may be vital to get a recognised external expert for the earliest design stage, in order to get confirmation that the approach is at least 'on the right lines'. In order to do this effectively, he or she needs to be told:

• who the intended learners are, and if possible, the expectations about their education/skill level at course entry;
• how many learners might use the materials, and in what circumstances;
• what the course will cost and whether learners will be sponsored;
• whether tuition and counselling will be available, and if so, in what form;
• whether the course will be assessed or leads to a qualification;
• the aims of the course and its behavioural objectives, if there are any;
• the date by which the expert's comments are to be returned.

At this stage the most helpful comments are those concentrated on overall design rather than detailed execution, and the kind of questions you might include in your brief to the expert are fairly self-evident:

— Are the course aims and objectives appropriate? (taking into account intended learners and context of learning).
— Does the course appear likely to achieve these aims?
— Should additional material (topics, examples, information, etc.) be included? Is anything redundant, inappropriate?
— Is the course design likely to encourage learning?
— What further changes would you recommend?
— How much tutorial/counselling support is likely to be needed?

— How does this course compare with other relevant courses/
materials in the field?

The expert does not provide blanket approval, but comments (or
should do) on fitness for purpose. You need to make sure that
she or he knows what the purpose is and the learners context,
at least as planned. Apart from finding out any obvious omissions
or misconceptions in the course design, it may be useful to have
the approval of an expert on record, should you find yourself
needing to justify your course to an outside body at any stage.

The 'advanced draft' stage

When materials have been thoroughly drafted, there may be time
to get more detailed comments from someone who combines
experience of the target population of learners with knowledge
of course content. (Your initial external expert may or may not
be appropriate for this role.) It is important to bear in mind other
desirable qualities when choosing readers. Are they so
overburdened with work elsewhere that they are unlikely to
complete the job to your timescale? Are they generally sympathetic
to open learning or suspicious of it? Will it be difficult (for either
or both of you) if they have to give you negative criticism? Can
they empathise with a learner's approach or are they 'too expert'?

Assuming you can find readers who seem likely to do the job
you want, the next stage is to brief them. They will need a written
account of the relevant background information and what their
task is. Here is a starting list of categories of information they
may need:

• A description of intended learners and the course, as outlined
above for the 'external expert'.
• The questions to be answered as they work through the
materials.
• The scale of changes to the materials that is possible; is there
time for a complete re-write or only minor modification?.
• The date by which comments should be returned.

Even though readers may be asked only a few questions, it will
help in the organisation and use of their comments if they are
provided with structured reporting sheets, of the kind shown in
figure 12. This example shows that at this stage in materials
development, questions on the effectiveness of the content can
be asked. Readers may also be able to pick up very small-scale
problems on the text and are helped by being given sheets on
which to record the page and line number against the comments
they make.

Figure 6.12: Sample questions for eliciting reader comments

Example: *A Case-study on the Relocation of Textile Production to East and South-East Asia*

1. Does the case-study achieve its aims of

   a) analysing the extent to which relocation has occurred? _____
   b) suggesting reasons for this relocation? _____

   c) analysing the effects in First and Third World countries? _____

2. Do you think the aims of the case study should be changed? _____

3. Bearing in mind the use of the case study in the course, what are its main strengths and weaknesses? _____

(A proforma would include space for reader response to each question.)

If there is a course team, it may be helpful for someone else to read through the comments submitted by readers as well as the author of the material, and to present an overview of feedback so that the group can decide more easily on changes required. (See chapter 8 for further details.)

Evaluation of existing materials prior to use

In some circumstances evaluation of existing materials will be required before offering them to learners. A deliverer of open learning may want to check out materials others have produced, not in order to revise them but to help decide whether they can be used effectively, in the local circumstances in which the deliverer is operating. Local experts — tutors or trainers — can be asked to evaluate the material using checklists of the kind suggested above. The North East Open Learning Network has developed a detailed version which local staff complete for course materials the unit may decide to offer, and which they might tutor. An extract of the range of questions included is shown in figure 13.

Figure 6.13: A proforma for assessment of the quality of existing open learning materials

Extract from the tutor proforma used by North East Open Learning Network.

EVALUATION OF OPEN LEARNING MATERIAL

By completing this form, you are helping to ensure that the Network delivers only good open learning programmes, that only those who can benefit from a particular programme are enrolled and that these receive all the support they need.

A PRACTICAL INFORMATION

---

1. How many study hours do the authors estimate the 'average' learner takes to complete this package?

---

2. How many do *you* estimate?

---

3. What media are used?

---

4. What equipment is necessary to complete the package?

---

5. Could you estimate how much access to the equipment is required, whether the learner needs access to it at all times or, for example, just for one or two sessions (Give as much detail as you can).

---

6. In information given on reference material, text books etc that the learner should have read or have access to? Give details.

B EDUCATIONAL CONTENT OF THE MATERIAL AND THE SUPPORT REQUIRED FROM THE NETWORK

---

1. What prior knowledge or experience does the material assume of the learner?

---

2. Does the material have clearly stated objectives?

---

3. In your view does the material meet these objectives?

---

4. Who do the producers of the material identify as their target audience?

---

5. Do you consider the material is suitable for this target audience?

---

6. Can you identify any other groups who might benefit from this package?

---

7. On average how much tutor support should be provided. Please try to specify whether it would need to be face to face, by telephone, by mail, etc and how it is broken down (e.g. 2 fifteen minute face to face sessions at beginning and end of package, telephone tuition as required, 1 assessment to be marked, etc.)?

8. What is the nearest equivalent to this package in existing work? (i.e. nearest f/t or p/t course, year and subject area)?
C IS IT GOOD OPEN LEARNING MATERIAL?
1. Does the material call for a reasonable level of participation from the learner?
2. Are all instructions and the path through the material clear?
3. Is the presentation visually attractive?
4. Is the style of the written material friendly and stimulating?
5. Are other media used well?
6. Will the material motivate/communicate with its intended users?
D SUMMARY
1. What is your overall impression of the material?
2. Are there any modifications/improvements you think would be desirable before the material was used in a Network programme?
3. Would you be interested in acting as a tutor for this package?

(Layout not in a format that would be used in practice, where space would be left for tutor response and other items of information)

Source: Erland Polden, NEOLN

Tutor commenting during materials presentation or delivery

The crucial difference between this and the preceding section is that materials are being used by learners and feedback can take into account the learner experience. For this reason it is assumed that tutors will be used. If there are no tutors, comments can be elicited by peers but the procedures will be similar to those outlined in the preceding section on readers.

The Open University originally used a quantitative approach to tutor feedback. This was set up in the first years when there were fewer courses and a much greater similarity among them. It was possible therefore in the early 1970s to design a proforma which could be analysed by computer. Data from tutors on each course in its first year of presentation were collected after each assignment marked. Each tutor on a full credit course therefore might complete and return up to eight feedback forms with pre-coded responses. Although this approach is no longer used by the OU, it may be worth considering if a uniform proforma for all courses is feasible. It does allow comparisons across courses as well as within courses for different reporting periods. Tutor feedback at the Open University is now course-specific and oriented towards open-ended comments, as illustrated in the example in figure 14.

Figure 6.14: Extracts from a tutor report form used for E355 Education For Adults
(Open University, Milton Keynes)

Report on the first part of the course: Block A: Concepts of Adult Education

In this section we would like your view on Block A of E355. You may wish to consider the academic content, the teaching strategy adopted or the balance and integration of the various parts. We would also welcome any information you may have on student difficulties with the material.

Question 1 a) Do the text and readings provide an overview of the education of adults as a field of study?

b) Have students reacted favourably/unfavourably to using source readings and commentary rather than the more usual OU course units?

Question 2   The First Assignment

a) How many finally registered students have you been allocated?

b) How many submitted the first assignment?

c) What was your assessment of the suitability of the first assignment?

d) Were there any common student difficulties?

e) Were there any problems in grading or making teaching comments on this assignment?

Source: Ryan, OU

In contrast, a closed-ended approach using ratings is being used by the Birmingham Open Learning Development Unit in its evaluation. Tutors are being asked to rate learning materials according to a four point scale, where 1 is low and 4 is high. some of the characteristics picked out for rating are as follows:

Clear objectives	1	2	3	4
Initial impression	1	2	3	4
General layout	1	2	3	4
Visual cues	1	2	3	4
Readability	1	2	3	4
Activities — relevance to the learner	1	2	3	4

Twenty-one such features are listed in all, and space left for the tutor to suggest other features if they feel something has not been adequately covered. (See Case Study D, chapter 2)

The use of one tutor form for all courses was eventually discontinued by the Open University for two main reasons. The use of computer analysis of returns delayed the receipt of the results by individual course teams, who needed them within the first few months of course presentation, when changes are made for the next year's presentation. The uniform proforma was also less and less useful to course teams whose courses differed so widely, with innovations like audio-cassettes, case study materials, non-assessed assignments and so on, replacing the more uniform nature of the foundation courses in the early days of the University.

Furthermore, course authors found quantitative information on its own not very enlightening. It may be important to know that, for example, 40% of tutors think unit 1 needs changing while 60% do not, but it is at least as important to know what tutors actually said about unit 1 — and who says it! Whereas feedback from learners is usually anonymous, there are good reasons why peer and tutor feedback should be identifiable. After all, such individuals are chosen on the basis of who they are and what they are doing, therefore at some stage it may be important to know whose feedback it is that we are reading. This does not necessarily mean that what the head of a training department says counts more than feedback from an ordinary trainer, or that the tutor who happens also to be a Professor of Sociology at Manchester University gets more weight than an OU tutor with 15 year's experience, but otherwise unemployed. It all depends. The important point is that authors/course teams/delivery projects need to interpret results; and knowing who says what is part of deciding what action to take as a result of getting feedback.

On the whole, Open University tutors have chosen to sign their reports, although this is not mandatory. Most people recognise that feedback which is so destructive that you would rather not put your name to it is not very useful anyway.

One of the problems with analysing and responding to peer feedback is that it can be mutually conflicting, or indecisive. It is probably the exception rather than the rule on OU tutor feedback for example, to find a clear majority of tutors all saying that something was excellent, or so bad that it must be changed. Peers and tutors also have difficulty restricting comments to changes modest enough to be made in the time available. Their comments amount to saying 'You've got it all wrong; what you should really be doing is this, which is how I would do it....' Unfortunately it is usually too late to throw everything out of the window and start again. Although conflicting views in feedback can never be avoided, feedback of this latter kind (i.e. which is wrongly focused), is a

Figure 6.15: A summary of tutor feedback: February-April, on a project based course

Begin Sat	Study week	Assignment	Comments on contact with students	Comments on course materials
21 FEB	1		*Establishing contact with students* • Most contact by letter or phone, but some face to face meetings. Some emphasis on the importance of early contact to sort out major difficulties and quickly establish a pattern of contact.	*Printed course materials* • tutors generally satisfied with the printed course materials. A typewritten format would suffice? • main reservation is that the printed material does not adequately prepare students for the reality of research.
28	2			
7	3		Suggestions • use of report form to stimulate regular contact, ensure students provide phone numbers, place firm onus on students to initiate contact.	Suggestions More attention to: • Planning and timing of activities • problems of small numbers of respondents/limited quantitative data • guidance on role, aims, content, presentation of assignments • increase option choice
14 MAR	4	Formative Assignment 01 (Mar 17)	*Purpose of student contact* • possibly less emphasis on choice of option than might be expected? Many students already have firm ideas or choice is restricted. • discussion tended to focus on project feasibility, strategies, methodology. • choice limited for students who do not live in a large conurbation or near second home area?	*Assessment structure* Seems to have worked fairly well. Timing good. Some doubts about the formative assignments – possible overlap between first and second, role of the eighth needs clarification.
21	5			
28	6			
4	7			Suggestions • improve assignment guidelines for students • clarify relationship between assignments – how much reiteration of early work needed in later assignments • use assignment 02 as a dry run for 02/04 • reduce number of assignments – drop either 01 or 02
11 APR	8	Formative Assignment 02 (Apr 14)	• TMAs generally considered useful – get ideas on paper, consider nature and availability of data sources, focus for tutor/student discussions. • some reservations: 1) Course Notes for 01 ambiguous – justification of choice or reasons for interest in topic area, 2) some have decided on project before 01, 3) tendency for 01 and 02 to overlap, 4) 02 due date clashes with Easter Holidays. • suggestions – set 02 three weeks before 03/04, better guidance on scope, style and content of assignments.	
18	8			
25	9			

TMA – Tutor marked assignment

Source: P. Kelly, OU

waste of everybody's time and can be avoided by better briefing of those asked to provide it, and more tightly constructed questions on the proforma.

As with reader comments, feedback of this kind can often be used more effectively if a summary is provided. Figure 15 gives an extract from one prepared for a third level guided project course in geography. This illustrates the potential of tutor feedback during presentation to communicate the learners' experience of the course as well as tutor opinions on materials. Most of the information is oriented towards contact with students and assignments, with quite a lot of suggestions for changes and additions which could improve the course for the next cohort of students. A summary of this kind does not replace the full comments by each tutor; the course team still need to read through these and form their own impressions. But the summary gives the group as a whole an overview which helps focus attention and decide what to do.

Conclusion

The evaluation of learning materials offers an area rich in different approaches towards and examples of evaluation. This chapter pretends no more than an introduction; a starting point rather than a definitive statement. The evaluation of course materials may, on the face of it, appear more straightforward than the evaluation of tuition and counselling. There is at least a tangible product – the materials – to which all the various responses can be related. However the tangibility of the product can be misleading, obscuring the reality of the learner's perspective. For the learner, the materials are the starting point of a process of study which is unique to the individual. It seems unlikely that any two learners will see the course and the course materials in exactly the same way. In this sense there are as many 'courses' as there are learners of the course.

I am not suggesting that evaluation should attempt to substantiate the uniqueness of each individual's experience, for that would prove overwhelming rather than illuminative. It is necessary to find ways of aggregating response so as to provide an overview and pointers to action. What is important is that these (usually quantitative) data are firmly tied to the learning context to which they relate, in terms of the characteristics of learners (their experience, age, qualification, work status and so on) and their reasons for studying the course. There may be a degree of uniformity in both areas in the case of on the job training provided by a large company for a specific task. In many other examples of open learning, both learners and their motivation are likely to be diverse. Even if it has not been possible to record this kind of information for all learners as a matter of routine, it is possible to illustrate the nature of the diversity by interviewing a small number of learners and providing the kind of case studies which Roffey Park Managment College, for example, has included in its various newsletters for students.

Finally, a reminder of the importance of different perspectives on the effectiveness of materials. Evaluation is more often like reading a detective story than searching for the holy grail; piecing together different pieces of information and following up clues, rather than a long trek till we find 'the truth'. When it comes to course evaluation, there isn't 'one truth' but many truths, and the task is to decide on priorities and to build up an account of the process of learning which is reasonably representative rather than comprehensive of all experiences. The dangers of relying solely on feedback from tutors, supervisors and other practitioners have already been elaborated. There are also dangers in using learner feedback in isolation, especially if only closed-ended quantitative data are available. Where support staff or sponsors have been involved, their perspective should be added, to complement that of the learner and perhaps, to place it in context.

Further reading

Gibbs, G., and Haigh, H. *A Compendium of Course Evaluation Questionnaires* Oxford Polytechnic. Standing Conference on Development Services, Occasional Paper 17.

A very useful set of checklists and ideas for course evaluation, which can be adapted for an open learning context. Most of the teaching it refers to is not materials based, but there are approaches which could be relevant to many forms of open learning. Has a useful opening discussion on the design of feedback and questionnaire items.

The Open University, *Professional Development in Education: Designing Effective Self-Instructional Materials for Adults.* Centre for Continuing Education, the Open University, Milton Keynes.

Includes workshops and a comprehensive pack of materials on developing your own self-instructional material, with sections on evaluation and feedback, for text and non-text components.

PART III THE PROCESS OF EVALUATION

Introduction

Although evaluations come in many different shapes and sizes, they can all be said to incorporate three *types of activity*:

— planning and design (and re-design)
— data collection and reporting
— data analysis and usage.

I prefer to see these as types of activity rather than as distinct stages, one following after another, because in practice, (especially in formative self-evaluation) they overlap. We may, for example, plan to use data progressively, so that early findings will be being analysed while later findings are still being collected. And early findings may suggest a re-design of initial plans. So, although each is treated separately here, in practice they often occur together, with more or less of each activity at different times.

The chapters in Part III are not intended to provide a manual on how to do evaluation. In particular, there is little point in adding to the existing literature on carrying out interviews, postal surveys and questionnaires, because the same *principles* apply whether these data collection methods are used in open learning or conventional education and training. The *application* of these methods in open learning does raise a number of practical issues, which are included in chapter 7. It is the social organisation and the use of evaluation findings which do raise important issues, and these have not, I believe, been sufficiently explored in the evaluation literature, and these are the focus of chapters 7 and 8, where they are explored in the context of open learning, developing some of the points made in chapters 1 and 2.

If there is a key question in effective evaluation I would suggest it is '*Who is it for?*' followed closely by the related question '*What is it for?*'. We may think the answers so obvious that the questions are never posed. But one of the purposes of evaluation is to reveal assumptions, including assumptions about who wants evaluation and why.

If evaluation is to be for practitioners and learners, it follows that they should be involved in defining its goals and the form it is to take. I have suggested a team approach as the one most likely to encourage all participants to feel that they can make a useful contribution to evaluation and that it is in their interests to do so. I think this is especially important where the role and status boundaries between different categories of staff in an organisation are very clearly marked. The risk in this situation is that evaluation is perceived as solely a management function, perhaps even imposed by management. However this is an area where rigid generalisations would be misguided. It may be possible to achieve the goals of equality and collaboration without a team approach, in some circumstances. Clearly practitioners themselves need to work out a form of organisation appropriate and acceptable for themselves.

Turning next to the use of evaluation findings, I think it is probably a justifiable observation that the last thing most people think about is how they are going to use the results of an evaluation when they have them. This is a great mistake, and doubtless contributes to evaluation's lack of impact on practice and, as a consequence, low motivation to evaluate unless required to do so by others. It is perhaps not surprising that evaluation (and also research) are not applied to practice when so little — if any — thought goes into the process of how their findings might be used on completion. There appears to be a naive reliance on the presentation of data in a final report, which reliance has withstood the evidence of decades, that this *alone* is an ineffectual tool for the communication and use of the results of an enquiry.

The professional evaluator may have little capacity to influence this end of the process, in any case. But here is where the practitioner-evaluator scores. He or she is at least one of the users of the evaluation, and the evaluation team includes those who take decisions about the open learning system as a whole, at least on a day to day basis. The practitioner evaluator is in a position not only to *ask* the key questions about who is going to use the evaluation, for what and by whom, but *can provide the answers too*.

Although 'planning' comes logically prior to 'use of findings', it is often at the end of an evaluation, during the difficulties of using the findings in some way, that we see the full force of those injunctions about the necessity of good planning. At that point, it may be much easier to see what should have been planned, as well as why. For this reason, you may find it helpful to read chapter 8 first, or to re-read the planning section of chapter 7, after reading chapter 8.

7 Planning and data collection

Main themes: *What is the role of evaluation in an open learning system and who is to define it? The importance of the social process through which evaluation is implemented and the desirability of a team approach. How the team might operate. The functions of the team. What do practitioners need out of evaluation? A possible strategy for planning evaluation, combining regular baseline evaluation with issue-specific evaluation. Practical issues in data collection: routine records, feedback, interviews and questionnaires.*

The social organisation of evaluation

Evaluation was defined in chapter one as 'a recognised process' of judging the effects and the outcomes of a learning process. There is a clear implication here that both learners and practitioners should know that evaluation will take place, and has a role to play, in the organisation of which they are a part. The question is, *what* role will it play, and *who* is to define its role? I have suggested answers to both questions. First, that practitioners and learners should define the kind of evaluation they want. Second, that evaluation is for development: for the development of learning and the learner's experience; for the development of services and the quality of the curriculum the institution offers, and for the development of the competence and the careers of practitioners. Evaluation is a process through which not only quality can be improved, but new developments initiated.

It is not necessary that *all* practitioners should subscribe to this suggested role for evaluation. What matters is that a collaborative decision-making process is set up, through which a definition can be agreed by all those concerned, together with procedures for its implementation. An 'evaluation team' is one way of achieving this.

The evaluation team

The size of the team obviously depends on the number of staff involved. It may be necessary for large groups of staff to be represented by one or two individuals, with a system for consultation and reporting back to the larger group. Some such system will certainly be needed for learners and probably also for corporate sponsors. It may also be desirable to invite one (or more) 'outsider' to join the team for particular meetings, if not as a full member; people who are experienced evaluators or peers who can bring a degree of objectivity and clear sightedness because they are not close to the day to day organisation of the system.

The overall goal of the team is to decide on the role of evaluation and to set up procedures through which it will occur. The team will need to meet regularly, and there may be sub-groups working on specific tasks, or delegation to individuals of some items. Some members of the team are likely to be more intimately concerned with all aspects of the evaluation than others, but the team should resemble more the working of a small group than a large committee. It is probably undesirable therefore to have more than about a dozen members, or to include anyone as a full member who does not have a direct interest as a user of the open learning system. External interests can be consulted and kept informed by other mechanisms.

Although the team may rightly wish to avoid formality, it is important to discuss how it will proceed and make conscious decisions about that rather than decide by default. The following suggestions are offered as (it is hoped) a helpful beginning.

Planning Tools and procedures

Minutes and chairing

An evaluation team may not be designated as a formal committee but it is still desirable to minute meetings, again creating a record of decision making which can be open for scrutiny. Minuting — and chairing — meetings can (probably should) be shared round the group. The approach to minuting should also be decided: should debate be summarised, or only decisions noted? Should points for action be highlighted and staffing indicated? Minutes can help to structure the work of a group, if used constructively.

Equality of contribution

Everyone in the group needs to feel that they can contribute to the discussion. At the first meeting especially, everyone can be asked what they would like out of an evaluation, and what they think ought to be done. This can be listed as in a 'brain storming' activity without judging whether the desirable is feasible. (It may provide the basis of a bid for more resources in future, to enable projects which are impossible at the moment.) This is a useful strategy to convince all members of the group that their ideas are worth hearing. If 'evaluation' is an off putting word for some people, 'monitoring', or 'developing the quality of our service', can be used instead.

Information needed by the team

The team needs information on which to make decisions and papers need to be provided for meetings on items such as these:

— criteria set by an 'external' body — e.g. progress reports required by a College's senior management, or the Training Commission's Code of Practice, 'Ensuring Quality in Open Learning';

— decisions already taken e.g. a college principal may have already specified that data should be collected on use of rooms, number of learners allocated a tutor etc;

— resources available for evaluation, if any. For example, there may be a budget for 'temporary secretarial' help part of which could be used for evaluation. Cassette recorders might be available for interviewing. The telephone budget may be sufficient to cover local calls to ex-learners or to drop-outs for follow-up. Tutors may be prepared to record tutorial attendance or to conduct a group discussion 'out of hours';

— sources of funds to which application could be made;

— calendar of activities already scheduled for the unit, with space to add possible evaluation tasks;

— list of data which are already collected routinely by the administration e.g. number of enquiries and content of query, student name, address, telephone, course(s), etc.

Information may not always be available for each of these items, in which case the planning group will have to use estimates. It is particularly important to have access at an early stage to a calendar of activities, on which tasks of particular staff are recorded. This provides a reminder of deadlines and duties at a glance, and is an essential working tool both for planning and for implementation. A calendar or flowchart of this kind often needs to be built up starting from completion dates — 'if we need this for that committee meeting we shall have to have data analysed by 10 days earlier, therefore feedback forms need to go out by . . . ' It may only be at this very detailed planning level in fact that goals can be shown to be feasible or not. For this reason it is useful

to work with a blank calendar to hand which the group can use
to try out its ideas from the beginning.

An evaluation plan

The immediate output of the team should be an evaluation plan
— a definition of the role of evaluation and of the means by which
it is to be achieved. This may have to adopt a format to suit the
stylistic requirements of a particular college or sponsoring body.
It may be a very long document or only a single page if resources
allow only the most basic form of evaluation. Whatever it looks
like, a plan ought to be a record of decisions about each of the
following, (not necessarily in this order):

- who evaluation is for — which individuals, groups, committees
  etc. within the open learning organisation concerned;
- who is in overall charge of/co-ordinating evaluation;
- membership of the evaluation team, how often it will meet
  and mode of operation;
- the goals of evaluation;
- what the evaluation findings will be used for;
- the objectives of evaluation — i.e. how goals will be achieved;
- the methods used to achieve the objectives;
- staff resources required to achieve them;
- equipment, consumables, travel, temporary staff costs;
- what reports/records will be produced and when;
- any other outcomes;
- a calendar of activities and the staff assigned to them;
- membership of the planning/steering group.

Once an evaluation plan has been drawn up and the evaluation
is underway, there may not be a need to meet again until results
are available. This obviously depends on the duration of the
evaluation and its scale. Members of the planning team may be
in touch daily in any case, so that formal meetings are unnecessary.
Any changes to the plan still need to be recorded, however.

Summary

An evaluation team should be established to initiate and co-ordinate
the evaluation and use of findings. The group's tasks include the
following:

- decide on membership and the status of the group;
- make decisions about goals and objectives;
- decide on action and allocate tasks;
- decide how the evaluation will be monitored and co-ordinated;
- draft an evaluation plan;
- record decisions and minute discussion.

A strategy for planning evaluation

Evaluation which can be integrated into the regular work of practitioners has to satisfy a number of criteria, otherwise it will be squeezed out by tasks perceived as more important.

First, it must relate to *a realistic assessment of what practitioner interests are.* Although these can only be defined locally (by the evaluation team) they are likely to include interests such as the following:

— implementing more effectively the programmes for which practitioners are responsible, thereby improving the quality of learner experience;
— meeting demands set by management or imposed by an outside body;
— justifying the value of the unit's work;
— promoting the careers of individual staff.

I begin with practitioner interests because evaluation as an arena of activity (often non-activity) demonstrates the effects of a phenomenon which Argyris and Schon have characterized as the disjunction between espoused theory and theory-in-use. (Argyris and Schon, 1978) The espoused theory is the one we say we believe in; the theory-in-use is the one which is embodied in our actions, and which may be admitted to or evident in 'off the record' conversation rather than public, attributable statements. The analysis of institutional interaction may suggest a disjunction between espoused theory and theory-in-use. Applying this to evaluation, lip service may be paid to its importance but a low priority assigned to it in practice. This must reflect to some extent a perception that evaluation is not in the interests of the practitioner because it is not intrinsic to carrying out the job, or to other goals which do have a high priority.

One of the aims of chapter 2 and of Part II has been to modify that perception by showing how evaluation can be done so as to feed into practical decision making and ultimately create a more effective environment for the learner. Thus might be achieved the first practitioner interest listed above. The strategies this involves need be very little different, if at all, from those which might be required by the governing body of an organisation or by an external agency; they therefore feed into the second interest of practitioners listed above. Similarly, such evaluation can contribute towards career promotion, even when pursued co-operatively by a group, as suggested here. The ability to organise a coherent account of a programme's progress and outcomes is itself a demonstration of competence. In addition, evaluation offers the practitioner in education an opportunity for writing and publication otherwise unavailable because of the lack of time for research.

I would also argue that evaluation makes practice more interesting although that is less easy to generalise to all practitioners because it reflects individual attitudes and interests so directly. And it must also be admitted that evaluation is not in the interests of practitioners seeking to reduce their workload, for whatever reason. However pragmatic the strategies we adopt, they do require *some* time commitment.

The second main criterion evaluation must satisfy is that *it must operate within the constraints of the open learning unit concerned.* Practitioners will make a number of requirements of any evaluation strategy, some of which are likely to be generally applicable, and can be listed.

Evaluation should be

- robust — in that it does not break down under pressure from peaks in work load;
- flexible — capable of being adapted to different courses, systems and learners, and
- user-friendly — makes realistic demands on staff and resources.

It is not easy to devise a strategy which will meet all the needs for evaluation, satisfy practitioner interests and operate within their constraints. In doing so it is helpful to consider a distinction which applies to most open learning systems. Such systems often require two kinds of information: regular, baseline information, and information about particular courses, learners or issues which will vary from one year or planning period to the next. We are usually in a position to predict the former, as a continuing requirement, but unable to predict in advance all our needs for the latter.

Figure 7.1: The components of evaluation

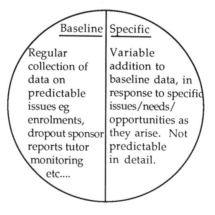

We may feel confident that we shall need certain kinds of information whatever learning opportunities we provide, and can set up procedures to collect it from the beginning. Thereafter, these will need to be reviewed and developed so as to incorporate all programme work as it grows and, in all probability, diversifies. The less predictable needs for information will occur in response to more immediate goals, and reflect decisions taken to find out information about a particular issue: a course, or group of learners, or tutor performance. What is done therefore will vary according to the goal at the time and the resources needed to carry it out. (See figure 1) The implication is that resources must be allocated for *both* baseline and issue specific data, but that the difficulty of specifying the latter in advance may mean that not all needs that arise can be met, in every year, whereas resources for baseline evaluation should be adequate to cover the known activity on a regular basis.

It also follows that different courses or aspects of provision will be evaluated to differing extents. Although figure 1 shows a circle neatly divided, this would be unlikely in practice. Taking the course as an objective for the moment, figure 2 shows a course which has findings available from regular baseline evaluation only — Course A; Course B shows a small addition of course specific evaluation and Course C, a large addition — where the course specific component contributes the bulk of the findings. These two kinds of evaluation are not of course unrelated or easily separable. Indeed as often as not, *it may be evidence provided by regular baseline evaluation which suggests that a one-off follow-up study is needed.*

Figure 7.2: An example of the combination of baseline and issue specific evaluation

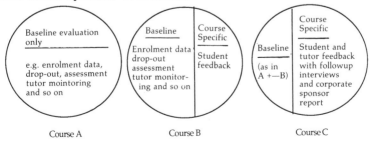

Course A   Course B   Course C

This distinction between baseline and issue specific evaluation appears in different forms in a number of the publications which refer to evaluation for open learning. Twining for example makes a similar point when he says this:

> *Evaluation involves judgements based on the analysis of data which can be collected automatically by standard monitoring techniques or by specially commissioned surveys. As the latter can be expensive and time consuming (and hence slow in providing feedback) we believe that there is considerable merit (especially when a new system is being designed) in systematic planning of standard collection and processing of data. Specially commissioned surveys can then be used to study in depth specific problems revealed by analysis of this data.*
>
> Twining (1982) p.149

Twining's terminology sees the distinction as between 'data which can be collected automatically by standard monitoring techniques' and data which require 'specially commissioned surveys'. Birch and Latcham introduce the concepts of 'instrumental evaluation' versus 'interactive evaluation' (taken from Becher and Maclure, 1978) but the underlying idea is familiar. They suggest that instrumental evaluation can be used to provide performance indicators.

> *A case has been made for the routine collection of data on enrolment, withdrawal and 'failure' patterns and the calculation of actual to planned ratios and wastage and pass rates. It has been argued that the comparison of these ratios against some pre-determined 'satisfactory' level of performance gives some leads as to the effectiveness of a course. This sort of formal monitoring comes close to what Becher and Maclure (1978) have described as* **instrumental** evaluation. The pre-set criteria which are most used in this style of evaluation are those which describe intended student learning.
>
> Birch and Latcham (1985) p.53.

They contrast this with 'interactive evaluation', which has the potential to avoid the limitations they identify as pitfalls of instrumental evaluation, i.e. that it over-emphasises managerial values and ignores unintended outcomes. By contrast, interactive evaluation 'is open-ended: the problem, the issues and the criteria of success are not pre-defined, nor are the techniques of investigation pre-determined, rather they are those which seem *best suited to the issues as they emerge'.* (Birch and Latcham, 1985)

These distinctions are similar rather than identical with those I have made between baseline and issue specific evaluation. Baseline evaluation for example might involve more than 'standard monitoring techniques'. Although we can make rules of thumb, there is no rigid distinction between baseline and issue specific evaluation in terms of quantitative versus qualitative data. Many of the measures practitioners are always going to want will be quantifiable, (as indicated in figure 3) but they may also want qualitative information, such as end of course open-ended reports from corporate clients, or monitor comments on tutors. Equally, specific evaluation may be designed so as to generate additional statistical data as well as qualitative findings (see figure 4).

However, there is some common ground between baseline evaluation and performance indicators, and this is an important point in the current climate where there is a drive to establish common criteria by which the comparative performance of different institutions can be judged. This can provoke understandable defensiveness within institutions, because indicators do not constitute either a neutral information-gathering instrument, or necessarily an agreed measure of performance.

As Schuller writes in his introduction to 'Towards a Continuing Education Audit':

> *Performance measurement is a major issue today in many parts of the public sector. There is concern from various quarters — that the service provided should be efficient and effective, and should be seen to be so, as far as this is possible. The question of how performance is to be measured, — by whom and using what instruments — is a matter of less agreement.*
>
> Schuller (1987)

The misunderstanding and mis-use of performance statistics is still apparent in conventional education. In an article on this subject in the THES, Gray makes a humourous point of the fact that statistics can as easily mystify as inform. He comments on the joint Committee of Vice Chancellors and Principals/University Grants Committee publication of a 200-page volume of Statistics: 'University Management Information and Performance Indicator Statistics'. After reviewing eight other Universities, he comes to Cambridge:

> *Cambridge: I have reserved my comments on the other ancient university till last. While the great strides the department has made in recent years are, indeed, common*

knowledge, few can have appreciated the scale of Cambridge's achievement. As reported by the working party, their performance in recent years suggests, contrary to popular belief, that it is perfectly possible for a department to have rock-bottom expenditure on teaching while sustaining a high research profile.

The figures show that in 1984/85 the department's performance was already impressive. Average expenditure per student was the lowest in the country at a mere £1,390 each, a good £1,000 a student below the national average; meanwhile, their staff-student ratio was by far the highest at 19.9 to 1. Yet, despite these apparently crippling handicaps, the department was able to achieve a research income of £14,650 per academic head.

Their achievement was the more striking when placed alongside that of departments rated as 'outstanding'. Leeds, for example, despite its established reputation and extensive list of publicly-funded research projects, apparently managed in comparison 'only' £8,840 research income per academic and with a far more favourable staff-student ration of 12.1 to 1.

It is the improvement *in Cambridge's performance between 1984/85 and 1985/86 which is most impressive of all, however; 76 more students were taken on, enabling a further reduction in expenditure costs per student to be achieved. At an amazingly cost-effective £1,270 per head, the cost of a Cambridge student was exactly half the national average and the lowest by a considerable margin.*

The student-staff ratio, meanwhile, had soared to an almost unbelievably high 23.9 to 1, double the national average. Yet, despite these developments which would surely have brought any other department to an immediate halt, the department marched on, sustaining its research income at a prodigiously high £14,000 per academic head.

THES, 11 December 1987

Clearly there is a long way to go before performance indicators of even conventional modes of delivery of education can be reliably collected and fruitfully used. Their value can in any case be overstated, or misunderstood. As Theodossin argues, a performance indicator is just that — an *indication* i.e. *'it directs attention to, without providing explanations, leading to conclusions or offering solutions.'* He defines performance indicators as 'symptoms or features which flag up an underlying reality, or, more accurately, a particular perception of reality, since the reality may be differently viewed'. He identifies the essential danger in the use of performance indicators as

> . . . *a possibility of forgetting that data so collected has no*
> *talismanic properties in itself. Indeed, it is useless unless it*
> *forms the basis for appropriate action. By appropriate action*
> *is not meant merely acting on bad news, i.e. confronting*
> *low retention rates, low Student Staff Ratios, high unit costs,*
> *but also acting on good news, i.e. high retention rates, high*
> *Student Staff Ratios, low unit costs . . . . If the use of*
> *performance indicators results in data which is merely the*
> *basis for staffroom or corridor gossip and anecdote, then*
> *we shall clearly be wasting our time.*
>
> Theodossin (1987)

It is easier to argue the case for performance indicators when used, as suggested here, for purposes defined by the institution from which they were generated. Schuller in this context proposes an audit rather than statistics alone, and his definition of the goals and findings which characterize such an audit, come close to my definition of baseline evaluation here. He quotes the FEU definition of an audit as 'a systematic review of the performance of an institution, a group of institutions or parts of an institution producing a profile of performance covering both quantitative and qualitative measures, leading to professional judgements, conclusions and recommendations'. Its key characteristics he lists as follows and all are equally applicable to regular baseline evaluation:

(i)   *It should be a process encouraging dialogue and debate,*
      not the unilateral imposition of rigid standards;
(ii) *It should be geared to the development of good practice,*
      not the punishment of past performance;
(iii) *It should include qualitative information which requires*
      interpretation, and not pretend to produce only self-evident
      truths;
(iv) *The instrument itself should be subject to regular revision*
      and refinement.

Schuller (1987).

Regular, baseline evaluation

Figure 3 shows a compilation of the kind of information, most, but not all, of it quantitative, which open learning providers might see as providing a *baseline* they can specify in advance as essential for judging the effectiveness of their work on a continuing basis (and including requirements which might be imposed by the wider institution or an external body). The value of these measures is not that they provide the whole story but that they are *indicative* -they *map the terrain of interaction between learners and institution*

Figure 7.3: Regular, baseline evaluation

*A list **indicative** of the kinds of data open learning practitioners might need to collect routinely for baseline information.*

About learners

- Number of enquirers
- number of enrolments/users, by name and address listing
- Demographic data – age, sex, previous education, qualifications, occupation/ employment status
- Source of information about centre/programme
- Reasons for enrolling
- Course(s) bought and tutor/counsellor responsible
- Number of attendances at workshop/centre
- Assignments completed and grades awarded
- Number sitting an examination
- Number and grade of passes awarded. Percentages of course passes and failures
- Number of dropouts
- Reasons for drop-out.

About staff

- Number of academic, administrative, technical and other staff
- Demographic data (as above) plus competence listing
- Workload – part-time/full-time/student loading/hours worked
- Courses tutored/counselled
- Staff development: meetings attended, courses, in-service training
- Monitors' reports on assignment marking and turn-round time
- Feedback from learners, corporate clients, etc.

About marketing

- Number of enquiries/enrolment/purchases generated by different publicity media
- Number of corporate clients, their training officers/contact name, number and type of employees.

About courses

- Number of individual/corporate users
- Drop-out and pass rate (if associated with an examination)
- Amount of tuition and counselling provided
- Learner ratings for degree of use, helpfulness and satisfaction
- Corporate client feedback (where relevant)

About facilities

- Rate of usage of workshop/study centre
- User ratings for satisfaction/convenience etc.

(inputs) and provide *clues about the cumulative effects of individual actions* (outputs). They do not offer self-evident truths, indeed can lead to misleading conclusions if taken out of context and used in isolation. Their utility increases however with the accummulation of findings over a period of time, so that trends can be identified and individual indicators compared with their previous levels. *Baseline evaluation should be cumulative.*

Although regular, baseline evaluation logically comes first, since it provides the framework within which any other kind of evaluation occurs, it is desirable that there should be one unified process of evaluation rather than two separate activities, and that the planning and management of baseline and specific evaluation should occur together. Although baseline evaluation may take the greater proportion of time in the first few years, thereafter the balance might shift towards issue specific evaluation. However baseline evaluation systems can never be completely taken for granted once in place. For example, while the existence of student and tutor records means that these do not have to be planned every year, there may be changes which require minor adaptations or updating to routine systems. There may be continuing procedures but they will lose their utility if fixed in concrete and never reviewed.

Issue-specific evaluation

Specific evaluation is an add-on activity either in relation to a particular course (as in figure 4) or some more general issue where baseline evaluation suggests the need for a follow-up survey or investigation.

Some aspects of specific evaluation can therefore be planned in advance (perhaps annually) when it is known what courses or programmes are being offered and the size of budgets available for evaluation. It may be that a new course is being introduced in one year and that a strong case can be made for putting more evaluation resources into that course, because others have been evaluated previously and baseline evaluation will be adequate to pick up any unexpected problems or changes in their learner population. Alternatively, analysis of the patterns of learner drop-out rate provided by baseline evaluation may suggest that some leaners are not getting the support they need, when they need it. In response to these findings a decision might be taken to re-design counselling provision and provide a 24-hour answer service for learner problems. A specific evaluation would need to be set up to monitor use of the service and evaluate its outcomes.

Figure 7.4: Issue-specific evaluation

*A list **indicative** of the kinds of information which open learning practitioners might need to collect on occasion, or for some but not all courses.*

Example: Evaluation needed for a review of a course prior to updating or
replacement.

Learner feedback

•   Postal questionnaire to previous year's students to check on ratings for use, helpfulness and difficulty. Attitudinal questions on applicability to work/ contribution to employment. Suggestions for how to improve the course.

•   For learners currently using the course, insert feedback questions into each module on time spent studying, objectives achievement and areas of difficulty.

Tutor feedback

•   Ask tutors to write a report on the changes required for the new course, focusing particularly on design, assessment and case studies included. Tutors should give reasons for their views, where possible drawing on learner experience with the 'old' course.

•   Organise group discussion of new course outline.

Corporate client interviews

•   Design a semi-structured interview for supervisors and trainers to elicit views on changes in job requirements and the way trainees develop their skills.

Learner performance

•   Extract data from baseline evaluation files on numbers enrolled, number and percentage sitting the examination, percentage passing, over each year the course has run.

Other needs for specific evaluation may crop up unpredictably, and require an ad hoc investigation set up using any resources available at the time. Marketing may uncover a request for local training which requires an immediate follow-up. Or learner feedback may suggest that there is insufficient practical work offered on an existing course. Both of these would require immediate investigation to provide evidence on the basis of which an appropriate response could be made. The evaluation team would need to meet specifically to decide what evaluation was possible in the circumstances and in the time available, and allocate the tasks of implementation and reporting back with findings.

Summary

Effective planning of evaluation requires that practitioners have a strategy for evaluation which both meets the interests of practitioners and can be carried out within the constraints of their working context. In devising such a strategy it was suggested that practitioners might consider their needs for evaluation in relation to

(a) those which they can specify in advance on a continuing base, with confidence, and
(b) those which are less easy to determine in detail, in advance, and which are likely to differ from year to year (or appropriate budgeting period).

Suggestions were made about the likely content of (a), baseline evaluation, and the possible content of (b), issue specific evaluation.

Data collection

This section explores some of the practical implications of using different methods of data collection. Issues to do with the content and design of the instruments (interviews, questionnaires, etc.) used are dealt with in Part II as a whole, and can also be followed up in the further reading suggested.

Although the goals and design of evaluations are immensely varied, reflecting differences in context and in what is being evaluated, the means used for data collection commonly involve one or more of a small number of types:routine records, feedback, interviews and questionnaires. Each of these main categories can be further sub-divided, and the boundaries between them are not always clear cut. Nonetheless they represent familiar ways of collecting data with some fairly clear differences in implementation, and these will be brought out in what follows.

Routine record systems, or monitoring

Monitoring, or the routine recording of information, is not always easily distinguishable from feedback, and is often used to refer to practices essential for the effective implementation of a system, whether or not it is evaluated. It includes therefore learner and tutor records, log books kept by receptionists of enquiries about courses, attendance lists at tutorials, and so on. Monitoring can be defined as any regular form of checking or recording which is, or can be used for generating data in an evaluation.

If the checking process is already happening as a routine, little if any additional time for data collection may be needed. This depends on how systematic the monitoring in place is already, and how effectively it is recorded. It may be necessary to design a new form of log sheet or attendance record and to discuss with the monitor the use to which the records will be put.

Some examples of formats for monitoring records are shown in figures 9 and 10 chapter 4 and figures 2 and 6 in chapter 5. The principle is to keep the design simple and robust — if records are manual, thin card may be preferable to paper, and the record needs to be intelligible and meaningful to a third party. Clear, self-explanatory records are an essential basis for evaluation. Since a number of different records may be collected over several weeks/months, each requires filing systematically.

Monitoring can provide very effective indicators of how a course or group of learners is progressing — *if it is analysed regularly*. This is often not a routine activity, and therefore time for this does need to be budgeted specifically. Even where data are held on computer, time needs to be allowed to analyse printout, and perhaps to relate a learner number to demographic data — name, address, age, sex etc. This can be estimated by a pilot analysis of a small number of records and extrapolating from that.

The analysis of records in a proactive fashion may already be a routine managerial procedure but if not, such a procedure needs to be set up. For evaluation purposes, it also needs to be recorded together with the results of any action taken, so that an explanatory file is built up and can be incorporated in end of programme reports. Obviously the amount of time this takes will depend on the size of the programme, among other factors. However, without regular analysis, monitoring is of little use for formative evaluation.

Feedback

Feedback can be defined as any form of coherent response from users of a programme, indicating their reaction to it. Some feedback is likely to happen 'spontaneously' and much 'seat of the pants' judgement relies on it: 'I've asked my students and most seem to like the course', or 'we've had two letters now complaining about that tutor; better investigate further'. Informal feedback however, is useful mainly for gathering clues and impressions. Finding out more reliably about user response requires a more formal and controlled approach.

One of the most economical means of generating sound feedback about open learning is to design a proforma which can be included in a routine mailing of course material or handed out to users of a centre. The format may look similar to a questionnaire or it may take letter form; the style must be dictated by circumstances. What matters is that the questions can be answered *in a reasonable time*, and that they do not constrain the response so much that the users get no opportunity to explain what might have been important to *them*. This means keeping down the number of questions, leaving plenty of space, and including encouraging phrases such as: 'Anything else you would like us to know'.

Although designing a feedback instrument or proforma may be much less ambitious than designing a questionnaire, always get as many people to read a draft as possible — including learners if possible. Phrasing and layout can nearly always be improved and two or three interpretations of it will provide some clues.

The next major decision is when to distribute the proforma . Ideally, users should know *before* they begin to use a programme that their views will be sought. This alerts them to the issues they will be asked about and starts them thinking along the right lines. However this is not essential; learners can be asked about their experiences at any time up to a few weeks after completing a course or programme. Obviously the more immediate their experience, the more detailed and reliable we may expect their responses to be. And the more respondents are forced to rely on long-term memory, the more we must look only for general impressions. If what we want is fine detail, such as 'how long did it take to study chapter 2?' this probably needs setting up beforehand by getting the agreement of a few learners to keep a diary of study times.

Whether users are asked for feedback early or late, you will probably need to send at least one reminder letter. However you should not discard feedback simply because of low response rates. Feedback does not assume the principles of survey design based on random samples where it may be very important to achieve a response rate of at least 80% and preferably higher. Course feedback at the Open University has often had to rely on a much lower response rate than that. Providing this is made clear to the user, the data can be interpreted accordingly, and compared with the impressions gained by the kind of informal feedback mentioned at the beginning.

Feedback is usually much more time consuming to analyse than it is to generate, that is if we ignore the time it takes the user in making a response. Even if there are less than 10 responses, it may take several hours to read them and decide how they can best be used. A larger number of responses requires some simple numerical analysis of pre-coded responses, and perhaps post-coding of open-ended responses. It may be possible for some of this to be done by secretarial/clerical staff but the framework needs to be designed by the 'author' of the proforma.

Feedback is typically used for generating reactions:

— on draft course materials, whether from peers or prototype learners;
— from learners who have used course materials;
— from tutors on courses they have 'taught' if not authored;

— from sponsors/employers of learners who have taken open learning courses.

Interviews

Interviewing of any kind is a distinctly labour intensive means of data collection, but it can provide the richest findings of any method and the basis of real understanding of the perspective of the interviewee. Three of the tasks in interviewing can be particularly time consuming

— arranging an interview appointment;
— carrying out the interviews;
— analysing interview notes, tapes or transcripts.

The amount of time this takes depends on the length of each interview and whether travel to each interview is involved. The time can be reduced by using telephone interviews, but whether that is a feasible option will depend on the content of the interview.

Notwithstanding the effort involved in interviewing, it is often used effectively when one or more of these circumstances apply:

— when the cost of course production/re-make is sufficiently expensive to justify in-depth coverage of issues;
— as a means of exploring the *range* of responses and attitudes as a basis for questionnaire design at a later stage;
— as a follow-up to more quantitative data, to provide case-studies of particular perspectives;
— where interviewees are easily available;
— where a limited number of fairly precise issues need to be checked out and can be handled easily over the telephone;
— where there is at least one member of staff with good listening skills and the ability to interpret a range of divergent responses.

Sampling

This is not the place for an introduction to formal sampling techniques for which there are excellent guides already in existence (see further reading). It is important to remember though, that in interviewing as in mail surveys, we are taking a *sample* of the total population unless we interview everybody. We need to consider, therefore, what the relationship is between our sample and the total population of learners.

This implies that we have relevant information about the total population — how many there are, which course(s) they have bought, their age, sex, occupational status and perhaps educational and training qualifications. Assuming we have at least some of these items of information, it is necessary to define our sample of interviewees accordingly. If, for example, a course of 70 learners has only 12 women, yet 8 out of the 10 we have interviewed are women, we have (whether by accident or design) used a sample highly representative of the women's reaction, and very weak in relation to the reaction of the men who are also the majority of learners. This may be the intention, but if so it should be clearly signalled so that the user of the feedback remembers that this is feedback largely obtained from a minority sub-set of the total learner population.

A very much less obvious example — and one which is sometimes harder to pick up — is the influence of existing qualifications and experience. Where materials and courses can be bought 'off the shelf' or without the learners having reached some mandatory level of experience or qualification, there is likely to be a range of existing skills and abilities in the total population of learners, which will affect their reactions and may produce roughly identifiable sub-groups of response. As course evaluators we may need to find out whether such sub-groups exist, and one way to begin is with interviews of learners whose characteristics differ according to categories we are interested in; it may be education, occupation or some other feature like participation in voluntary work, length of time unemployed, place of residence, and so on.

Types of interview and the timing of interviews

Interviews are generally considered to be either structured, semi-structured or unstructured. The structured interview is one where the interviewer uses a carefully worded questionnaire and pre-coded responses as a means of recording interviewee answers. It is important that the same question is asked in the same way in each interview and that the interviewer need use very little specialist judgement in coding the responses.

Many of the areas investigated in evaluating learning and teaching are difficult if not impossible to specify in advance in such detail, and it is for this reason that the semi-structured interview is most often used here. This requires a framework of questions common to each interview, but with considerable judgement required of the interviewer to follow up and probe responses, as required.

Unstructured or depth interviews refer to lengthy (sometimes two hours or more) dialogues between a trained interviewer and interviewee, the purpose of which is to explore highly complex issues, or deep seated emotional responses. It does require a highly skilled and aware interviewer and is not usually an appropriate method therefore in evaluation by practitioners.

Issues of timing are self-evident, but easy to forget. Responses are influenced by the mood of the interviewee at the time, and by the usual processes of forgetting. It may be necessary to remind interviewees about the early stages of course work, if interviews occur at the end of a course; responses can be unduly influenced by what is uppermost in the mind, unless attention is directed elsewhere. Bell et al provide a neat summary of this area, and a hint of some of the emotional states to be avoided; doubtless there are others:

> *It is not always possible to do anything about such circumstances, but grossly unsuitable timing should be avoided, and* people should not be interviewed when markedly upset or euphoric *unless this emotional condition is the subject of or central to the enquiry.* (emphasis added)

> Bell et al (1984)

Interviewing skills

Although interviewing can be developed into a highly skilled performance, it is possible for the non-specialist practitioner to use interviews effectively for course evaluation and development, by giving forethought and reflecting on other people's accounts of interviewing as well as their own. Helen Simons has written effectively about her practical experience on the SAFARI project at the UEA Centre for Applied Research in Education, which studied the effects of the curriculum reform movement in the 1960s, on the context of the school, the classroom and relations with the LEA. She says . . . *'I think one of the most common errors in open-ended interviewing is failing to listen, either by asking too many questions or interrupting to confirm one's own hypotheses. A second related error is seeking closure too soon by accepting the initial response too readily, summarising erroneously or by asking questions which give the interviewee a plausible response without committing him (sic) to reveal what he really thinks or feels . . .'* (Simons, 1977)

Interviewers need to be able to tolerate a pause in speech which they probably would not tolerate in conversation, where we tend to fill the gap and 'help out' the speaker with a phrase or two to prevent embarrassment. However in interviewing this is often a mistake because, when we do tolerate a few second's silence, the interviewee can go on to say something we could not have predicted, or which was difficult for them to say but significant for the evaluation.

This is particularly important since one of the strengths of the interview is that people can be asked about their *feelings* as well as their opinions. A package of materials may get very high ratings for 'clarity', 'ease of use', 'difficulty' and so on, but if it makes learners feel patronised or talked down to, they will find learning difficult and be put off using something similar again. This is exactly the sort of finding that might be missed by a mail survey but picked up in careful interviewing.

One final word about interviews concerns rules of conduct in their use. Whether we tape an interview or write up a report of what was said, the result represents a very personal account of the interviewees' reactions. Accordingly evaluators ought to abide by a number of rules and the following list is suggested as a starting point:

1. Interviewees should not be put under *any* pressure to be interviewed or to finish an interview if they do not wish to do so.
2. If the interview is not going to remain anonymous, the interviewee should be aware of that before agreeing.
3. If the interviewee wishes, he or she should be allowed to listen back to the tape. If the interview is written up, a record should be sent for checking first.
4. Interviewees should know how interview data will be used before they agree to be interviewed.

Face to face interviews

These will be more time efficient for the interviewer if interviewees attend the same site as the interviewer, and can be interviewed there.

The semi-structured format is likely to be the most useful approach, and, like all interviewing, requires preparation. However small-scale the interview programme, this will require several hours at least and ought not to be done in isolation. Spend an hour or so explaining the draft schedule to someone with knowledge of the learners or the programme, and incorporate any amendments. If possible, arrange to pilot the schedule and amend it accordingly.

The length of each interview depends, of course, on what and how much you want to find out, but few useful interchanges can be done in less than half an hour, and anything longer than one and a half hours is straining the good will of the (normally unpaid) interviewee. It is safest to assume that the analysis of a completed interview will take at least half as long again as the original interview, working from notes taken by the interviewer at the time. If the interview is tape recorded for full play back afterwards, analysis will take about twice as long as the original interview. Writing a report of a series of interviews will take time in addition.

Telephone interviews

Telephone interviews can generate a lot of useful data in a short time, if there are a small number of specific issues for follow up, and easy access to the telephone numbers of interviewees. Most people will not want to spend much more than half an hour on a phone call, especially if not pre-arranged, so telephone interviews should usually be restricted to topics which can reasonably be covered within that time.

Time should be budgeted for a high call failure rate, and calls may need to be concentrated in the evening, when more adults are likely to be in. This is also a very tiring form of interviewing so three to four interviews an evening would be a reasonable maximum to aim for before fatigue sets in. Keep a card with all the questions to be asked on one side, so that it can be seen while listening, and have a separate pad on which each interviewee's responses can be jotted down during the call. Spend time after each call filling out what will, inevitably, be a scribble of notes made while listening carefully and asking the next question. Don't be afraid of a pause though, while you ask your listener to allow you to finish a note before asking the next question. And, as in the comments on interviewing in general, don't be afraid of a few second's silence, if you want the interviewee to expand a point they have made. It is more useful to you to allow *them* to fill the pauses, if possible, rather than to do it yourself.

After the interview, you need to budget time as before, for analysing notes and writing up.

Group discussions

These are a very economical way of gathering impressions. You may be able to get a group of learners to spend perhaps an extra half an hour or more of their time at an open access workshop, tutorial or resource centre, discussing their reactions and opinions with you. Depending on the method you use to record the discussion, you need to budget about half a day to write a report and draw conclusions from such a discussion.

Group discussion can also be used to generate feedback and reactions from practitioners and sponsors involved in programme work. Case study A at the end of chapter 2 provides a very interesting example of the use of workshops for this purpose. Both flip chart summaries and individual questionnaires were used there to document findings, so that group reactions could be checked against an analysis of individual response.

Questionnaires

As commented earlier, the dividing line between a feedback form and a questionnaire may be a fine one. The fully fledged professional questionnaire is however, very time consuming. Its value lies in the opportunity it provides to generalize about a large number of individual reactions to commonly expressed issues. Such questionnaires require several weeks preparation by a practitioner, clerical resources for mailing and reminder letters and again several weeks analysis by a practitioner. Large scale surveys of this kind may be possible in collaboration with statistical services in a college or some external bureau for computer processing of questionnaires. Otherwise they remain on the fringes of concerns here, as likely to be too time consuming for most regular purposes.

However, this does not rule out the use of less ambitious questionnaires which can be used very effectively to collect views and experiences from a local population of learners. Many microcomputers have software which can be used to process pre-coded responses, and if the number of questionnaire returns is low enough, this can also be done manually (see Mitton in the Further Reading section for chapter 2, for an excellent guide to different methods of processing questionnaire data).

Part II contains many examples of the kinds of questions which have been used in evaluating open learning, and it is certainly crucial to get the questions right, if the maximum benefit from doing a survey is to be reaped. It is so often in the design of such questions that one realises afresh the capacity we all have to use language in a way which makes our meaning less rather than more clear. The question which, to us, looks perfectly straightforward and an expression of exactly what we mean, turns out to have several possible meanings when we see how respondents have answered it, and none of their meanings is quite what we intended. Unfortunately, by this stage it is too late to do anything about ambiguities or omissions in the questionnaire. The moral is, always pilot a questionnaire before using it. Even if a group typical of the eventual respondents cannot be arranged, ask two or three colleagues to work through it. They will certainly pick out some if not all of the pitfalls.

The appearance and design of a questionnaire is almost as important as the phrasing of questions and pre-coded responses. Try to make it as attractive and easy to complete as possible. Obviously, from the respondent's point of view, the quicker it is to complete, the better, and some people take advantage of this by an eye-catching appeal on the first page: 'Just 60 seconds of your time' was used by the NEC evaluators. (Case Study C) It may be possible to find other means of catching the respondent's attention and increasing the likelihood that they complete and return the questionnaire. Using coloured paper is one option, especially if more than one questionnaire is to be sent to learners. The OU piloted a Study Skills Package during the late 1970s, which required a rather elaborate questionnaire as part of its evaluation. The evaluators used an elephant logo to emphasise their request to learners to remember to fill in the questionnaire after completing each section of the package. The logo took on something of the status of a mascot and 'the elephant questionnaire' was easily distinguishable from all the other information OU students received. Respondents were asked about their initial reaction to the Study Skills Package (SSP) for example, and one respondent commented : 'Looked interesting . . . (the) elephant was sweet — became a friend. Other people got irritated with it and it became a shared joke among others doing the SSP.'

Conclusion

This chapter has focused on issues of strategy and planning in evaluation, with practical pointers about particular data collection methods which need to be borne in mind during planning. Though evaluation may often be led by a manager, it should not be seen merely as a sub-set of the manager's role. After all, evaluation may show the need for changes in what the manager does which may not happen if evaluation remains in the 'private' domain of the manager. The definition in chapter 1 designated evaluation as a *public activity* i.e. one that is known to be happening, including by those whose performance is being evaluated, that is recorded as an activity of the Open Learning unit concerned, and that has records or reports capable of being made public, if not published.

There is no obligation to produce sophisticated reports, but there is an obligation to be 'open to inspection'.

Evaluation should be planned and co-ordinated therefore by a group, or a team, as suggested here. Those immediately involved need to decide on the membership of the team, how often they will meet, to whom report and what relationship they have, if any, to the existing management structure of their organisation. It is also important to decide whether to include one or more colleagues who can bring a degree of 'objectivity' to bear, or who have expertise in relevant research or evaluation processes. It may also be useful to establish links with other institutions.

Although 'planning' is another area with a large theoretical literature which is beyond our concerns here, the evaluation team may need to remember what planning in these circumstances often involves:

— *Trade-offs:* that is, the more detailed the data we collect, the more analysis it may need and the greater the risk that it might not be used: the more time we put in on monitoring correspondence teaching, the less we will have for following up drop outs, and so on.

— *Having a strategy but engaging in tactics.* The one certainty about planning is that it won't happen according to the plan. The receptionist will fall ill and two week's data will be missing. Or take-up on a course is so low that sending five students a questionnaire can hardly be justified. These kinds of contingencies are the norm, not the exception and it is important not to allow browbeating because 'plans were not carried out'. They hardly ever are carried out exactly as envisaged, and *tactical* changes have to be made when unforeseen circumstances render *the strategy* (i.e. the original overall plan) inoperable. The strategy is nonetheless essential; without that there are no tactics, just reactive behaviour.

Further reading

DE304 Research Methods in Education and the Social Services. Open University, Milton Keynes.

A course available either for study as a student, or materials may be purchased through OU Educational Enterprises, Cofferidge Close, Milton Keynes. Includes a thorough account of data collection methods which can be used in evaluation; sampling, design of surveys and interviews.

Oppenheim, A.N. (1986) *Questionnaire Design and Attitude Measurement*. Gower Publishing Co. Ltd.

The classic work on questionnaire design, originally published in 1966 by Heinemann. Covers among other things question-wording, checklists, inventories, rating scales, attitude statements and the quantification of questionnaire data. Aims, in the words of its preface 'to prevent some of the worst pitfalls and to give practical, do-it-yourself kind of information that will point the way out of difficulties.'

Association of Principals of Colleges (1987) *Management of Open Learning Support Centres*. Available from Central Manchester College.

A training pack based on text, video and audio materials. Although oriented towards procedures for setting up Open Access Centres especially in collaboration with the Open College, it does have a useful section on setting up an information system, which is of general interest, and includes guidelines on how to set up a basic computer system.

8 Analysing and using evaluation findings

Main themes: *What do the users of evaluation need findings for? What practitioners can do to facilitate a constructive use of findings, considering the needs of users, notably: the learner, author, receptionist, tutor, manager. Factors which influence the extent to which evaluation is applied to practice: planning, contextual factors, interpretation of data, staff development, communication skills and consultation.*

Evaluation users

The reader may be understandably surprised to see a chapter devoted to the use of evaluation findings. If practitioners and learners are collaboratively involved in evaluation, as suggested in the preceding chapter, does this not resolve the problems in applying evaluation to practice? To some extent, yes. When it is the same group of people who both evaluate, and maintain the system and the learning being evaluated, the problems of communicating results and their significance for practice are much reduced. But they are not removed altogether, if only because, even with a team approach, there is likely to be a need for delegation and a degree of role specialization. All the members of the team cannot be equally involved in all the data collection activities, and some of the major activities may be carried out by one or two people, on behalf of the rest. So the need to communicate remains, both within the team and any 'external' audiences involved — sponsoring bodies, corporate clients, college management, board of management and so on.

However, the problems of communication are not restricted to issues of clarity and presentation. They derive from the demands made by the different tasks to which evaluation is to be applied, and include problems of interpretation, selection and analysis of material. Furthermore, the social context within which evaluation is used by particular individuals or groups also has an influence.

All of these factors can be illustrated through the consideration of particular users and user contexts. Figure 1 lists a number of potential users of evaluation findings and a selection of situations in which they might reasonably expect to make use of them. What kind of information is likely to be of most use to them, and in what form? What kinds of support might they require in order to make the best use of findings?

The learner

Where the individual learner is evaluating his or her own learning, there may be little need for communication to a wider group. A group may discuss the purpose of the sessions they have been involved in, with no need to record their joint reflections; they may simply come to a decision about how to spend future sessions. However, a written record can be necessary to keep track of the process of self evaluation in distance learning, and probably in other forms of open learning, to record progress at key points in the course. This could be done in a journal or portfolio kept by the learner.

The Bury College example in chapter 3 offers a simple record of the learner's estimate of the time taken to complete each assignment and the grade their work might achieve. This facilitates the tutor-learner exchange subsequently. It may also be helpful for a counsellor to review with a learner the self-evaluations they have made during a course, as part of the decision about further study at the end of the course.

The learner's interest in other forms of evaluation is likely to be strongly instrumental — to improve the information on which he or she makes a decision, or to bring desirable changes to the teaching process. In the former, information may be communicated by guidance staff and publications. Where learner feedback suggests changes to teaching, these will probably require either a written report of findings to make the case, or an accepted decision making process which represents learner experience, as illustrated in Case Study B, the trainee centred programme review team, at Sumlock Calculating Services Ltd.

Summary

- the productiveness of self evaluation can be increased by records the learner makes, at key points;
- information to aid individual decision making should be presented in terms accessible to the learner;
- changes to teaching systems will probably require either a written report or learner involvement in the evaluation process.

Figure 8.1: Indicative list of potential users of evaluation of findings

User	Some of the possible uses for which evaluation required	Needs findings when . . .
Learner	Judging whether this course is appropriate – likely to be interesting, at the right level, relevant to a professional exam, etc.	Pre-course: on application and before enrolment/ starting
	Getting any necessary changes made before the end of the course – e.g. better access to workshops, more contact with trainer/tutor, etc.	On course, sufficiently early to make any changes required
	Deciding whether to continue study/training, and which route to take	End of course
Author of learning material	Adjustments to an existing draft (major re-write unlikely unless feedback suggests draft is badly 'off target')	At minimum 2 weeks before handover to editor/ printer: much longer if author working part time
Receptionist in Open Access Centre	Advising applicants of the guidance facilities available on courses and the expected number of hours of study each requires	As soon as possible after the first group has completed a course, and before the next application period
Tutor	Adjusting standards of grading and commenting to meet the expectations of the institution and the needs of learners	After marking first batch of assignments, and regularly thereafter
	Deciding what to cover in sessions with learners, and effective approaches to facilitation	In time to make changes to benefit current learners (assuming it is the tutor's own sessions which have been evaluated)
Manager of an open learning centre	Deciding whether to change the allocation of resources among several courses, having appraised their relative effectiveness	During the planning period for resource allocation in the next financial year
	Checking the efficiency and effectiveness of tutors employed to mark learner assignments	Mid course, or immediately, if routine checks uncover an obvious problem
	Progress report to senior management and/or corporate client on the effectiveness of a new course	Towards the end of the course, in time for a report to be circulated to the appropriate committee/ group meeting

The author of learning material

As chapter 6 makes clear, authors may be able to make changes to material at various stages in its development, some of them at a point where learners have not used the materials and only feedback from peers or experts in the field is available. Ideally, the author needs evidence of learner performance in assignments or examination, job performance if relevant, and qualitative feedback from learners and tutors or trainers. There are problems however in using each one of these sources of information. Feedback from experts and peers may be mutually conflicting; learner performance data may show something is wrong but not precisely what; learner feedback reveals particular problems but not what would be better instead; tutor feedback can be split into two (or more) camps, with strong supporters of the materials in one, detractors in the other. Such dilemmas may not *always* occur, but they are familiar, and although they can be resolved usually by more detailed investigation, this is not always possible.

Notwithstanding the difficulties of making sense of these various findings, authors can be helped in a number of ways to make intelligent use of them. First, they should be available in time. This may be obvious, but one of the greatest difficulties is to get feedback to the author in time for it to be read, digested and the changes required to be made. Second, someone other than the author, with no personal interest in the text in question, should do a preliminary analysis of any qualitative feedback, identifying any themes and the number of responses on each. Where there are any noticeably positive or negative views, these should be noted. If possible, all the qualitative responses should be typed up (or a representative selection if there are too many) so that the author can read through them and compare his or her reactions with those of the disinterested reader. If there are quantitative data available from pre-coded responses, or performance data, these should be used to qualify and interpret other feedback.

Authors should also have access to the original proforma or questionnaire returns since reading through even a handful can help give a better feel for the response and generate ideas about improvements. if the author is also the evaluator, this will happen anyway but if this is the case, some overview analysis as suggested above is still necessary. One can be unduly influenced by a minority of strongly worded negative (or positive) results, into thinking that the reaction *overall* is negative or positive. It can be surprising sometimes to do a numerical check on positive/negative/neutral responses because it may show that an impressionistic reading cannot be justified, or anyway overstates the case.

The context in which authors attempt to get directions from evaluation findings for how to improve their material is also very important. The author's ego is involved in this, and should not be ignored. There are many points in favour of a group of supportive colleagues meeting with the author to discuss the findings and then agree on a list of changes, which is minuted. Such a group can help sort out the most important points to take not of, since it is rarely possible to respond to all the points that have been made. Even more important, they can reassure the author about *the good points which can be built on*. It takes energy and self confidence to revise materials as well as to produce them in the first place, and both can be sapped by negative criticism.

If a group meeting is inappropriate, other steps can be taken to support the author. If the evaluation has been carried out by an open learning manager for example, rather than the writer her/himself, it is desirable for the evaluation findings to be handed over with an explanation of how learners were selected and the format and intentions of the report. (It is assumed authors would have been involved in the planning stage and therefore be aware that an evaluation was being done.) If this cannot occur face to face, then a covering letter and telephone call can be used for the same purpose. Where someone else has analysed learner comments, it is also very helpful to authors to discuss findings with them. Printed reports are best kept short, and *conversation* used as an additional means of communicating the subtleties of response and preventing misinterpretation and offering encouragement.

Summary

— authors need feedback early enough to digest its significance and work out how to take it into account;
— author morale can collapse if feedback is presented without adequate support;
— responses from anything more than say 10 readers or learners will need analysis by someone who knows about the course/materials area;
— authors need both quantitative and qualitative information: performance data, where available an *overview* (quantitative or otherwise) of general reaction through feedback or evidence of the learner's experience as a whole, and some direct *examples* of feedback, perhaps organised within a framework of categories of response;
— authors need to understand the context of evaluation and be able to discuss findings with others.

Receptionist in an open access centre

One of the main reasons receptionists may need evaluation findings is to improve the information they provide to applicants/enquirers about courses. It is probably unlikely that they will learn about some of the information they need, as part of their regular function — items such as exam success rates, average length of time for course completion, the suitability of courses for particular learners, and so on.

At some stage therefore, evaluation findings will need to be analysed so as to identify information which receptionists can use, to discuss course choice/suitability with enquirers and learners. Both the format and the context of this communication are important. The conventional report of findings is not much help to a receptionist, who needs two things:

1.   to understand the significance of information which may have little *personal* meaning for him or her (in this sense a contrast with the author in the preceding section);
2.   to have ready access to findings *in a form he or she can use directly*, with enquirers and others.

This implies the need for both a *record* of the relevant information, and a meeting to discuss its status and how it can be used. The record needs to be integrated with existing information on courses, or kept in a form easy to access during conversations with enquirers, whether face to face or by phone. The wording needs to be precise enough to be read out without giving a misleading impression — for example it would be misleading to say 'this course can take twice as long as the number of hours stipulated', if only two out of 50 learners had had that experience.

Evaluation findings should not be handed over without comment. The receptionist should have her or his attention drawn to them by discussion of how the information has been generated, how it might help enquirers and how it relates to existing course information. If the findings are tentative/incomplete, this should also be discussed. The receptionist may be able to add useful information, or may have important questions to ask, which should be aired. It would be most useful therefore to schedule a meeting *before* a record is finalised. The discussion may show the need to make changes, perhaps even that the receptionist produce the final draft, in a form most suited to his/her needs.

Summary

Receptionists who have not carried out the data analysis themselves need:

— a record of findings, in a form which can be accessed easily and used directly with enquirers and others;

— to discuss the significance of findings and add any comments from their own experience;

— to contribute to the design of the final record or report.

Tutors

One of the most important factors in the use of evaluation by tutors is the degree to which the findings reflect the individual tutor's performance. Those which do so require handling differently from those which do not. Aggregate data about the progress of learners in general, where particular tutor groups are not identified, might be discussed by tutors in a group. Drop-out for example might follow a common pattern across all tutor groups, and tutors could be alerted to the action they might take during the period of greatest risk.

Other kinds of feedback are much more sensitive because they reflect on individual performance; two of the main examples being monitoring reports on the quality of a tutor's correspondence teaching, and learner feedback on the quality of a tutor's face to face teaching. Because of their sensitivity, there are good arguments for allowing the tutor to handle the feedback in private at least initially, with the option of discussion with an experienced colleague, who might also have access to the same feedback. Where tutors are newly appointed, discussion is especially important, both for reassurance and to clarify expectations.

Where there are written reports on the individual's performance, these require phrasing with the same care used in good teaching by correspondence. The aim is to open a dialogue through which the tutor feels encouraged to examine and to develop his or her tutoring competence.

Some of these areas can of course be touched on in a less personal way by the discussion of findings of the kind included in chapter 4, where a sample of Open University students was surveyed for their attitudes towards tuition and their evaluation of its effectiveness on the courses they had taken previously. A brief summary of the findings, with perhaps a comment from one or two tutors on their implications, is desirable in this context; tutors need a record they can keep and enough information to form their own judgements, and to raise any issues which concern them as a result. Tutors can also discuss findings of this nature in a group, with the ease which comes from knowing that none of them is being judged as an individual. Group discussion offers an important opportunity for tutors to find out how their colleagues tackle common problems, and can create support for changes in approach, if these seem desirable.

Many of the findings from evaluation are not clear cut, and sharing qualitative experience in discussion is an important way of drawing conclusions from them.

A number of the measures discussed in chapter 4 can be used in staff as well as system appraisal, although only correspondence tuition monitoring is regularly used for this purpose by the OU, for example. The willing collaboration of tutorial staff is vital for effective evaluation and can be forfeited by mis-use of indicators. None of the indicators discussed in chapter 4 measures educational effectiveness directly, but they can be helpful in structuring discussion with tutorial staff themselves, to identify priority areas for staff development or system change.

In addition, the evaluation of the effectiveness of a particular cadre of staff may be complicated by legislation on such matters as contractual requirements and dismissal proceedings. Irrespective of any action necessitated by these considerations, it may be desirable to maintain a file for each tutor and counsellor/advisor which indicates role/duties undertaken and any relevant indicators associated with performance. The staff concerned should know whether files of this kind are kept and the conditions under which they might have access to them. One possibility for example is that a tutor and manager might review the file together, during an appraisal or staff development session. A tutor ought to be free to add comments or other evidence he or she considers relevant for their record, before or after such sessions. Individual files need at least three main categories of information if they are going to be used for appraisal effectively.

1.   Work experience sufficiently detailed to indicate skills and competence of the individual. Perhaps for new staff, a list of skills/performance they'd like to improve.
2.   Records of attendance at staff development or training sessions.
3.   Evidence relevant to performance appraisal: this could include size of workload, feedback, learner exam performance, monitors' reports (see preceding section), unsolicited letters from students/clients etc.

Summary

— evaluation findings which reflect directly on individual tutor performance require sensitive handling, allowing time for private reflection on feedback as well as the opportunity to discuss its implications with an experienced colleague;

— evaluation findings which do not identify the individual's performance can be more easily communicated in writing,

but group discussion can have an important role in motivating any changes in approach;
— where evaluation findings are added to individual tutor files, tutors should be aware of these files and, at minimum, invited to comment on or add to them.

Managers

A manager of an open learning system has a major role in the use of evaluation, because he or she is likely to have overall responsibility for the implementation of effective evaluation procedures. Thus a manager may take an equal rather than a dominating role in the regular work of an evaluation team, but still carry the responsibility of ensuring that evaluation is initiated, implemented and used. It is likely to be a manager therefore who ensures that all the users discussed up to this point have access to findings in an appropriate manner, and take any action which is agreed as a result. Also managers are themselves direct users of evaluation to the extent that findings reflect on managerial issues of resource deployment, staffing and policy decisions.

In relation to the use of evaluation by others, managers have a key role in the content and design of written information, and the interpersonal process through which it is communicated. They need to demonstrate an awareness of the various requirements (introduced above) of different users. This may mean spending time in consultation with a user before finalising a report, and possibly employing someone else to draft whatever material is required.

Even where there is no need for documentation of findings for others, managers still need to consider whether they will have the time to analyse data themselves, during the periods in which they plan to use it. It is easy to be overwhelmed by raw data, whether in the form of student records, interview tapes or user feedback reports. If these require analysis at a time when other managerial tasks are also imperative, it may be necessary to identify someone capable of doing a preliminary analysis of raw data beforehand, which a manager can then analyse further and make use of.

Evaluation results may point strongly towards the need for changes in other peoples' work roles or behaviour. There are usually more productive ways of doing this than by announcing a 'fait accompli' — 'we've done an evaluation and it shows it would be better if you were available by phone every week-day evening' . . . Meetings to *discuss* the implications of findings *before* a course of action is finalised can have two very desirable pay-offs:

- a more creative use of the data — people often come up with new ideas which can be an improvement on existing interpretations. Even if they aren't, its desirable to check them out.
- greater commitment to the changed role/behaviour — since this comes out of discussion and decision making with those who will make the changes, rather than being imposed on them.

Evaluation is also very likely to have implications for the actions of a manager, and this is where the manager needs the support of the evaluation team. The team may be reviewing baseline data of the kind suggested in chapter 7 — number of enrolments, completions and exam performance per course, average rate of tutor turn-round per course, end of course reports by corporate clients, and so on. The evidence may suggest the need for important policy changes — course re-design, improved marketing or a change in the sector from which learners are drawn. The team can ensure that the implications for management are realised and recorded, without necessarily replacing the existing decision making structure. If the team is small, it might be wise to strengthen its expertise for key meetings of this kind, where there are data covering a significant period during which trends can be identified and outcomes assessed. Another manager or experienced colleague from outside the immediate unit might be asked to read the relevant findings and to begin a team discussion by providing his or her own interpretation. This might be desirable for a number of reasons. It can help prevent the myopic effect of getting too close to findings and failing to see points which a relatively uninvolved outsider may pick up. It may also help to decide which are the most important findings, for early action, and to preserve a degree of objectivity.

It is also likely to be a manager who is required to draft reports to committees or funding bodies, and time needs to be scheduled specifically for this. Presenting all the available findings, especially as part of a long narrative description of 'how the evaluation was carried out', is unlikely to be the best approach. Committee or Board members are likely only to skim read a big report, and if there are no cues in the layout to help them extract the main points, they may give up the attempt to read it completely. It is probably worth remembering that few people will want to spend more than half an hour on any one paper for a committee meeting. They *will* be encouraged to read a report however if it meets at least the minimum requirements of good presentation: an opening summary of the recommendations arising from the evaluation, (if there are any), a summary of the main findings, a contents page, clear headings and numbered paragraphs.

Summary

Managers

— are responsible for ensuring that the process through which *other* practitioners use evaluation is effectively implemented;
— may need additional help/specialist skills in data analysis and presentation for particular purposes;
— need to schedule time to familiarise themselves with findings and think about their implications;
— require the support of the evaluation team at meetings to discuss the implications of evaluation findings for manager action and decision making;
— may need to strengthen the evaluation team's discussion of outcomes and performance data, by involving an experienced outsider.

Making the best use of an evaluation

The foregoing analysis of how different categories of open learning staff are likely to be involved in using the results of an evaluation suggests that a number of factors influence the effectiveness with which evaluation can be used for the development of practice. I shall comment on each in turn.

Planning

The effective application of evaluation to practice is a process which requires planning as much as does data collection, because, as we have seen

— the *timeliness* of evaluation findings is important; they need to be available at times which fit in with the existing schedules and deadlines of users, otherwise their likely effect on practice is much reduced;
— analysis needs to be scheduled and may need extra staff if it clashes with workload peaks elsewhere, or requires skills otherwise unavailable;
— A variety of different documents may be required, calling for careful, often time-consuming work;
— one or a series of meetings needs to be arranged to discuss interpretation and implications of findings and negotiate follow-up action.

Contexts — politics, interests and identities

The context in which an evaluation takes place becomes especially crucial during the use stage. Are there a large number of users, and are different work roles involved? Or is the main user a manager, with an important committee or external body to influence? Whatever the circumstances, they cannot be disregarded because they condition *the quality of attention* people will give to evaluation results, and the way they are likely to interpret and respond to them. If there are many different users, then a number of (probably overlapping) contexts need to be taken into account.

This means that the role of the evaluation team is as vital for the use process as it is for goalsetting and planning. The team offers a forum which can operate so as to protect and support individuals, as well as to initiate action designed to improve the performance of individuals or the unit. The team can offer both a degree of public accountability and collegial support.

There are some occasions where this may become particularly important. If evaluation produces findings which are politically sensitive, a team is in a better position to promote or negotiate action than an individual. *The existence of a team approach is an important strategy for the depersonalization of evaluation issues.* It offers a forum through which conflicts of interest can be identified if not resolved.

Interpretation of data

The raw data of an evaluation needs some kind of analysis or, at minimum, collation, in order to provide information for a user. What kind of analysis, and how much, depends on two things — the kind of data and the needs of the user. Open-ended comments may simply need typing up so they can be read easily, or there may be so many that someone needs to analyse the responses and organise them into categories, or topics. Questionnaire responses will need to be tallied and perhaps descriptive statistics prepared. Analysis may be handled manually throughout, or there may be a need for computer resources.

Turning to the user, one needs to ask 'What counts as information for the user?' 'How much information can this user reasonably handle?' This may reveal for example that authors must have access to learner comments if they are to understand *why* there was difficulty with their material, and thus be able to apply the findings. Or it may show that a receptionist needs the demographic data on respondents — needs to know whether those who took longer to study a course were older learners or not, or whether for example most of those 'unable to find a course to suit my interests' were women or a pretty even distribution of men and women.

Users can also fail to apply findings if there are too many to absorb in the time available. If too much data has been collected, it may be better to analyse only a proportion of it so that it can be used rather than attempting to use all of it, which may simply prove overwhelming. It may be possible for example to analyse only two or three questions on a questionnaire rather than the whole thing; or to sample one in five feedback sheets returned. Providing the limitations of the data are clearly noted, this may be a useful tactic to make sure something is salvaged from an unwieldy evaluation.

Having transformed raw data into information of various kinds, there is still the question of meaning, which can be characterized again in the form of questions. 'What does this mean?' 'Does it matter, and if so, what do I/we do about it?'

In the case of performance indicators, aggregate data may need to be disaggregated so that differences between the performance or ratings of different groups can be explored, or the ratings of one course against another compared. Disaggregation is necessary, because average measures across a whole body of learners may conceal disturbingly low values among a sub-set, or fail to identify the need for further investigation to find out why a particular course has very much lower ratings than others. The difficulty of interpreting the significance of the measured values thus revealed is not easily resolved; two approaches are commonly used.

First, it may be possible to compare the performance data with other similar courses or institutions, and with internal data for previous years. This allows *relative* judgements to be made: course x in 1988 is better or worse than y, or the performance of course x in 1985 and 1986. The second approach is to decide on a value as having an *absolute* significance for the programme or unit concerned: for example it might be decided that any drop-out rate in excess of 25% over a whole course would not be acceptable and would be investigated further; or that appropriate improvements be made to any facilities rated 'poor' by 20% or more of the users.

> *When one is dealing with human perceptions, information is neutral until one attaches a value to it. This is true for both providers and clients. Thus an SSR (Student Staff Ratio) of 17 to 1 is neither high nor low, efficient nor inefficient, until someone decides that it is one or the other, and the act of decision is essentially political. To an MPhil thesis supervisor, 17 to 1 might appear mean; to an infant-school teacher it might seem generous. In each instance, what is acceptable/unacceptable will be in part a function of precedent.*
> *Theodossin and Thompson (1987 p27)*

Using evaluation involves us heavily in *interpretation* of the meaning of findings and *judgements* about their significance for what we and others might do in future. Both processes are likely to be more effective if undertaken collaboratively — certainly with those whose work is involved and possibly also with others less directly involved. It may be very difficult for example to see any recommendations for action from some findings, but these may develop as a result of discussion. And even if they do not, to conclude that no change in action/programme is required is still a positive use of an evaluation.

Staff development

It will be clear from the above points that one of the key uses for evaluation is staff development. Evaluation can be integrated into an existing programme of staff development, or may be used to initiate one. The purposes of staff development however are broader than the use of evaluation findings, and include the need to motivate staff, giving a sense of belonging to a unit concerned for their interests as well as for 'efficiency'. If an evaluation suggests for example that learners do not find tutor comments very helpful, or that a receptionist is not perceived as 'welcoming' by many enquirers, resources need to be offered to the groups or individual concerned to help them to reach the same self-appraisal willingly, and then to determine and carry through the changes required.

Evaluation may also reveal more intractable problems; it may highlight an inappropriate appointment initially, or the failure to resolve problems already well identified and understood. Sooner or later evaluation will raise issues which should be handled through management processes rather than by an evaluation team. Boundaries are rarely clear cut, but the team should be aware of some of the obvious points of demarcation between management and evaluation systems, and have procedures for identifying the proper scope of their actions.

Communication skills

Most of the forms of usage discussed here have involved two things — discussion, and some more permanent record of findings. Practitioner-evaluators need to be good communicators — or to hire people who are. They should be prepared to get advice about the layout and format of written reports, which may take a variety of forms — a committee paper, an aide-memoire, information on enquirers, statistics for tutors, reports for authors and so on. On occasion, it can be very effective to present data in some other form. Interview extracts on tape can be played back for a few minutes and make a much greater impact than text alone. Overhead projector slides can also make sure that all in the audience are focusing on the same information at the same time. This can be be an effective way of communicating messages, however small scale the evaluation.

Oral communication skills are also necessary, in one to one and group meetings, in order to gain attention for the results of an evaluation and to shape the interactive process of their use.

Consultation and collaboration with 'outsiders'

Practitioner-evaluators need to be able to demonstrate some degree of objectivity, particularly in the methods of data collection and analysis that they have used. Objectivity also matters in the analysis and interpretation of findings and it can be valuable to engage one or more colleagues who are not personally implicated in the programme evaluated, to act as an advisor on the evaluation team. Their involvement may not be necessary throughout; perhaps only at meetings where each year's evaluation is planned, or where there is a major review of findings relevant to the unit or operation as a whole. Whatever the circumstances, such consultation strengthens the status of the work, because it constitutes a public form of checking, and a demonstration that the evaluation process is recognised and open.

Apart from objectivity and openness, consultation can be very helpful in the development of links, albeit informal, with other evaluators. A colleague from a different area of the institution may agree to act as a 'sounding board' for ideas and problem discussion, and also keep evaluators in touch with other developments within their own organisation which may be relevant. Another option might be to form links with other open learning centres/units to discuss findings from a number of different evaluations. Even where there is no direct collaboration, it helps to make an evaluation more interesting when it can be related to local issues or a common problem. The 'blinkers' of our own institution can restrict our ideas, and collaboration, even on an informal basis, helps to 'open up' thinking and generate new ideas.

Conclusion

The use of evaluation findings is a complex social process involving many different kinds of activity, notably planning, management, consultation and collaboration, data analysis and presentation, meetings, materials design and production, and staff development. Practitioner-evaluators need to possess many of the skills these activities require and to be able to enlist others to contribute the skills they do not possess, and at times when they are working on other tasks.

The process of using evaluation findings is typically unexamined and under-emphasised in the evaluation literature. This may be because professional evaluators are not often involved in using evaluation for the development of learning and teaching. For practitioners this is likely to be one of the most important reasons for undertaking evaluation in the first place, and it is essential therefore that they allocate sufficient time and resources for this stage, and take into account those factors which influence the effectiveness with which evaluation can be applied to practice.

Further reading

Theodossin, E. and Thomson, C. (1987) *Performance Indicators: Theory and Practice*. Coombe Lodge Report Vol. 20. No. 1. Further Education Staff College, Coombe Lodge, Blagdon, Bristol BS18 6RG.

After a general discussion of the use of performance indicators, it includes a case study developed out of one of the projects of the Responsive College Programme in Further Education colleges. This project involves the development of questionnaires on Student Perceptions of Colleges. Data from the use of these questionnaires in colleges across the UK are used to discuss the analysis and interpretation of performance indicators, from the perspective of a college manager.

Sagar, E. and Strang, A. (1985) *The Student Experience: A Case Study of Technicians in Open Learning*. Roffey Park Management College, Horsham, Sussex.

Reports the result of interviews with 17 students who had just started a three-stage engineering course, which normally takes three years to complete. The interviews explored the students' first experience of open learning relevant to their work, and the results are presented here in a way much more likely to encourage their practical application, than would a conventional report. The use of colour, drawings, layout and succinct analysis is excellent.

Conclusion: Beyond quality control, towards excellence?

One of the assumptions I have taken for granted throughout this book is that many aspects of quality in open learning cannot be achieved and maintained *without* evaluation, and I have certainly stressed the importance of quality control as one of the purposes of evaluation. I also think that a legitimate argument can be made that, at this stage in the development of open learning, quality control is a priority. Unfortunately the danger with this position is that evaluation is seen as *nothing more than* quality control – or indeed, as a means of exerting *control* rather than constantly improving quality. Under this approach, the kind of evaluation which has a key role in the *development* of learning and teaching is quietly forgotten. It would be regrettable if this were to happen. One of my objectives up to this point has been to demonstrate something of this developmental potential of evaluation, and thus to counter narrow and restricted versions of its meaning.

However, narrow and restricted versions of evaluation do exist, and it may be that the pressures on all forms of education and training, currently and for the foreseeable future, are more likely to encourage the narrowly instrumental than the creative and the developmental approach to evaluation. There are important issues for practitioners here, which I shall review in outline, in conclusion.

Beyond 'mere' quality control?

Quality control, and the evaluation which contributes to it, is not a temporary phenomenon, if it is to be effective. Having achieved a standard of practice we feel reasonably happy about from evidence during one period, does not release us from the need to evaluate in future. Standards once reached do not maintain themselves automatically, and evaluation is the spur to action which not only maintains standards, but improves them.

The emphasis we put on 'mere' in 'mere quality control,' does of course reflect the definition we have of 'quality' in the first place.

Some organisations and some individuals within organisations set
such high standards for quality that, were they to achieve them
in, say, 90 per cent of what they do, they might justifiably claim
to have achieved excellence. The Open University monitors all
its part-time tutors at least once every year, using demanding
criteria (indicated by the categories in figure 7 chapter 4) to judge
the quality of each individual's correspondence teaching. Merely
by having such a system the Open University has demonstrated
a commitment to quality in one area of its operation which is
probably unrivalled. 'Quality control' in this instance does not mean
merely checking that the process (tutor commenting on student
assignment) is up to standard, it means encouraging the tutor to
reach *the highest standard.*

First, there is a quality threshold which all tutors must reach.
Any tutor who does not grade and comment adequately on a script
is followed up and may ultimately not be reappointed. Any student
whose tutor has been consistently late in returning assignments
during the year, is 'flagged' by the computer and the examination
board may take this into account in making final awards at the
end of the course. But second, in commenting on the quality of
a tutor's comments on a script, the monitor is seeking to encourage
the best practice in correspondence tuition, not just an acceptable
minimum. For a good monitor, this will involve appreciation of
the good practice already in evidence, as well as suggestions for
improvement.

However, evaluation of this routine form of quality control in
the OU has suggested improvement which, when fully achieved,
constitutes in my view an example of open learning evaluation
being used for the achievement of excellence, not merely good
practice. Surveys of part-time staff, together with evaluation of
their training (Thorpe 1985), have repeatedly shown up a weakness
in the feedback link to part-time staff. The monitor's evaluation
is communicated automatically to staff tutors whose responsibility
it is to take appropriate action where tutors are shown not to
be reaching the high standards set. Until recently however, the
monitor's comments were often not communicated to the majority
of tutors, whose performance was seen as at least acceptable and
often of a very high standard. Evaluation showed that experienced
tutors in particular had little or no feedback on the quality of their
teaching (unless of course it was not adequate) and would have
liked such feedback.

As a result, most faculties now send the monitor's comments
direct to the tutor, as well as to the staff tutor who in this instance
has the line manager role. The monitor writes as a peer, in a
manner intended to encourage the tutor to reflect constructively

about his or her own practice. The tutor is free to reply, if there is a difference of opinion or emphasis, or simply a wish to discuss teaching/learning issues. This development of the original quality control system in my view represents a form of excellence. To have institutionalized a regular system of *commentary and communication about the quality of teaching* is an unusual achievement, certainly in further and higher education. Its purpose is not merely the narrow one of identifying bad practice, but of recognising and encouraging the good.

It is also possible to envisage ways in which a naive or over-simple use of evaluation findings can inhibit creativity. Feedback from learners on one course might show that project work was found 'too difficult' or 'too time consuming'. These findings could be used to argue *against* the inclusion of a project on another course, where differences of context and design might very probably lead to positive rather than negative learner reaction. The failure of a teaching strategy in one context does not guarantee its failure in all contexts. Evaluation of a good idea, badly implemented, does undoubtedly make it more difficult to try again with the same idea, unless the results of the evaluation are not widely known.

It is also possible for evaluation to inhibit creativity if there are pressures to homogenize teaching style, and to make it conform to an approach which appears to cause few problems or strong reactions in learner feedback. I think there has been a change in this respect among Open University course teams at least, which reflects the accumulation of years of experience with a very wide range of subject areas and course designs. It is probably true to say in the early years it was thought important that all units should achieve as near as possible a 'house style' of impersonal clarity and rationality, and that the course materials as a whole should have a uniform style. There is now a more sophisticatd grasp of the difficulties of writing good teaching material, and of the indissolubility of style and content. Perhaps more important has been the realisation that for many students, differences of style can be stimulating and that units which give a sense of the personality behind the writing can make as positive a contribution to learning as others which do not.

On the whole though, I see little evidence of evaluation's having had a negative influence of any significance in the past. If the provision of education and training has evinced little imagination or creativity, I think it unlikely that an over-rigid institutionalization of evaluation, or an over-emphasis on it could be cited as a cause. There may be a greater danger of this in the future and it is to this issue that I turn in conclusion.

Towards excellence?

It will be a progressive feature of open learning if more evaluation takes place than occurs presently, and obviously I would prefer that such evaluation adopts the constructive and self-critical approach I have tried to embody in this text. In fact I think it likely that there *will* be a lot more evaluation in (say) five years time, but the causes of any increase are likely to come from external pressures upon institutions and individuals, than from the power of a text such as this one to persuade.

Unfortunately these pressures are more likely to push evaluation into the quality control corner than to encourage its full potential for institutional and individual development. I referred earlier to one of these pressures – the movement towards using performance indicators to judge the comparative efficiency of institutions of further and higher education. There are also financial pressures following cuts in government funding and the probability that the passing of the Education Reform Bill will introduce tighter control by government of the way funds are spent. Appraisal of academic staff is being introduced across the public and private sector, and although appraisal *can* be developed as a constructive procedure for both staff and institution, there is an equal possibility that it increases defensiveness at a time of threat to employmnent and job security.

The danger for evaluation in this context is that it is used narrowly as either a tool for personal or institutional justification or as a means of managerial control. If this is to be avoided, practitioners need to develop an alternative model, whether incorporating the features introduced in chapter 1 or an alternative approach. It takes a model to kick out a model; that is we cannot expect that a developmental approach to evaluation will come about merely by pointing out the shortcomings of a narrowly instrumental or control oriented approach. There must also be a conception of what should be developed in its place and examples which suggest how it is achieved.

I have outlined what for me are *key features* of a desirable model of evaluation but am in no doubt that these need to be further fleshed out and developed in practice, so as to demonstrate how the generalities might be variously developed in different contexts. The key features I have stressed relate more to the *purpose* and *process* of evaluation than its content – that it should be a *collaborative* exercise, undertaken in the interests of *all* those engaged in the teaching/learning process, and open to their inspection, not 'owned' by management. As to purpose, I take it as axiomatic that evaluation is for development – of learning and the quality of learners' experience, of service and the quality of the curriculum the institution offers, and of competence and the careers of staff employed by the institution.

For me therefore, the achievement of excellence in and through evaluation is more to do with whether and in what manner learners and practitioners are involved and how results are used, than with technical excellence in interviewing or questionnaire design. Technical excellence is an important goal and practitioners need to be aware of their limitations and prepared to reduce them by learning from the more experienced and professional evaluator. Rigorous methodology however is pretty valueless as part of a process which leads to little or no improvement in practice or in understanding, or which even alienates people. Evaluation needs to be developed as a resource for the learner and as an essential aspect of excellent practice. Prior to rigorous standards of data collection and analysis is *commitment to the evaluative process itself* which, at bottom, is a commitment to two main ideas: first, that our understanding of teaching, training, learning or any of its associated activities is not perfect, and that we should continue to push forward that understanding, however long our experience 'in the trade'; second, that our practice can always be improved and that this requries that we are open to, and reflect on, evidence about the effects to which we have contributed through our practice as a professional.

The improvements in evaluation that I would like to see derive from this. Evaluation, if it occurs at all, is too often 'sub-contracted out' to one person or a small sub-group. Accepting that some tasks need to be delegated and everybody cannot do everything, ways need to be found to integrate the processes of evaluation into routine communication and activities so that all staff are aware of their commitment to the evaluation process rather than assume that it is someone else's responsibility.

Second, much greater attention to the use of findings is required in the planning and design of evaluation. This is almost certain to involve a readjustment in the proportion of time accounted for by each of the main phases in an evaluation, with perhaps less ambitious data gathering and much more time allowed for the analysis and discussion of findings and for the planning of follow-up action.

Third, it seems to me inescapable that, if evaluation is really going to push forward our understanding of learning and teaching and thus aspire towards excellence, it has to be communicable beyond the immediate context in which it occurs. This requires a greater willingness among practitioners to publish what they do and to discuss its implications for different institutions and sectors. If evaluation is (as I have argued it should be) central to excellence, it is as important to find out what other practitioners have learned from their involvement in evaluation, as it is to read accounts of the latest developments in provision. This certainly requires that evaluation goes beyond mere statistical checks and measures, and takes responsibility for exploring learning and illuminating the relationship between teaching/training and learning.

I have attended in this concluding chapter to longer term goals for the evaluation of open learning where in earlier chapters I focused on goals and approaches which might contribute an achievable good practice in the more immediate future. I am aware that, because open learning has taken many providers and deliverers into a selling relationship with corporate clients, some readers will not wish to look further than their immediate future in responding to what the market appears to want now.

However, open learning may be the current 'buzz phrase' in education and training but it is unlikely to be 'the last word'. If there *is* a long term future, it is only in terms of a continual development of new and better ways of learning, certainly not of re-packaging old ideas and products. Open learning is no longer a new idea, and if it is going to achieve the promise with which it was heralded, none of us can afford to avoid evaluation for development. Without it, we may find ourselves judged only by an imposed set of performance indicators, and subject increasingly to external views of 'what the market demands' rather than asked for our professional expertise on what might be desirable and effective. 'There is no such thing as a free market any more than there is a free lunch; all markets are socially constructed.'[1] And if you see yourself as a professional in open learning, you are likely to want a role in constructing the market for open learning, whether your 'paymaster' is government, the corporate sector, or the individual citizen – and in all probability a combination of all three. This requires practitioners who can speak cogently and with confidence about the quality of the open learning they provide, and the ways in which it might best be developed. Both require a firm foundation in evaluation.

---

[1] A. H. Halsey, Professor of Continuing Education, Oxford University Extra Mural Studies. In a public lecture at the Open University, January 13th, 1988.

References

Argyris, C. and Schon, D. (1978) *Organizational Learning : A Theory of Action Perspective* Addison-Wesley Reading, Massachusetts.

Ashton, P. M. E., Henderson, E. S., Merritt, E., Mortimer, D. J. (1983) *Teacher Education in the Classroom: Initial and In-Service* Croom Helm

Ballard, A. (1987) Community Education and the Limits of Openness in *Beyond Distance Teaching — Towards Open Learning*, Hodson, V. E., Mann, S. J., Snell, R. (editors) OU Press, Milton Keynes.

Becher, T. and Maclure, S. (1978) *The Politics of Curriculum Change* Hutchinson.

Bell, J., Bush, T., Fox, A., Goodey, J., Goulding, S. (editors) (1984) *Conducting Small-scale Investigations in Educational Management*. Harper and Row, in association with the Open University.

Birch, D. and Latcham, J. (1985) *Managing Open Learning*. Further Education Staff College, Coombe Lodge, Blagdon Bristol.

Bradshaw, P. (1987) Feedback Forms and Forms of Feedback in *Open Learning*, Vol 2 No 2 The Open University with Longman.

British Association for Counselling (1985) *Counselling : Definition of Terms in Use with Expansion and Rationale*, BAC, Rugby.

Byrne, C. (1979) Tutor-marked assignments at the Open University: a question of reliability. *Teaching at a Distance* No 15. The Open University, Milton Keynes.

Clarke, A., Costello, M., Wright, T. (1985) *The Role and Tasks of Tutors in Open Learning Systems* Industrial Training Research Unit, Hobson St., Cambridge, CB1 1NL.

Cox, R. (1978) *University Teaching Methods*, Centre for Higher Education Studies, Institute of Education, University of London mimeo.

Field, J. (1987) Report on Proposed new TMA Routing Procedures. Mimeo: internal report available from the author, The Open University, Milton Keynes.

Field, J. (1983) Course Research Researched in *Feedback and Evaluation in Course Presentation and Development* Teaching at a Distance Institutional Research Review No. 2.

Fotheringham, H. (1976) Post-Experience Counselling: A small survey in Seven Study Centres in East Anglia Mimeo. Open University Regional Academic Services, Milton Keynes.

Gibbons, S. (1984) 'Bailing Out' : A report on research carried out into student response to a regional publication sent to students who withdrew from courses in 1983. Mimeo. OU East Anglian Region, Cambridge.

Grundin, H. (1980) Audio Visual and Other Media in 91 Open University Courses. Results of the 1979 Undergraduate Survey. IET Papers on Broadcasting No 149. The Open University, Milton Keynes.

Henry, J. (1978) The Project Report Volume 1. Findings and Recommendations. IET, The Open University, Walton Hall, Milton Keynes.

Jenkins, D. (1978) Alternative Educational Evaluation and the Open University in *Teaching at a Distance* No 12.

Kaye, T. (1987) Computer Conferencing and Electronic Mail, in *Open Learning for Adults* Thorpe, M., Grugeon, D.

Kelly, P. (1978) Strange Encouters of A Counselling Kind. Mimeo. Open University, Regional Academic Services, Milton Keynes.

Kelly, P. (1979) Interim Report on the RAC1 Associate Applicant Record Form. Mimeo. Counselling Research Papers, Regional Academic Services, the Open University, Milton Keynes.

Kelly, P. and Swift, B. (1983) Tuition at Post Foundation Level in the Open University. IET/SRD Paper No 247, The Open University, Milton Keynes.

Lawless, C. and Crooks, B. (1985) Report on the Annual Survey of New Courses 1985. Mimeo. Student Research Centre Report No 4, IET, The Open University, Milton Keynes.

Lawless, C. (1987) Report on the Annual Survey of New Courses 1986 Student Research Centre Report No 6, IET, The Open University, Milton Keynes.

Lawless, C. (1988) Report on the Annual Survey of New Courses 1987 Student Research Centre Report No 13, IET, The Open University, Milton Keynes.

Lewis, R. (1985) *How to develop and manage an open learning scheme* Open Learning Guide 5, Council for Educational Technology.

Manpower Services Commission (1987) Open Learning Case Studies: B&Q.

Melton, R. and Scanlon, E. (1983) Learning from evaluation for S101 in *Feedback and Evaluation in Course Presentation and Development*, Teaching at a Distance Institutional Research Review No 2.

Nathenson, M. and Henderson, E. (1976) Developmental Testing: A New Beginning. *Teaching at a Distance* No 7.

Nisbet, J. Broadfoot, P. (1980) *The Impact of Research on Policy and Practice in Education* Aberdeen University Press.

Nixon, K., Holmes, S. and Coleman, T. (1975) Customer Contact Skills Training for Staff at Heathrow Airport. An Evaluation Report. *Training Research Bulletin*, Vol 6 no 2.

Parlett, M. R. and Hamilton, D. F. (1972) Evaluation as Illumination: a new approach to the study of innovatory programmes. University of Edinburgh, Centre for Research in the Educational Sciences, Occasional Paper No 9.

Rowntree, D. (1981) *Developing Courses for Students* McGraw-Hill.

Ryan, S. (1987) Using Audio tape to Support the Learner, in *Open Learning for Adults*, Thorpe, M., Grugeon, D.

Sagar, E. and Strang, A. (1985) The Student Experience: A case study of technicians in Open Learning. Roffey Park Management College, Horsham, Sussex.

Schuller, T. (1987) Towards a Continuing Education Audit: Warwick Indicators for Performance Measurement, University of Warwick.

Simons, H. (1977) Conversation Piece: The Practice of Interviewing in Case Study Research in *Safari : Theory in Practice* edited by Nigel Norris. Occasional publications No 4 Centre for Applied Research in Education, UEA, Norwich.

Simpson, O. (1977) Post Foundation Counselling, in *Teaching at a Distance*, No 9.

Strang, A. (1987) The Hidden Barriers in *Beyond Distance Teaching – Towards Open Learning* edited by Hodgson, V. E., Mann, S. J. and Snell, R., SRHE/OUP Milton Keynes.

Taylor, E., Morgan, A. and Gibbs, G. (1982) Students' Perceptions of Gains from Studying D101, The Social Science Foundation Course. Mimeo Study Methods Group Report No 11, IET, The Open University, Milton Keynes.

Theodossin, E., and Thomson, C. (1987) Performance Indicators: Theory and Practice. Coombe Lodge Report Vol 20, No 1. Further Education Staff College, Coombe Lodge, Blagdon, Bristol.

Thorpe, M., Grugeon, D., editors (1987) *Open Learning for Adults* Longman, Harlow.

Thorpe, M., (1979a) The Student Special Support Scheme: A Report in *Teaching at a Distance*, No 15.

Thorpe, M. (1979b) 'When is a Course not a Course?' *Teaching at a Distance* No 16

Thorpe, M. (1983) Post Foundation Tuition: Measures of Student Usage and Tutorial Attendance. Mimeo Regional Research and Development Papers No 10 Regional Academic Services, The Open University, Milton Keynes.

Thorpe, M. (1985) Part Time Staff Learning on the Job, in *Teaching at a Distance*, No 26.

Thorpe, M. (1988) *Module 1: Approaches to Adult Learning.* Diploma in Post Compulsory Education (Part B): The Open University, Milton Keynes.

Twining, J. editor (1982) *Open Learning for Technicians* ST(P) Handbooks for Further Education, Stanley Thornes (Publishers) Ltd.

Tyler, R. (1949) *Basic Principles of Curriculum and Instruction* University of Chicago Press.

Unit for the Development of Adult Continuing Education (1986) The Challenge of Change: Developing Educational Guidance for Adults. National Institute of Adult Continuing Education, Leicester.

Woodley, A. (1987) Understanding Adult Student Drop-out in *Open Learning for Adults*, edited by Thorpe, M. and Grugeon, D.

Woolfe, R. (1988) *Module 3: Counselling. Diploma* in Post-Compulsory Education (Part B): The Open University, Milton Keynes.

Index

Accredited Staff Training Centres, 17, 25–28
administrator, 17
appraisal, 202
assessment, 6, 20/1, 22, 51, 57/58, 126/7
assignments, 20, 57/8, 67–76, 83, 108, 121,
    137, 148, 184
audit, 22, 167
author, 17, 185, 186/7

Birmingham Open Learning Development
    Unit, 22, 33–40, 149/50
Bradford and Ilkley Community College, 45,
    78/9, 121, 123
British Association for counselling, 90
broadcasting, 20, 66, 103, 133

case study, 63, 96,
collaboration, 12, 197, 202
corporate clients/sponsors, 3, 4, 24
counselling, 18, 47, 52, 61–5, 88–118, 120,
    133, 144
counsellor, 48/9, 51, 78/9, 190
    tutor-counsellor, 91, 95, 100–2, 110–13
course evaluation (see also materials), 35–8,
    47–9, 169, 173, 185, 119–23
course team, 122/3, 146, 210

data collection, 6, 12, 157, 164, 171–81
diary/journal, 27, 55/6, 57/8, 96, 173
distance education/learning, xi/ii, 79
development, (see also staff development) 3,
    25, 198/9, 202
developmental testing, 130/1
drop-out, 58, 81, 91, 107–14, 169

evaluation, definition of, 2, 5–7, 24
    need for, 1–3, 4/5
    purpose of, 5, 18/19, 155
    types of, 7–10
    formative, 5, 9–11, 172
    summative, 5, 9–11
    self-evaluation, 51–59, 90/1
    quantitive, 131–9, 148, 152/3, 165, 186/7
    qualitative, 140–2, 165, 186/7, 190
    baseline, 162–9
    issue specific, 162–4, 169–71
    plan, 6/7, 160–71, 193
    team, 156–160, 194
    use of findings, 155/6, 156, 183–98, 201
    interpretation of data, 194–6

examination, 6, 20/1, 121, 126, 132, 134–6

feedback (questions), 55, 83/4, 123, 130–2,
    142–52, 159, 172–4, 200
flip charts, 26/7
Further Education Unit, 46, 50

groups, 55, 178
guidance, 89/90

helpfulness ratings, 132–7

Industrial Training Research Unit, 62–5
International Extension College, 44
interviews, 5, 45, 96/7, 98/9, 114/5, 140,
    141/2, 174–8, 198, 200

learner, 1, 4, 20, 21, 49, 51–9, 92, 93, 102,
    109, 121, 123, 124–8, 140–2, 144/5, 152/
    3, 155, 166, 169, 184/5, 203
learner feedback, 57, 127–42, 143, 150

management, 5, 49, 172, 202
manager, 17, 25, 45, 185, 191–3, 194
Manpower Services Commission/Training
    Commission 4, 17, 24, 50, 56, 57, 62,
    119, 125, 159
marketing, 168, 170, 192
materials, 5, 22, 25–8, 66, 91, 119–53, 201
    production, 120–3, 144–6
    delivery, 131–152
mentor, 17
monitoring, 5, 6, 12, 75/6, 78–86, 95/6, 103,
    164, 171/2, 200/1
motivation, 54, 109

National Extension College, 33–8, 179

open learning, xi, 1–4, 19–23, 94, 124/5, 166,
    204
Open Tech, 38, 45, 54
Open University, xi, 20, 22, 40–3, 45, 49, 50,
    55/6, 58, 79, 95, 96, 102/3, 105, 108,
    121, 130, 132, 137, 141, 180, 200, 204
Optis, 25–8

performance indicators, 4, 6, 13, 21, 83, 92,
    94, 104, 117, 123–5, 126, 164–9, 190,
    198, 202
politics, 193/4

practitioners, ix–xii, 3, 11–13, 16, 17, 18, 22, 23, 49, 59, 155, 203, 161

questionnaires, 25, 27, 45, 66, 97/8, 115–7, 133–40, 153, 155, 179/80

rating scale, 60, 101, 133
receptionist, 17/8, 49, 185, 188/9
record/proforma, 57, 95/6, 148, 150–2, 172–4, 184
response rate, 133, 175

South Manchester Community College, 79
staff development, 3, 27, 189–91, 191/2, 196
supervisor, 17, 25–8, 124–6, 161/2, 168, 183, 197/8, 203
surveys, 25, 45, 66, 109, 132, 155, 200

team, 20, 22/3, 31
trainee, 26/7, 32/3, 125, 184
trainer, 17, 25, 54, 124/5
tuition, 47–9, 61–87, 91/2, 104, 120, 133
    correspondence, 69–76
    face to face, 76–85
tutorial attendance, 77–85
tutor, 5, 17, 20, 57, 66–86, 94, 121, 123, 140, 148, 185, 189/91, 200/1
tutor feedback, 142–52, 186

UDACE, 89

workload, 137–9
workshop, 26, 78/9, 104, 153

YTS, 17, 25–33